THE HOAX THAT I

JAMES LI

Creative Texts Publishers products are available at special discounts for bulk purchase for sale promotions, premiums, fund-raising, and educational needs. For details, write Creative Texts Publishers, PO Box 50, Barto, PA 19504, or visit www.creativetexts.com

The Hoax That Let Jesse James Live
By Bud Hardcastle

Published by Creative Texts Publishers, LLC
PO Box 50
Barto, PA 19504

ISBN: 978-1-64738-042-7

THE HOAX THAT LET JESSE JAMES LIVE

BUD HARDCASTLE

CREATIVE TEXTS PUBLISHERS
Barto, Pennsylvania

FROM THE PUBLISHER

More than a century ago, one of the most famous men in America was the outlaw Jesse James. Equally cheered and hated by the populace of his time, Jesse was in many ways the embodiment of the post-Civil War era. His legend was born of the war between the states and depending on whether one's disposition was pro-union or pro-confederacy; Jesse may have been considered either a demon or an avenging angel. For more than fifteen years, Jesse was active as an outlaw on the national stage and neither the Pinkertons, nor the law, nor even the US Government could bring him down. According to history, that feat was reserved to be accomplished by a member of his own gang, whom he trusted. On April 3, 1882 in a little four room house in Saint Joseph, Missouri, we are told that "the dirty little coward" Robert Ford shot an unarmed Jesse in the back of the head while he was up on a chair straightening a picture on the wall.

Although quickly arrested and deemed a coward by the public for shooting an unarmed man in the back, many felt as though Jesse was so dangerous that this was the only way that Ford *could have* taken him out. Those that hated Jesse believed Ford to be a hero and thought him justified for ridding the populace of such an evil menace. This view would ultimately prevail as, although Ford was charged with murder, he was eventually pardoned and set free. But justice was not to be denied to the James family and word on the street quickly spread that Jesse's brother, Frank James, who was himself a hardened member of the James gang and a feared killer in his own right, wanted revenge and was on the trail of Robert Ford, hunting for blood. As fate would have it, it was inevitable that the two men would meet and meet they did. However, far from the expected crescendo of blazing guns and shattered bodies, the meeting between the two men, consisting of both murderer and avenging brother, simply resulted in them sitting down having a quiet chat before shaking hands and departing one another's company. Sometime later, Frank James himself would quietly surrender to Missouri Governor John S. Marmaduke. James was pardoned and became free to live out his life as an ordinary citizen with no consequences for his many crimes.

This pretty much ended the chapter for Jesse James until many decades later, in 1948, when *The Lawton Constitution* newspaper shocked the world with the headline "Jesse James is Alive". The story featured in the newspaper was based on the claims of an old man who used the name J. Frank Dalton. Dalton claimed that it wasn't Jesse James that was killed that night and that there was a whole lot more to the story than anyone knew. Among other things, he claimed that a man named Bigelow had been killed in his place and that the "death" of Jesse James was all part of an elaborate ruse. A loyal confederate to the bone, Dalton claimed (according to some) that he was the treasurer for the *Knights of the Golden Circle,* a pro-confederate group that was robbing banks to fund a second civil war where *"the South will rise again"*. Dalton claimed that he and the James gang had agreed long ago that if he were ever to live to be one hundred years old, he would come clean and reveal himself.

Obviously, these claims sparked tremendous interest and thousands of people from all over the country came to meet the old man. At the time, he attempted to prove his claims by producing vintage photographs he claimed to be of the James family and also by leading a group to buried artifacts that supported his claim. What is incredibly unfortunate, however, is that there remain almost no records from this period on the man J. Frank Dalton. Now old and infirm, he fell into the care of an unscrupulous group of men that attempted to profit off of his story by charging for admission to see him.

Likewise, one of the men began writing his story but not only was he not a writer but he also decided it would be a better story if he was Jesse's grandson, which was obviously not true, and which made the effort quite ridiculous. The modern reader therefore is left with virtually no records of the claims made by J. Frank Dalton that he was Jesse James.

However, there was also among the curious throngs that came to see J. Frank Dalton a young woman that made the journey by the name of Ola Mae Everhart. Ola was born on March 7, 1916 and as a young woman she had always heard from her family that she was related to Jesse James. When she heard that the notorious outlaw was allegedly alive, she was determined to meet him. She went to see him and once in his presence, she began the conversation by stating the names of her grandparents. Dalton immediately recognized the names and acknowledged them as being his relatives. This short exchange would become the basis of a special relationship that would last for many years and that would culminate in Ola becoming a caregiver for the aging Dalton.

Sometime after Dalton passed away on August 15, 1951, or perhaps prior, Ola began making notes of her conversations with Dalton in hopes of someday proving that J. Frank Dalton was indeed the famous outlaw Jesse James. Upon her death on November 27, 1988, her husband, Aubrey Everhart, gifted her notes to Bud Hardcastle, of Purcell, OK in exchange for a promise that he would someday prove the truth about Jesse James.

For more than 40 years since that day, Bud Hardcastle has kept his word and has conducted research in order to find the truth. Among his many talents, Bud is a treasure hunter and has found more physical archaeological evidence than anyone living that the story of Jesse James and the Knights of the Golden Circle are real and verifiable. Among those in his line of work there are none more suited than Bud Hardcastle. Bud is the descendant of pioneers that made the "run of '89" to get their share of a 2,000,000-acre tract of land offered up for settlement in Oklahoma in 1889 and his great uncle was Deputy US Marshal John Swain. John Swain's wife was the first woman in the Oklahoma Hall of Fame.

Ola's information has been in his possession for more than 40 years and he has diligently studied it for clues to help with his research. Now, for the first time, he is publishing the story that Ola told him in its entirety. When one reads this account, it is reasonable to keep in mind that Ola was neither a detective, historian, or forensic investigator. She was a southern lady who was convinced based on stories from her family that Jesse James was her relative and she also convinced by J. Frank Dalton that he knew those same stories which meant to her that he must be Jesse James.

Regardless of one's opinion of J. Frank Dalton, this work should be recognized as an extremely rare firsthand account from someone that intimately knew J. Frank Dalton and his claims of being Jesse James. What follows is not a carefully laid out apologetic that will conclusively prove the case that J. Frank Dalton was Jesse James but what follows is a story from a southern lady that knew him well, and which may very likely reveal details that may be followed up on and researched as Bud Hardcastle has been doing for more than 40 years.

Regardless whether one believes that J. Frank Dalton was the outlaw Jesse James and regardless whether one appreciates the firsthand perspective of a twentieth century southern woman who dedicated her life to caring for a man she believed to be a living American legend, one thing is certain; like his forefathers before him, when Bud Hardcastle makes a promise and gives his word, it can be relied upon.

Dedicated to Ola May Everhart, her husband Aubrey for his help, patience and understanding while she was recording her memories, and to William A. Tunstill who helped with research and to the many friends who helped and encouraged her to keep going.

CHAPTER ONE

As I write this book, it is not to show that Jesse and Frank James were Outlaws. That fact has been known for years. Many, many books and movies have been written about them, their robberies and about the killing of Jesse James by Bob Ford.

To the best of my knowledge and ability, I will, in the following pages, share the first-hand account of J. Frank Dalton as told to Ola Everhart and recorded by her in her notes, which were given to me by her husband Aubry with the understanding I continue her research and tell her story. After almost forty years, I'm thankful that I can say it has now been done.

J. Frank Dalton claimed that the killing of Jesse James, in St. Joseph, Missouri on April 3, 1882 was a hoax. A hoax that enabled the real Jesse James to live almost 70 extra years. During which time he was a law-abiding citizen. Robert Sallee James, a Baptist Minister, married 16-year-old Miss Zerelda Dalton who, after the death of her father and her mother married a Mr. Cole, she and her sisters became known as "the Cole girls." Robert and Zerelda were both born and raised in Kentucky.

After their marriage, they lived for a while near Adairsville, Kentucky and it was there on January 10, 1843 that a son was born to them and named Alexander Franklin James. A girl was also born to them there and named Mary. Her exact birth date I don't know but, Jesse James told Ola Everhart that his sister Mary was a beautiful girl and was in the bloom of young womanhood when she died at the beginning of the War Between the States.

Robert and Zerelda went to Missouri to visit relatives and decided to leave Kentucky and move to Missouri. They settled in the little community called Centerville in a log cabin, which was common at the time. Centerville was the principal trade point for the surrounding country and boasted of about 250 inhabitants.

It was there on November 25, 1845 that another child was born to the family. A girl, named Susan Lavenia, called Susie. Then, on September 5, 1847, another child was born, a son, named Jesse Woodson James. Jesse told Ola, "I was named Woodson for my uncle Drury Woodson James, my father's youngest brother."

Robert James was a circuit riding preacher and also a farmer. Of course, they had slaves who did the farm work because the Reverend James was busy with his church work and was away from home a lot. Zerelda had a faithful slave woman who helped her in the house and with the four children. In 1849, when the gold rush hit in California, Reverend Robert James got the gold fever, and leaving his poor wife and the four children on the farm in the community of Centerville, Missouri, he climbed in the wagon with his friend Mr. William Sallee of St. Joseph, Missouri and went to California. Drury Woodson James lived in California and naturally the two brothers were together when Reverend Robert James reached there.

Travel and the mail was very slow in those days so it was some time before Zerelda heard from him. In fact, it wasn't until Mr. Sallee returned to Missouri three years later, which was 1851, and went to see Zerelda and the children that she learned that her husband had, so Mr. Sallee told her, died four months after they got to California. He was buried in an unmarked grave near Marysville, California in 1850. Jesse was not yet two years old when his father left home and went to California, so naturally he never remembered him.

After Reverend Robert James death, Zerelda married Benjamin Simms, a neighbor, on September 30, 1852. But that marriage didn't last long. He was too strict on the James children to suit Zerelda. Simms died not long after they separated and in September 1855, Zerelda married Dr. Reuben Samuel who was a native of Kentucky. They had four children. A girl, born December 26, 1858 named Sarah Lavenia Samuel; A boy, born December 25, 1861 named John Thomas; A girl named Fanny Quantrell, born October 18, 1863 and Archie Peyton born on July 26, 1866.

In 1858, Zerelda and Dr. Samuel bought a farm. The farm contained 350 acres of land and on it was a log house built in 1858. This farm is located about three and a half miles northeast of where Kearney, Missouri is now, on the Greenville Road. As of 1882, the house, a formidable but very unprepossessing structure, stood fully a quarter of a mile from the road. As stated earlier, it was built in 1858 of log but it was later weatherboarded. Frank James was 15, Susie was 13 and Jesse was 11 when Zerelda and Dr. Samuel moved there.

Approaching the house from the road, you opened a gate, followed a well defined path through a wooded pasture and over a small ridge which concealed the house from view, and passed through another gate into the yard proper. The house, a one-story and a half high in frame had an "L" containing three rooms in the rear, with a small pantry extending out from the farther end with a porch between the pantry and the main building and in front of the rooms in the "L".

The place was evidently put up with an eye to strength and protection. All sides were finished with loopholes put in after the war, after the style of the block forts in which the whites in the olden times used to keep a lookout for hostile Indians. Those appeared to be small apertures from the outside but investigation revealed the fact that they were made especially for business, being cut in the logs in the shape of triangles. One corner focusing on the small hole through the outer wall. The reason for this was obvious – it gave full sway for the movements of a rifle. For instance, a person on the inside, putting the rifle barrel through the hole and by moving the stock in the wide space which formed the base of the triangle is enabled to cover a wide range of the country on the outside without any chance of being hurt himself in case of a scrimmage.

Passing the front gate a yard distant, a distinct view could be had of the premises. The house fronts the east. A yard containing an acre of ground surrounds it, in which were located an ice house, smokehouse and chicken coop, and other outbuildings, a barn, which was comparatively new in 1882 and large enough to stall six horses, was located about a hundred yards northwest of the house and was the best building on the premises. A small branch ran through the

3

yard some seventy-five yards east of the house. From this description it would be seen that the casual observer would fail to see anything peculiar about the house other than in any ordinary farm house, and only a close inspection revealed the fact that it was well fitted to stand a regular siege.

It was in this farm home that the James children grew up with their mother and step-father Dr. Reuben Samuel. In 1868, when the Hannibal and St. Joe railroad was built through that part of Clay County, the town of Kearney was laid out, situated twenty-four miles northeast of Kansas City. Old Centerville was a quarter of a mile south of Kearney.

The new town was named in honor of Phil Kearney, and as of April 1882, contained 600 inhabitants. The principal street, in fact the only street, extended from east to west, and was lined with business houses on both sides, mostly frames, only one or two brick. The country surrounding was rick, fertile and beautifully rolling.

Many writers have written that Jesse Woodson James was born on that farm near Kearney. How could he have been when he was born in 1847 and the town of Kearny was not laid out until 1868? Jesse was 20 years old at that time, nearing 21. He was, just as he told Ola, born at Centerville, Missouri not Kearny, Missouri.

Preceding the War Between the States there was lots of trouble between Kansas Jayhawkers, the Red Legs and the people in Missouri. Missouri was a divided state, half Southerners and half Yankees. The Jameses and Dr. Samuel, of course, were Southerners. The Jayhawkers and Red Legs would come over into the southern side of Missouri and burn barns, steal cattle and horses and mistreat the womenfolk before running back to Kansas.

The War Between the States started January 21, 1861. Young Charles Hart, a school teacher, who was a native of Kentucky soon was to become known throughout the land. His desire was to stay neutral in the war but soon learned that wasn't to be. Some Yankees came to his house one night and wanted to know how he stood. His reply was, "Well gentlemen, I prefer to stay neutral and continue teaching school here."

They said, "Well you can't do that. You've got to state your allegiance."

So young Charles said, "Well, as you know, I am from Kentucky. I have a brother in the Confederate Army so naturally my allegiance is to the South."

So, the next evening they came back and by force took young Hart out on the street, tied him to a tree and beat him terribly. When he got over that, he was understandably very angry. He quit teaching school, changed his name to William Clarke Quantrell and, with the training he had received in Military School in Kentucky, put together an independent army of guerrilla raiders who fought for the South. Many of Quantrell's men were young but they were well trained, brave and were excellent marksmen and horsemen.

Much has been written about Quantrell and his men during the war. Some correct and some incorrect. They have been portrayed as cruel, savages and so on. To quote Jesse James, "It was war, and although some call it the Civil War, there wasn't a damn thing civil about it. It was war and war is hell."

Frank James joined Quantrell's outfit in 1861 at the age of 18. Jesse wanted to join but was told he was too young, so he stayed on the farm and helped with the field work. Jesse told Ola, "One day some Yankees came out to our place, mistreated my mother and step-father so bad, then came out in the field where I was plowing and wanted to know where Quantrell's men were camped. I told them I didn't know. I didn't but I wouldn't have told them if I had. They got mad as hell and one of them damn near beat me to death. Cut the blood out of my back with a whip. I went running to the house with blood running down my back. That picture you've got of me when I was 14 years old was taken in Liberty, Missouri, that's how I looked and how old I was when that damn Yankee damn near beat me to death. That was in 1862 before I was 15 years old in September."

It takes a big brave soldier to whip a 14-year-old boy like that who was out working in the field. Then Jesse said, "They came back to the farm one morning a while later. I was out in the field plowing. They asked me again where

Quantrell's camp was and about Cole Younger in particular. It was Cole's birthday and my mother was fixing him a nice birthday dinner because she knew if he could, he'd be coming by and could eat. When I told them that I didn't know where Quantrell's camp was, one of the Yankee's threw a rope around my neck and, pulling me half-running behind his horse out to the barn, threw the rope up over the hay lift and pulled me up, then they rode off. My mother was watching and as soon as they rode off, she ran out to the barn, cut the rope with a butcher knife, and helped me into the house.

"That happened like this morning, and it was late tomorrow evening before I really realized just how close to death I came. As soon as I was able, I got on my horse and went and found Quantrell's camp. I showed them and told them what had happened. So, on the 8th of March 1863 at the age of 15, Quantrell took me into his outfit. I was placed under the command of Captain Anderson. Bloody Bill Anderson. We went through a lot, but I can say this: Quantrell's men were the toughest group of men and boys that the Civil War produced. I was with Quantrell's outfit at the burning of Lawrence, Kansas. One of the damn Red Legs let himself down in a well that day to keep from getting shot."

Jesse carried the rope burn scars on his neck for the rest of his life.

Jesse said, "In 1865, I was riding a bay mule and a Yankee shot at me and hit me in the forehead. The only reason that it didn't blow the whole top of my head off was that it hit at a glance and the Yankee just didn't have the powder load strong enough. It knocked me out and the mule I was riding took me back to camp and stopped right in front of the camp.

"That was the only time I ever got shot that I didn't know anything about it. It didn't hurt much, just knocked me out and since then, I've had this sunk place in my forehead. I got out of Quantrell's outfit April 5, 1865 then the war closed April 9, 1865.

"I was leading several Quantrell men as we was riding into Lexington, Missouri to surrender. Some Yankee soldiers was there in town and one of them refused to honor the white flag of surrender that I was carrying, opened fire and shot me in my right lung and just under my right lung. An injury that caused me much suffering. Still bothers me at times. Has ever since it happened. It was quite some time before I was able to be up and about much after that. Governor Silas Woodson was the Governor of Missouri during the War Between the States. But from 1861 to 1865, the capital of Missouri was at Marshall, Texas."

Aubrey asked him, "Is it true that Quantrell had a black flag?"

He replied, "No! That story is definitely fiction. We fought under the Confederate Flag." Frank and Jesse were both young when the war was over. Frank was 22 and Jesse was not yet 18.

Jesse told Ola, "After the War Between the States ended, me and Frank wanted to and tried to come back home and live quiet, normal lives but we were Quantrell men and public sentiment wouldn't let us. We had to live some way, so we turned to outlawry. It's not the life to live. Not the life we wanted to live. Before we started into outlawry, me and Frank made a pledge to each other, that if one of us was killed, the one remaining would avenge his death and by golly we would have too.

"We were accused of a lot of things we never done. Of course, we done a lot of things we never got caught at too. If a bank or train was robbed in one state and we were in another, they'd say the James boys pulled the robbery. If two banks were robbed in two different places and we were miles away, the first thing that was said was, 'The James boys done it again!' We were accused of lots of things we never done and was nowhere around when and where it happened, but we got the blame just the same.

"It's mighty bad to be hunted like animals day and night. We holed up in the daytime and traveled at night sometimes. It was safer that way. When I slept, I slept on my back with my hands crossed across my chest with a gun in each hand.

"Our negro cook, John Trammcl, was a handy man and looked after the horses for me and my men. He was a good and faithful old man. I thought lots of him and tured him. I made it my business to see that old John had a farm near Guthrie, Oklahoma when he got old and that's where he lived out his life.

7

"When me and Frank got grown and after the War Between the States, we went out to California and stayed a while with my uncle Drury, my father's youngest brother, at Paso Robles. Drury Woodson James owned Paso Robles, California which lays on the old Spanish Trail, El Camino Real, half way between San Francisco and Los Angeles. His home was located at 939 Spring Street in Paso Robles. He owned a Spa and also owned a 30,000-acre ranch. The La Panza Ranch. Me and Frank worked on his ranch while we were there and I went to town regularly and took the hot springs baths at his resort hoping to heal the old gunshot wounds in my right lung. It did help me. We used our true names while we were at uncle Drury's. While we were in California, we tried our best to find our father's grave in or near Marysville, but we never could find it."

Jesse didn't say what year that was or just how long they stayed in California. From the research that William A. Tunstill and Ola conducted since 1981, it looks as if their father, Reverend Robert James didn't die as reported by Mr. Sallee. He deserted his family in Missouri but Frank and Jesse never knew it. So, it would be impossible to find a grave that was never there in the first place, wouldn't it? The boys really loved their mother and thought lots of Dr. Samuel. Jesse told Ola, "A better man than Dr. Samuel never lived."

Then thinking back, he said, "Back in my outlaw days I was riding along one day and when I got close to a creek, I heard a black man hollering down in the creek bed. There was a rise in the road and when I got up on it and looked down, I saw two white men whipping a black man something awful and he was begging for mercy." He didn't say just what he done or when and where; he just said, "Them men couldn't beat anyone else when I rode on."

Out from St. Louis, Missouri on the old highway between Flat River and Leadwood, Missouri in a little community called Mitchel and Gumbo, on highway 8 out of Flat River, was the old Blue Goose Saloon. Jesse used to speak of it often. That he used to go there and things that happened.

He said, "One time I was in the old Blue Goose Saloon standing at the bar drinking a drink of whiskey. There was a man standing on each side of me. I didn't know either one of them. But all of a sudden, one of them reached across me and cut the other one's throat. God-O-Mighty I got out of there mighty quick! I'll tell you that!

"I went to Arizona and lived with the Sioux Indians a while. They taught me how to take leaves and berries and made dye and dye my hair. I wore my hair real long and braided. Sometimes I dyed it brown, sometimes black and other times white. I always kept it real nice, neatly braided and wore the braids in different ways. Then sometimes I wore it short. I wore a false mustache at times and then at other times I'd cut my real mustache in different styles.

"In 1869 I went to Chicago and lived a while and while I was there, I joined the Masonic Lodge and the Odd Fellows Lodge. I am now a 33rd degree Mason." Then added, "But not under my real name, of course."

Ola asked, "What name did you join under?"

After a bit he replied, "Well, I was John Franklin."

He told Aubrey and Ola that he wanted to talk with some masons and some Odd Fellows too. He was in the hospital in Austin, Texas at the time due to a bad spell of pneumonia. So, on Saturday night October 7, 1950, Aubrey and Ola went out to the hospital to see him as they did every night and Allen Mozingo, his brother Cecil Mozingo and Ben Mewis, met them there. They all went up to Jesse's room. Allen was a Mason and when he got in the room and started talking with Jesse, he told him he was a Mason and gave his lodge number there in Austin, Jesse said, "I am a Mason, too. Masonic Lodge number 60, Chicago, Illinois and have been a Mason ever since 1869." Allen told Jesse what degree Mason he was and Jesse said, "I am a 33rd degree Mason."

After their talk and hand shake, Allen was very satisfied that Jesse James was just what he said he was, a 33rd degree Mason. Cecil Mozingo and Ben Mewis were both members of the Odd Fellow's Lodge in Austin, Texas. They walked up to the bed and started talking to Jesse, checking him to see if he really was an Odd Fellow. Ben told Jesse that he was an Odd Fellow and what lodge and lodge number.

Jesse said, "I am an Odd Fellow, too. Lodge number 24," and gave the name of some park in a suburb of Chicago, Illinois. "I joined the Odd Fellow's in 1869."

Then Ben started asking him the questions that are always asked when a person is being checked to see if they are a member. Jesse answered all of the questions and didn't have any trouble answering them. Ben was very pleased and said, "There is no doubt at all in my mind about this man being an Odd Fellow." In the room to hear the conversation between them was Cecil and Allen Mozingo, Aubrey and Ola.

Jesse and Ola were talking one day and he told her, "There was a Payne's Store in Missouri owned by Tom Payne. Tom married a Jones girl. Tom Payne's son married one of J.H. Taylor's girls. J.H. Taylor's brother Andrew Taylor came from Dallas County Missouri and is buried at Elmo, Texas, 10 miles from the Taylor home. Tom played the fiddle at the Taylor home with Bob and Jim Taylor. Tom Payne had a brother named George Payne and another named Ayers Payne. J.H. Taylor, whose wife was named Luiza, was a member of the James gang. Dick Sells was a member too."

There was a Real Estate agent in Austin, Texas whose name was Lloyd Payne. He called Ola one day and told her that he had a great-aunt who ran off from home and married a man who was a member of Jesse James' gang and they ever saw the aunt any more. Her name was Luiza. He said her folks would sit and talk and say, "Poor Luiza."

Ola told Lloyd Payne that she would talk to Jesse and then call him back. When she called back a few days later to talk with him about his great-aunt after she'd talked with Jesse, she learned that he had died of a heart attack a short time before.

While Jesse and Ola were talking one time he said, "In 1872, I went to Fort Smith, Arkansas and joined the United States Marshal for the first time as a Deputy Marshal. But I didn't stay in but about a year. I was John Franklin then too. Then I decided I wanted to be a doctor. J.J. McAlester, Chief Marshal at that time encouraged me, so I quit the force, went to Ann Arbor, Michigan and still using the name John Franklin, enrolled in medical school in the spring of 1873 at the age of 25. But I didn't stay long."

Before I go any further with this writing, I want to say that Ola was raised by the old school. She was taught from childhood that her elders were never called just Jim, Joe or John but aunt and uncle. So, although Jesse James was her third cousin, due to his age she called him "Uncle Jesse".

So, when he told her that he'd gone to medical school, she said, "Why Uncle Jesse, I didn't know you had studied to be a doctor. How come you quit?"

He looked at her, grinned and replied, "I couldn't stand the sight of blood."

They had a big laugh and then he said, "No honey, I soon realized I was not the temperament to be a doctor. So, I quit medical school, went over and enrolled in law school. I finished law school and passed the bar exam."

Ola said, "So, you are an attorney."

He replied, "Yes, I am, but I never did practice much." After a short pause he added, "Legitimately, that is."

Then he told Ola, "When I left Ann Arbor, Michigan, I went back to Fort Smith, Arkansas and, still using the name John Franklin, I went back on the Marshal force again and from then until the spring of 1874, I was a Deputy U.S. Marshal again under Chief J.J. McAlester."

In the spring of 1875, Jesse and Frank came to Texas. It is said, that on the 12th of May 1875, they robbed the Austin Stage Coach near Kyle, between Austin and San Antonio, Texas. Jesse neither confirmed nor denied it, so let the people think what they will.

He told Ola, "I went to Louisiana in the winter of 1875 and taught school at Calico Rock. I had a good many grown up pupils as well as children to teach in that school. Frank went over to Red Rock, Texas in Bastrop County and taught school. He stayed with some people there named Petty."

Then, he and Ola got to talking about some pictures of him and he said, "Ola, that picture you've got of me taken at Long Branch, Kentucky was taken in '73 or '75. I was 26 or 28 years old, can't remember exactly." He smiled and thought a minute or so then said, "There was another picture of me taken at the same time and there was a girl with me in it." He never said who the girl was or what became of the picture, just smiled when he told her about it.

He was thinking back to his days gone by and told Ola, "At first, we robbed banks before we went to robbing trains. But one time, back when I was an outlaw, me and the boys robbed a Stage Coach in Kentucky. We stopped the Stage, had all the passengers outside and was taking their money and jewelry. One of the passengers was a preacher and when I got to him, he said, 'Please don't take my watch. I'm a man of the cloth and I need it.' I looked at him and said, 'Why? The Lord didn't have a watch!' So, I took his watch."

Then he said, "We robbed the Nimrod Long Bank in Kentucky one time. I didn't know until after we'd robbed that bank that Nimrod Long had financed my father's way through Georgetown Baptist Seminary. But when I found out, I felt pretty bad about robbing it and I made it my business to see that the money was all returned."

He didn't say how he did it, just what he had done. Then he said, "That safe was not a combination safe. It opened with a key."

Another time while he and Ola were talking, he said, "Back in my outlaw days, I went to Brownwood, Texas. I went there fairly often because Bloody Bill Anderson, under whom I'd served while I was with Quantrell, lived a short distance from Brownwood and had for some time. Had a nice place there. And, Colonel James R. Davis and his wife lived there in town and had for some time. On one of these trips, I met Clay Allison there in town and while we were talking, I paid Clay for a horse that I'd killed of his father's some time before."

Jesse was very staunch about paying whatever he owed. There at Ola and Aubrey's house at 1103 East First Street in Austin, Texas they were talking with Jesse about back when he was young and a much-wanted outlaw he said, "One time we had stopped a train and while my men were robbing part of it, I was walking through the coaches taking the passengers' money and jewelry. I came to a seat where an elderly woman was sitting by herself and I said to her, 'Open your purse and give me your money!'

"She said, 'Mister, please don't take my money, I'm on my way to see my boy who was injured in the war and is in the hospital. I've just got barely enough money to get me there and please don't take it.'

"When she talked, I seen she was a Southerner but I said in a firm voice, 'I said open your purse anyway!' She did. I rammed my hand down in her purse, jerked it out, closed her purse right quick then walked away."

Then he looked at Ola and said, "Ola honey, she had a damn sight more money in that purse when she got off than she had when she got on."

In 1949, She and Jesse were talking one day in Austin, Texas about by-gone days and he said, "Ola honey there's been so many different stories told and written about me paying off the mortgage on the widow woman's farm, I'm going to tell you the straight of it."

She said, "Alright sir, I'd like to know."

He said, "Me and Frank and Cole Younger had been riding a good while and our horses needed water. So, when we came to this farm, we rode up to the windmill not far from the house, I got off my horse, went to the door and asked, 'ma'am can we water our horses?'

The woman said, 'Sure, help yourself.'

"While we were watering them, I heard somebody crying in the house and I told Frank and Cole, 'Something's wrong in that house. I hear somebody crying and I'm gonna go see what's wrong.'

"I went to the door, knocked and said, 'What's wrong lady? Can we help you?'

"She opened the door, I went in and she said, 'My husband was killed in the war. I don't have any money and the banker is coming out today to foreclose on the mortgage on our farm and I don't know what in the world me and my children will do.'

"Ola asked, 'How much is the mortgage on your farm?'

"She told me. I went out to the windmill, talked to Frank and Cole and between the three of us, we barely had enough money on us to pay off the mortgage. I took the money, went back to the house and said, 'Lady, we're gonna give you the money to pay off the mortgage.'

"She said, 'Oh but I don't know when I can pay you back.'

"I said, 'Oh you can pay it back when you and the children make a crop.'

"I set down at her table, wrote out a receipt then told her to copy it. She did, then I took the one I'd wrote out and destroyed it.

"I told her, 'Now don't you give that banker the money until he signs that paper. Which way is the banker coming from?'

"She told me and I went out, we got on our horses and as we rode off I told her, 'Now be sure you make him sign that paper before you give him the money.'

"There was timber and thick underbrush on each side of the country road. We rode down the road a ways, hid our horses behind some thick underbrush and just waited. After a while here come that damn banker and the Sheriff in a buggy. They went on by and we just waited. In a little while we heard them coming back. When they got even with us, we stepped out, stopped them and got all of our money back, plus a little extra for our trouble.

"They went on as soon as they could, of course, and then me and Frank and Cole got to talking. How could that woman make it and plant a crop without any money? So, we got on our horses, rode back to that farm, gave the woman some money then rode off. We never saw her again, but her and her children had a place to live and something to eat. We seen to that. And that is what happened and the way it was."

He didn't say when or where this was, just what happened. Ola always thought it was somewhere in Tennessee, but she didn't know for sure.

Jesse told her, "Ola, when the Pinkerton Detectives were called in to find and capture the James boys and their gang, particularly the James boys, Allen Pinkerton felt sure it would be easy and wouldn't take long to get the job done, but soon learned that he and his men were wrong.

"First and foremost, they didn't know how me and Frank looked and had no pictures to go by. We kept ourselves well disguised and therefore only relatives and close friends actually knew how we looked. Me and Frank have stood and talked to Pinkerton men. We knew who they was, but they didn't know who we was." Then after a bit he said, "They never caught us, but we caught several of them."

In 1949 when Jesse was in the hospital in Austin, Texas, he and Ola were talking one day. He got to thinking and talking about his outlaw days and said, "Them damn Pinkertons wondered a lot of times and so did the railroads, just how it happened that we always knew just which train was carrying money and which trains was decoys. What they didn't know was – we would ride into town in pairs, not in a group. We'd look the situation over. When the boys all got to town, I would take one of the boys, ride out of town a ways then I'd climb a telegraph pole, tap the line and read the Morse code. So, I knew what the train was carrying. I knew the Morse code well. The old Morse code, that is. Bring you some paper and a pencil when you come back out here to the hospital, Ola honey and I'll tell you the alphabet in Morse code."

So, the next day Ola did and he told her from A to Z. Much had been written about Jesse James robbing the Kansas City Fair. Well, the following is what Jesse James himself said about that robbery, while talking to Ola one day.

He said, "I had two good race horses and knowing there was going to be some races at the State Fair in Kansas City I took my horses and went to the fair. They would have some pretty good races, I figured. So, me, Frank and Cole Younger went. When we got there, they wouldn't let me enter my horses in the races and it made me as mad as hell, because I knew my horses was in good shape. So, I told Frank and Cole, 'By God I will get the money I could have won,' and me and Cole and Frank got on our horses and rode around to the entrance of the fairgrounds. I got off my horse, handed the reins to Cole and said, 'Wait here.'

"I walked up to the ticket window and said to the young man that was selling tickets, 'What would you say if I told you that I am Jesse James and to hand over that money box?'

He said, 'I'd tell you to go to hell!'

I said, 'Well that's just what I am saying!' And as I talked, I raised my gun, pointed it at his head and said, 'so hand over that money box and damn quick!' He handed it over when he saw my gun. I went out, got on my horse and we rode off. There was $10,000 in that money box. So, I got the money I could have won and a little extra besides."

He never said why they wouldn't let him enter his horses in the races. Just that they wouldn't. Jesse said, "Back in our outlaw days, me, Frank and our men were in the state of Louisiana riding along when we came upon some Yankee soldiers and learned that they were coming from New Orleans. And, that while in New Orleans, they had gone into a Catholic Church and stole a diamond-emerald studded gold cross from the church." He didn't say how he and his men managed to get the cross. Just that they did. And intended to return it to the church where it belonged. But they couldn't right then. So, they rode on to the little town of McCombe, near the Mississippi River and just a ways from there, stopped and buried the cross so they could come back later, dig it up and return it to where it had been stolen but they never got a chance to.

After Jesse came out with his true identity in Lawton, Oklahoma in 1948 he still wanted to go get that cross and return it, but he couldn't because of his age and a broken hip. In 1951 when he was there at home with the Everharts in Austin, Texas he told Ola, "Ola honey I sure would love to go get that cross and get it back where it belongs before I die." Bless his heart; he never got to fulfill that wish.

I'm sure you'd watched a western movie at one time or another and watched the posse trying to catch the train robbers. I have. So go with me if you will through the following. A fact, not fiction, that was told to Ola in 1949 by her third cousin, Jesse James, who was 101 years old at the time with a mind of a man 35 years old. They were talking and he said, "Ola, one time back when I was an outlaw, I had decided to rob a train. It was arranged where my men would wait until the time set for the job, where to meet the train and where to show up after the job was done. Then I got on my horse, rode on ahead to the town where the train would stop first after our job was finished.

"I was dressed in a dark suit, white shirt and tie and wearing a white linen duster over my clothes to keep them clean. Lots of men wore dusters those days to protect their clothes."

Just when and where this train robbery took place, he did not say. Just what he'd done. Needless to say, they never caught the James boys and didn't have any idea what they looked like.

A very good friend of Jesse and Frank James was Myra Belle Shirley. The daughter of Judge John and Elizabeth Shirley born February 5th, 1848 near Carthage, Missouri. They were Southerners. Judge Shirley operated Tavern near Carthage. Belle was almost 13 years old when the War Between the States started. The Shirleys were friends of William Clark Quantrell and his men and always made them feel welcome.

Belle wanted to do her bit for the South and she did. She delivered bullets and messages for the Quantrell men. The Yankees didn't suspect this young girl of being a messenger. She was pretty, she was an excellent rider, and she knew the country. She would go out close to the Quantrell camp and whistle to imitate a bird but incorrectly to let them know she was there. The important thing was to be sure the imitation was incorrect because if she'd done them correctly, others could work it.

Jesse told Ola, "In the latter part of 1864, Quantrell and his men came to Texas. It was the beginning of December when we reached Sherman, Texas and there was the bank broke into two segments. Part of them went to West Texas and the others went to Missouri. Except Frank and Quantrell. They went to Kentucky. I went back to Missouri."

Then he said, "Myra Belle was a wonderful person. I thought a mighty lot of her. She helped us a lot when I was with Quantrell during the war. She would bring messages to us and take messages for us. She was good with the signal we had worked out to whistle like a bird then one of us would go out to her and get the message or send one. She could ride like the wind and was brave.

"She saved my life one time. I had been shot, had lost a lot of blood but had managed to crawl and get to a little creek when I passed out. When I came to, I was in a room, in a bed and Belle was taking care of me. I found out from her that she had found me, had taken me to her house and tended to my wound. She was a wonderful woman, a wonderful rider and a good shot with a gun.

"After the war, Judge Shirley and Myra Belle moved from Missouri to Sherman, Texas. Us boys used to visit them there. Myra Belle was later known as Belle Starr. She owned a place on the Canadian River not far from Briartown, Indian Territory. A lot of us boys that was with Quantrell went to see her on her ranch there.

"Belle took some of her cattle to Dodge City, Kansas one time. The men that worked for her drove the herd and Belle rode in the chuck wagon. When they got to Dodge City, Belle told Blue Duck to sell the cattle so she could pay the men, while she went to town to do some shopping, then she walked off to town. When she got back to the wagon she asked Blue Duck, 'Did you sell the cattle?'

He said, 'Yes I did.'

She asked, 'Where's my money so I can pay the men?'

Blue Duck said, 'Well, I got in a poker game and lost all of it.'

That made Belle mad as hell. She said, 'That's my money and I'll get it!' She got her gun, went to the saloon and gambling place where he'd lost it, walked in and there was two men sitting at a table playing poker that had been in the game with Blue Duck a little bit before. She walked over to the table, pulled her gun and got her money back, plus a little extra for her trouble. I was standing across the street watching, just in case she needed some help. She went back to the wagon, paid the men then started in on Blue Duck and really raked him over. He sure didn't make that mistake again.

"I was on the ferry one time, crossing the Canadian River to Briartown, Indian Territory and I shot a button off an officer's coat. They said I done it deliberately, because I'd warned him not to follow me. But the lurching skiff caused me to miss him."

He didn't say who "they" was but Belle Starr lived near the ferry.

"In 1876, using the name Frank Dalton, I joined the U.S. Cavalry. Was in C – Company – 5th Regiment. I was in the troop that was sent to Custer, Montana to help General George Armstrong Custer. But we got there too late. Everybody was dead when we arrived. The Custer Massacre. June 25, 1876.

"Belle and Judge Shirley moved to Dallas, Texas. He bought a place out from town and lived there. Belle moved to Scyene, Texas where she owned and operated a Livery Stable. Scyene was then a suburb of Dallas. She was known for the elaborate clothes she wore, but lacking in women friends, though she always conducted herself as a lady.

"Bob and Jim Younger moved to Scyene and with them was their sister Henrietta who was the housekeeper and cook. All of them attended church and Bob sang in the church choir. Frank was working at a store in Wichita Falls, Texas and I was staying there at Belle's house.

"A Pinkerton Detective got to snooping around and I knew something had to be done. So, the Pinkerton man named Nichols was shot and killed. Belle told the folks that he was her husband. I left out and headed for the Indian Territory.

"Belle had seen that the Pinkerton man was buried then sold her Livery Stable and went out to the home of the Travis family at Lancaster, Texas. She stayed there for six weeks. They were close and longtime friends of Jesse and the Shirleys. Mrs. Travis had gone to school with Jesse in Missouri and knew that he was Jesse James."

Her son, DeWitt Travis, told Ola, "While Belle was there with us after Pinkerton Nichols was killed, she stayed six weeks then she got a letter from

Jesse. He told her where he was, so she caught the train and headed for White Horse, Indian Territory. Arriving there she went to a hotel and there met a nice-looking young man named Mr. Bruce Younger. He courted her and then they were married. A big wedding and a fancy one, there in the hotel lobby. Mr. Bruce Younger was none other than Jesse W. James."

In 1950, one time Jesse and Ola were talking when he was at home with her at 1103 East First Street in Austin, Texas. He got to talking about his outlaw days and though he didn't say just when or where the following occurred, just somewhere in Texas. Here's what did happen as he told it to her.

"Me and Frank had been riding quite a while. We were both getting pretty hungry and we knew our horses needed feed and water. We came to an old farm home, turned off the main road and rode up to the house. A young boy about 16 was out at the woodpile chopping wood and Ola asked him, 'Can we water our horses?' The young boy replied, 'Sure can. Help yourself.' He put his ax down and came over to where we were. While the horses was drinking I said to the young boy, 'Could we get some coffee and something to eat and some feed for our horses?'

"The boy said, 'My Pa has gone to town, but my Ma is in the house. I'll go get her.' He dashed in the house and came out in a little but with his Ma. I said, 'Ma'am, could we get some coffee and something to eat? We'd sure appreciate it.' She replied, 'Well we ain't got much, but you're welcome to it. So just come in. My boy will feed your horses.'

"We went in and then decided that while she was fixing our food, we'd go out and chop some wood, and did. The good was very poor and it was plain to see that the folks was pretty much against it. But we never let on, just looked around and ate what she offered. Not seeing any sugar on the table, Ola asked, 'Ma'am, could I have a little sugar for my coffee?' She said, 'You sure could if I had any, but I haven't got a bit. We're having a pretty hard time and I run out of sugar. Haven't had any sugar in a good while.'

"I said, 'That's alright, ma'am.' We finished our meal, thanked the lady for her kindness, got on our horses and rode off. We rode on to town, went to a grocery store and bought all the groceries we could put in two big feed sacks and a big sack of sugar, tied the sacks on our horses, got on and rode back to the farm house where we ate. We rode up to the front gallery, untied the sacks, put them on the gallery then got back in our saddles and rode off. One thing for sure, that woman had some sugar when we rode off. I seen to that."

Many, many writers have written over the years about the Northfield, Minnesota bank robbery that occurred on September 6, 1876 and they all say that Jesse and Frank James was in that robbery but that they got away. Well, while Jesse was at home with Ola in Austin, Texas one day they were talking and she said, "Jesse, I've read that you and Frank were both in that robbery at Northfield but both of you got away."

He said, "Oh honey, they write lots of things and they don't know anything about it. They are wrong. That was a Cole Younger project. Me and Frank was miles away from there. I was in Henrietta, Texas at that time with a leg injury and Frank was in Louisiana. No! Me and Frank was not in that robbery. They are all wrong and don't know what they're talking about."

While Jesse was at Meramec Cavern on Route 66 near Stanton, Missouri in 1949 he told Lester D. Dill, owner of the Cavern about how him and his men used to use the old Salt Peter Cave as a hide out, back in his outlaw days. Then, when he came back home to the Everhart house at 1103 East First Street in Austin, Texas in 1950, he told Ola, "Ola, me and my men used to use the old Salt Peter Cave as a hide out. It's called Meramec Cavern now of course, but it was originally called the old Salt Peter Cave back when I was young and an outlaw.

"One time after we'd pulled a robbery and they were after us, we headed for the old Salt Peter Cave and made it inside ahead of them. They figured we had to come out the same way we went in. So, they just waited at the entrance. What they didn't know was that there was a way out of the cave at the back. There was an opening just big enough for one man at a time on his horse to go through the passage way and out the opening. So, while the men were at the entrance, waiting for us to come out, we had gone out the other way and was long gone. There was brush around that opening so you couldn't see it and wouldn't know it was there.

I told Dill about the back opening us boys used. He just couldn't believe it. So, he hired some men to go around there where I told him, they cut all the brush down and found the opening. He never knew it was there until I told him. The men that was after us, wondered how we got out and got away, but never knew."

If you enjoy the western movies then I hope you'll find the following interesting. One time while he and Ola were talking, he started talking about the by-gone days and said, "Ola, back when I was an outlaw, we had robbed a train. The boys had gone on to our meeting place as arranged. All but me and Frank. We got on our horses and was riding in the opposite direction, going to a town when we met a posse of men coming toward us. When they got to us the Sheriff asked, 'Did you boys pass any strangers on the road as you was coming along this way?'

"I replied, 'No sir we didn't. What's the trouble? What happened?' The Sheriff said, 'Oh my God, the James boys robbed the train and we're looking for them! Would you boys like to join in and help hunt them?' I looked at Frank and we both said, 'Yes sir, we would.' So, Frank rode on the outside on one side of the posse and I rode on the outside on the other side. Ola, don't you know they'd have all dropped dead of fright if they'd known that the much-wanted James boys that they was looking for, was riding right along with them.

"Me and Frank rode where we knew we could take care of ourselves and each other, just in case we needed to. If any of the posse recognized us, they wouldn't have lived to tell about it because me and Frank were both good shots and fast shots. We'd learned that well while we were with Quantrell during the War Between the States. That posse never found the James boys of course and they didn't have any idea what they looked like."

He never told when or where this happened, just what happened. Another time, Jesse told about a tragedy that occurred in the James-Samuel family that embittered Jesse the rest of his life and understandably so. One night in January, 1875, some of the Pinkerton detectives sneaked up to the James-Samuel farm home and threw a homemade bomb in the window. The explosion of the bomb blew the right hand and part of the arm off of Jesse's mother and killed his little half-brother Archie Feyton Samuel who was only 8 years of age.

It takes big brave men to do such a cowardly thing with no consideration for the mother, the child and Dr. Samuel. They must have been thinking if it killed them all, so what. It had been written that the Pinkertons thought that Jesse and Frank were at home at the time and they were going to capture them. Really! Now in my opinion, if the Pinkertons had been as smart as they thought they were, they would have looked in the windows and listened a bit before throwing the bomb. Or did they want to get the entire family? The throwing of that bomb injured the mother the rest of her life and killed the innocent child, which made the Pinkertons murderers, pre-meditated.

Jesse told Ola about what happened and said, "Me and Frank were not at home at the time. As I told you, I was in Louisiana teaching school at Calico Rock and Frank was in Red Rock, Texas teaching school but when we heard about what happened at home we went home as fast as we could and when we got there and saw what happened we just went wild and killed every damn Pinkerton we could find."

CHAPTER TWO

The following was sent to Ola by her friend, Eugene Huff, who was born and raised in Missouri but then moved to Ohio. Mr. James Koger of Paducah, Kentucky, formerly of Nashville, Tennessee and now and then St. Louis, Missouri, said:

"Yes, I knew Jesse James – knew him rather well – for several years, beginning, if my memory be not at fault, in 1876. I made the acquaintance of Jesse James in Tennessee, when I was living in Nashville. I knew him in that city, and also in Humphrey's County, to the west where he lived for a couple of years on a farm in the bottom country.

"Of course, though, I did not know him as Jesse James. His name in Tennessee was Howard – J.D. Howard. Self-preservation was the pre-primary law of Jesse's life. All other laws faded and fell before that one. Jesse James was the most dangerous of all the border outlaws because he was the most desperately determined of them all to retain his life, which involved, in his case, retention of his liberty."

Mr. Koger told of an incident which, he thought, would serve to show "what a brave and fearless man" Jesse James was. "I think it was in the fall of 1878," said he, "when the State Fair was being held at Nashville. A handsome cash prize was offered in a competition to determine the most graceful rider. It was the gentlemen riders event. I recall that there were about thirty entries. I sat in the grandstand with thousands of others as the riders passed in front.

"Mr. Howard, mounted on his favorite horse, was one of the contestants, and he rode well up toward the front. Knowing him to be a most skillful rider, I took particular interest in watching him. The riders passed in review two or three times. When the event was over, I encountered Howard and asked him why he hadn't won the prize. 'Oh, I can beat any of these men riding,' he replied, 'but the judges had to give the money to one of these dudes.'

24

"Right under the eyes of the Nashville Police and Pinkerton detectives who were looking for Jesse James, to get the high reward offered! I think that was a rather remarkable exhibition of courage."

There can be no doubt that the adventure required a certain sort of courage. Jesse James frequently rode as his own jockey in horse races at county and neighborhood fairs, and sometimes he took the money. But in those instances, as at Nashville, a shrewd common sense is to be credited even more than the quality of courage. The outlaw knew that if he acted exactly like any ordinary citizen, he would be safer than if he acted otherwise. He knew that the detectives had no pictures of him and that none of them knew how he looked.

None of them would suspect that the notorious bandit would have the nerve to appear thus at a public event. For that matter, throughout his career, this man mingled with the general populace, wherever he happened to be, going and coming as other men go and come. In his way, Jesse was a wise man.

CHAPTER THREE

While Jesse and Ola were talking one time, he said, "In 1877, I was in Texas and I joined the Texas Rangers. I was stationed at Fort Concho at San Angelo, Texas. I was in Company C – Border Battalion."

"What name was you using?" Ola asked.

He replied, "Well, I was Benjamin Franklin Johnson."

Then he said, "In 1879, I was a Texas Ranger and war stationed at Abilene, Texas. Known at that time as Murphysville, Texas."

Ola asked, "What name was you known by then?"

He said, "Well I was known as Frank Dalton."

While they were talking, he said, "As I told you, in 1872 and using the name John Franklin, I went to Fort Smith, Arkansas and joined the U.S. Marshal force as a Deputy Marshal under J.J. McAllister, Chief Marshal at that time.

"Let me tell you, Ola. Fort Smith Court started in 1863. Powell Trakel was Judge for a while. But he really was a lawyer and not a judge. Fort Smith is located on the line of Arkansas, right outside of the Indian Territory and Isaac C. Parker "The Hanging Judge" was Judge for the Western District of Arkansas. There was railroad from Fort Smith to Little Rock, Arkansas that was built by convict labor. If a convict died or got killed, they just covered them up and kept right on working. U.S. Marshal Headquarters was at Fort Smith, Arkansas then. And still is."

Ola had finished feeding Jesse his breakfast one morning when he was there at home with them and after he'd finished eating and was relaxing a bit, he told her, "We were fixing to rob a train and took our time robbing it."

Then, looking at her, he grinned as he said, "Ola, you'll never know how shocked and stunned those passengers all looked as we were going through the coaches taking their money and jewelry. I still think about that and how amusing it was the way they looked."

That afternoon while they were talking, he told her, "I met Captain Thomason's son at Clay Allison's place near Red River on the Texas-Arkansas line and paid for a horse I killed of Captain Thomason's, some time before."

Jesse James lived at Kansas City in 1881 for a short time and occupied a house on the same block with the home of Con Murphy's father. Cornelius (Con) Murphy was County Marshal of Kansas City.

The Marshal would get his deputies together there every now and then, of an evening, and set out in search of Jesse James and his gang. Jesse got the habit of strolling over to father Murphy's on these occasions and asking Con how he was progressing in his search. Tradition has it that one night Con invited Jesse to go along and help catch Jesse James.

"No thanks," replied Jesse. "I'm kinda timid about such things, Mr. Murphy. But I'll set on my front porch, and if Jesse passes along maybe I'll recognize him. How does he look?"

"If I only knew," said the Marshal. "I might catch him. But that's just the trouble – nobody, who want him knows how the fellow looks."

Whereupon Jesse James smiled. It was his way of disarming suspicion, and it worked well. Jesse and Ola were talking one day and Ola asked him about his wife.

He said, "I married Zerelda Mimms in the Elms Hotel in Excelsior Springs, Missouri June 9, 1874. We were supposed to be married by my uncle, William James, but he couldn't get there. So, we was married by some preacher there in the hotel. My uncle William lived at Harlem, Missouri just across the river from Kansas City at the time. But sometime later, the river got up and washed the town of Harlem away. Zerelda died November 13, 1900 and is buried in Missouri."

In 1880, Jesse moved his family to Tennessee. They lived out at the edge of Nashville for a while and at this place they not only had a nice house but Jesse had a good place to keep his race horses and he fixed a nice track to train them on.

They then moved to Edgefield. East Nashville now, into a nice two-story house located at 711 Fatherland Street. Known as Jesse Howard at that time he traded at a store not far from where they lived and got to be friends with the store owners, Henry Priest and Wilson Waters. Jesse would come in the store, pick up a paper, look it over and call attention to a holdup that had taken place out in the west by the James boys. The next day or day after, he'd pick up the paper again in the morning and call attention to another holdup and say, "My, can't they get around fast." It would have been impossible to have gotten from one point to the other on horseback.

It was reported that Mr. Howard loved to play cards. One morning he came through. There was a string of stores, some four or five on Ridge Avenue at the time. "My store," said Henry Priest, "was fartherest from the river. And at the far end of it was a Livery Stable, and next door the old john Woods Saloon. Well, a young black boy come walking in from the Saloon and brought me a note. It asked me to loan Jess Howard a little money until he could go home. I didn't have that much money in my pocket of my own and I went to my partner Wilson Waters who was waiting on a lady, told him about the note and he said, 'Why Henry, take it out of the drawer and just make a ticket and put it in the drawer.' I turned to the boy and says, 'I'll be up there in a few minutes.'

"I took it up there, walked into the Saloon, into the back end, and then to the room to the left of it. I don't know for sure if there was four or five men sitting at the table but I think there was five. I walked up and Jess was sitting at the table. I touched him on the arm and he just turned his head and I handed the money to him. He says, 'Thank you.' I was on one side, he stuck it in his vest pocket and took his cards back in both hands. Set there a minute or two and he points across the table at one of the men and says, 'Don't you cheat that way anymore. Now don't repeat that!' It had been reported that he wouldn't play with you if you cheated. He says, 'Don't you cheat that way anymore!'

"They reached out and pulled the money off the table. But his hand moved and when it did, there was a blue-barreled pistol dropped across his lap. I don't know where it came from, but I never saw a man draw a gun so fast in my life! It made me commence to sort of back off. Well, they commenced to play on around then and the next time that hand was played out, he reaches out and pulls the money in. Well, I stood there, I suppose, five or ten minutes then went on back to my store.

"Oh, I suppose in half an hour or such matter, maybe longer, he comes walking in and says to Wilson Waters, 'Where's Henry?' Wilson just pointed at the back of the store. I was back in the office. He came right back to the office and gave me that money. As far as I could say, it was the same money. I don't believe he had ever unrolled it."

Frank and Annie lived there in Nashville under the name of Ben Woodson but Frank was called Buck. Him and Jesse would meet there at the store and visit. And, Frank used to visit Jess there on Fatherland Street. Bob Ford visited, or come there sick and was there at Howard's several weeks before they moved. He was about an 18 or 20-year-old boy. Mr. Priest, when asked in 1950 if Jesse James was the same man he knew in Tennessee, he replied, "Well, I believe it is, yes sir."

Frank James married Josephine Welch the first time. They had one daughter, born December 29, 1872 in Vinita, Indian Territory and named Mary Plina James. She was Frank's only daughter. Mary died in 1952. They had a son who was named Alexander Franklin for his father but called "Little Frank".

In 1881, Jesse moved back to Missouri and settled for a while at Excelsior Springs. Thomas T. Crittenden, whom Jesse had known for a good while, was running for Governor of Missouri on the pledge, "to rid Missouri of Outlawry." Jesse said, "I knew if I could help him get elected, he would listen to what I had to say. So, I contributed $35,000 to his campaign. Me and my family was living there in Excelsior Springs when he won the election."

In April 1881, Jesse decided to move to Nebraska. He read an ad in a newspaper about a farm that was for lease or sale near Lincoln so he wrote the man a letter regarding the ad and then changed his mind and decided to move to St. Joseph, Missouri.

Jesse said, "I went over to St. Joseph and rented a house at 1318 Lafayette Street. The rent was $15.00 a month and I paid two months rent in advance. I owned two good race horses and I was preparing to enter them in a forth coming race and rented the house so I could keep them in the stables.

"I went to Kansas City, Missouri one day and while there, I saw Charley Bigelow. We'd first met when we were in Quantrell's Outfit. I was with Bill Anderson's outfit and Bigelow was with Captain George Steiger's outfit for a short time, but not very long. The next time we met was in the suburban town of Memphis, Tennessee. When we met again in Kansas City, Bigelow told me that he wanted to go to St. Joseph, but had no place to live. I told him that I'd rented a house there, paid two months rent and that he could take his family and move in there and stay until he could find him a place. So, he took his family and moved there in that house on Lafayette Street but I reserved the stables for my horses.

"Bigelow was about the same size and age of me, and resembled me a great deal. Fact of the matter, he looked enough like me to be my twin. He was related to the Bigelow that the town of Bigelow, Missouri was named for. Charley Bigelow and his wife had two children, a boy and a girl about the same size and age as my two children.

"Charlie Ford had come to St. Joe when the Bigelow's did and was living in the house with them under the name of Charlie Johnson and a short time later, Bob Ford came to St. Joe and he too stayed at the Bigelow's, known as Bob Johnson. He was a young boy only 20 years of age.

"Old Bigelow was an outlaw. He was a member of the Slade gang. He paraded sometimes under my name. He'd do things and say he was Jesse James. In St. Joe, he was known as "Mr. Howard", but his actual true name was Charley Bigelow. Then he joined Pinkerton's and there I was with a price on my head. A $10,000 reward was offered for Jesse James – dead or alive."

After the Blue Cut train robbery in Missouri, Conductor Hazelbacker, in an interview with a reporter with the Kansas City Times on September 8, 1881, stated that he did not think the leader of the gang was Jesse James. Though the robber kept declaring he was.

A friend of Ola's, Mitchell Graves, worked for Jesse on Jesse's ranch in Canada. Mitch told me that Mr. Dalton, as Jesse was known there, was a mighty fine man to work for. They became very good friends. He said Frank Dalton seemed to know all about the James gang and could name them all, which he wondered about and thought how strange that he knew all of them. Then he read about Frank Dalton being the real Jesse James and he understood.

Jesse told Mitch about the Pinkerton's pulling a bank robbery in a town, passing themselves off as the James gang and when they didn't get any money, Bigelow, passing himself as Jesse James, shot a small boy on their way out of town. Jesse also told him how the Pinkerton's used to burn and steal and blame it on the James gang. This, they thought would make the people angry at the James gang so they would turn the James gang in to the Pinkerton's.

Mitch told Ola, "Yes, I saw the scar on Jesse's left shoulder, plus a few more. He didn't tell me how he got them. He did tell me about the James boys castrating some of the Pinkerton's for raping girls and trying to put the blame on the James gang. He said some of the Pinkerton's got down on their knees and begged not to be castrated, but it did not do them any good."

On July 4, 1881, the town's leaders in St. Joseph, Missouri was getting a parade together. Ozark Jack Berlin, who was also known by Jesse to be Pres. Webb, a good and longtime friend and another good and longtime friend who would later be known as Brushy Bill Roberts, who was also known by Jesse to the real Billy the Kid, was in town visiting with Jesse that day. One of the town's leaders asked Jesse, who was known as Mr. Thomas Howard, if he would like to ride in the parade and help swell it.

Jesse replied, "Yes sir!"

So, as the parade moved slowly down the main street, there riding along, was the much-wanted Jesse James with a price on his head and on each side of him was Brushy Bill and Ozark Jack, while the Pinkerton's and other laws were as busy as bees looking for him. But they didn't know how he looked. There he was, well dressed and gave the appearance of a well to do cattle buyer, with no thought by the on-lookers of him being the much-wanted outlaw and that under his nice dress coat that reached almost to his knees, which was the apparel of the well-dressed gentleman of that day, was a shoulder holster holding a fully loaded pistol.

The yard behind the house there on Lafayette Street was sort of down grade from the house to the stables and behind the stables was pretty heavy timber. So, on the night of April 2, 1882, the much-wanted Jesse James had a secret meeting with Governor Thomas T. Crittenden. They sat on a log in the woods behind that house and had a confidential talk for more than an hour. Colonel James P. Davis sat on a log a short distance away and kept watch, to make sure that they were not seen or heard.

On the morning of April 3, 1882, Jesse was out in the stables looking after his racehorses. Bob and Charlie Ford were in the house and in a little bit a shot was fired. Jesse told Ola, "I knew it wasn't a firecracker. I ran in the house and there was Bigelow on the floor deader'n a mackerel. I said to Bob, "Well Bob, looks like you killed him."

He said, "Looks like I did, Jess."

I said, "Bob, you tell 'em it's me and take care of Bigelow's wife and kids. I'm gone!"

Word spread like wildfire that Robert (Bob) Ford, who was using the name Bob Johnson at the time, had just killed the much-wanted Jesse James and soon the house and yard was covered with people. A man who knew the real Jesse James, was working on a house not far away. He heard the shot, rushed to the house, went in, looked at the dead man and knew it wasn't Jesse.

Jesse told Ola, "Those who knew me, kept their mouths shut. Those who didn't, accepted the man that was killed as being Jesse James. So I, Jesse James, was officially proclaimed dead. Shot by Robert (Bob) Ford on April 3, 1882."

While talking with him about that killing of Bigelow, Ola said, "Jesse, in books and movies, it always shows Jesse James stepping up on a chair to straighten or dust a picture when he was shot. Sometimes in the picture, there's a house and the words 'Home Sweet Home' and other times a horse or some other picture."

He replied, "Yes, I know, and that's all wrong. That house in St. Joe had ceilings so low, that I could stand on my tip-toes and reach up and touch them. So why in the world would I stand on a chair? If there was ever a picture on the walls of any kind, I didn't know it. Of course, I wouldn't, because as I told you before, I never lived there myself."

Ola said, "Well, I've always thought that that house looked a lot like the O. Henry Home in Austin, according to a picture I have of it."

He said, "You're right. It did a whole lot. But the ground sloped. There was quite a slope from the house to the stables."

Ola asked him, "What about this story I hear and read so much, about one finger on one of Jesse James' hands being cut off or missing for some reason?"

He replied, "Oh, they write a lot of things and don't know what they're writing about."

Ola asked, "Did Bigelow have a finger missing or part of one?"

He said, "Yes, Bigelow had almost the first joint of his first finger missing on his left hand. And the strange thing about it, is, that I've got a bad finger too. My first finger on my left hand is buggered up, but not any of it is missing. The damage to my first finger was due to me fooling with an old pistol when I was very young. That's one of my identification marks."

Charlie Ford was in the room with Bob when Bigelow was shot but Bob had done the killing. They went and turned themselves in and were placed in jail.

Jesse's mother, Zerelda Samuel was notified and went to St. Joe as quick as she could after she received the telegram.

Bigelow's body was taken to the Seidenfadden Funeral Parlor. When Mrs. Samuel arrived, went in and looked at the body, she said, "No gentlemen, this is not my son." She was taken out of the room, talked to by Colonel James Davis and told to identify the dead man as her son Jesse so he could have a chance to live a different and better life with no price on his head. So, she went back in, looked at the body again, broke down and cried, saying, "Oh yes! That is my boy Jesse!"

Jesse told Ola, laughing as he talked, "My mother just hadn't been briefed quite enough and she almost gave the whole thing way. So, she had to be taken out and briefed some more. She was a good actress. She just cried and carried on."

So much has been written about what took place between the 3rd and the 6th of April that I won't go into that. I will say that those who knew the dead man was *not* Jesse James the outlaw kept their mouths shut and those who didn't had nothing to tell and accepted the dead man as being Jesse James. Not a lot of people at the time knew that two of the main identifiers of the body as being Jesse James were two Quantrell men who had served with Jesse during the War Between the States and not only knew the dead man was not Jesse, but knew it was Charley Bigelow who had been with Quantrell a short time. Their names were Harrison Trow and Wild Henry Roberts. Wild Henry was the father of William Henry Roberts, later known as Brushy Bill Roberts, but who in truth and fact, was the real Billy the Kid.

Few people knew that the real Jesse James was downtown listening to the people. He was watching their reaction and listening to what they said. Folks from miles around were coming to town. Few people knew that Frank James, still a much-wanted man, was also down on the streets watching and listening and a number of Quantrell men were in town.

After Bigelow's body was placed in the coffin, Frank James, disguised as the best looking and most perfect looking undertaker you can imagine, with a Quantrell man on each side of him, walked in the Funeral Parlor and stood by the coffin a good bit looking at Bigelow. The smaller of the two men with Frank was none other than Fletcher (Fletch) Taylor.

At the inquiry, when the wife stated that the dead man was her husband, she was telling the truth. But, when she said that she was Mrs. Jesse James and that the two children were Jesse's, she wasn't. The truth is, Jesse's wife and two children were not even in the state. They were with some friends in Nashville, Tennessee visiting at the time.

When Mrs. Bigelow was asked, "Which one of your husband's fingers had part of it missing?"

She replied, "I don't know."

Then when she was asked, "How long were you married?"

She replied, "Seven years."

Now isn't that unusual that a woman was married to a man seven years, he had part of a finger missing and she didn't know which finger? It was his first finger on his left hand. Jesse had a buggered-up first finger on his left hand too but just buggered-up, none missing.

When he was just a young child, he got ahold of an old cap and ball pistol there at home, pulled the trigger and messed up the end of his finger and the fingernail. When it happened, he grabbed his finger and said, "Dingus! Dingus! Dingus!" Thinking he was saying "Damnit!" So, for a short time afterwards the family called him "Dingus", in fun.

On April 5, 1882, when excitement was high about the killing of the supposed Jesse James a Gazette Reporter wrote about Jesse James' body – that a well-known man on the corner of Fifth and Felix Streets in St. Joe that day had stated, Jesse James' body would be worth a fortune for display purposes.

No photographs of the mature Jesse Woodson James were available to the public before he was killed. Now, as there was no mature photographs of him available to the public before he was killed they didn't know how he looked. So only Jesse, his kin and close friends, which included the Governor, knew that the dead man was not Jesse James but Charley Bigelow, who had been claiming he was Jesse James and that the boy that done the killing was Jesse's cousin.

On the 5th of April, the funeral train carrying Bigelow's body, Mrs. Bigelow and her two children and Mrs. Samuel, Jesse's mother went from St. Joe to Kearney, Missouri where the body was placed in the Kearney House until the next day and on April 6, 1882 the funeral service was held at the Baptist Church. The church was so full of people that many of them had to stand and the yard was full of people. Among the coffin bearers, or pallbearers if you will, was J.D. Ford, Charles Scott, James Henderson, J.T. Reed, and William Bond. The sixth was a man whom no one had seen until just as the procession was about to start; he then came forward, his countenance stern, his eyes bright and piercing. Moving to the head of the casket he directed the movements of the others quietly, dumbly, yet with a countenance sad and commanding. His apparent age was about forty years, but his lithe, muscular figure seemed to deny such age. The real Jesse James was the sixth pallbearer. The Coroner refused to sign a death certificate for Jesse James. Then Jesse decided to sing at the funeral, and did, while Colonel Davis stood at his back to protect him. In the vast crowd at the church were several Quantrell men.

When the funeral service started, the Reverend R.H. Jones of Lathrop, Missouri read the passages from the book of Job beginning with "Man that is born of woman is of few days and full of trouble." He also read two verses from the thirty-ninth Psalm beginning, "Lord, make me to know mine end." After a fervent prayer by Reverend Jones the funeral was preached by Reverend J.M.P. Martin, pastor of the church.

Jesse told Ola, "You know Ola, that preacher said so many nice things about Jesse James, I could hardly believe he was talking about me."

Jesse's mother had the preacher announce, at the close of the funeral, that due to her boy John Samuel being so bad off at home and not expected to live, that she requested that nobody but relatives and close friends go out to the farm where the body would be buried in the yard near the coffee bean tree. John Samuel was Jesse's half-brother. What she didn't tell them was that Frank was out at the house and he was also a wanted man at the time. There was quite a good many Quantrell men at the burial and all of them armed; just in case anything went wrong.

Bigelow's body was buried in a grave that was eight feet deep instead of the customary six feet. After the friends and relatives left, then Jesse, after suggesting the wording to be put on the tombstone at Bigelow's grave, he and Frank went to Kansas City and with Bob and Charlie Ford in the adjoining room, they all spent the night in the Blossom House Hotel across from the depot.

Stop and think! You know that no man alive would spend the night in a hotel in an adjoining room to the man that had shot and killed his only full brother just a few days before. Particularly Frank James. For him and Jesse had pledged to each other that if either one of them was killed. The one remaining would avenge his death.

The next morning Jesse and Frank, Bob and Charlie Ford all walked over to the depot and Jesse caught a train and went to St. Louis, Missouri. From there he went to Memphis, Tennessee and then to New Orleans, Louisiana where he caught a boat and went to South America.

Jesse told Ola, "I went to the Argentine, stayed a while then went to Brazil. Fact of the matter, I went just about all over South America before returning to Texas."

Then he said, "When I came back, I went many places, done many things and I changed my name as often as I changed my shirt but I used the name Dalton, more than any, for that was my mother's maiden name."

Ola asked him, "How long did you stay in South America?"

He said, "I stayed there about a year or a little over. About a year and a half. I was in Buenos Aires in the Argentine a while and just about all over South America before I come back.

CHAPTER FOUR

In the April 7, 1882 issue of St. Joseph, Missouri Herald Newspaper, the following was published under the heading:

A Recent Midnight Ride

On the way down to the Samuels place, two weeks ago, Jesse James and Charlie Ford discovered one night, a short distance ahead of them, a party of horsemen. Without pausing for a consultation, Jesse commanded Charlie to draw his weapons and fall in behind him. He then put spurs to his horse and galloped forward, Charlie following closely at his heels. Just before overtaking the party, the latter turned aside and began to dismount at a farmhouse. Perceiving at a glance that they were innocent farmers boys, who had probably been out on a lark, Jesse dashed into their midst, and reeling in his saddle, called out,

"Hello, boys, don't you want something to drink? We've been over to Plattsburg. Excuse us, fellers, but we're drunker'n hell." Without waiting for a reply, he reeled, wheeled about and both dashed away in the darkness, whooping and yelling until they had passed out of hearing of the party, when they relaxed their speed and rode quietly on, neither mentioning the circumstances. Jesse was capable of assuming any disguise on the shortest notice and acting out any character to perfection. He had a keen sense of humor, and delighted to humbug people with whom he came in contact. He took special pleasure in engaging people in conversation and by adroit questions ascertaining their opinion of the James gang.

The real Jesse James had already left for South America when a nice tall white marble tombstone was placed at Bigelow's grave and on it was the wording: "In Loving Remembrance of My Beloved Son, Jesse W. James, Died April 3, 1882,

Age 34 Years, 6 Months, 28 Days, Murdered by a Traitor and Coward Whose Name Is Not Worthy To Appear here."

Jesse's mother planted flowers on the grave so if anybody bothered it, they would have to bother the flowers.

At St. Joseph, Missouri, April 17, 1882 – That morning the indictments came down against Charles and Robert Ford, charging them with the murder of Charley Bigelow who was passed off as being Jesse James. Robert was charged with murder in the first degree. It was the usual legal form. The indictment against Charles charged him with aiding and abetting his brother in the murder. The documents were handed to the Clerk at 11 o'clock, and a little before 12, the two boys were brought into court. The courtroom was well filled with spectators. Among them was Captain Ford, brother of the boys. At 12 o'clock Prosecuting Attorney Spencer arose and read the indictments and when he asked, "What plea do you make?" Both boys said, "Guilty". There was a hush in the courtroom for some moments. Finally, Judge Sherman spoke, "Under the circumstances" said he, "there is only one thing I can do and that is to pronounce sentence here and now. You have pleaded guilty to murder in the first degree and it only remains for me to carry out the provision of the law. It remains for others to say whether the sentence is carried out. Robert Ford, stand up."

Robert did as commanded.

"Have you anything to say why sentence should not me pronounced upon you?"

"Nothing," responded the prisoner.

"Robert Ford, you have pleaded guilty before the court to the crime of murder in the first degree, and it becomes my duty to pass the sentence of death upon you. It is therefore the sentence of this court that you be taken to the Buchanan County jail and there safely kept until the 19th day of May, 1882, and at that time to be taken to some convenient place and hanged by the neck until you are dead."

The same sentence was passed upon Charles Ford and then the two were taken back to jail.

Jefferson City, Missouri, April 17, 1882 – The Governor issued unconditional pardons that afternoon to Robert and Charles Ford, having received a telegram from St. Joseph that they had been convicted and sentenced for the killing of Jesse James.

From the *Sedalia Dispatch*:

Jefferson City, Missouri, October 5, 1882 – This evening at half-past 4 o'clock Frank James came boldly into Jefferson City and surrendered himself to Governor Crittenden. A reporter of the Sedalia Dispatch was early upon the grounds and had a brief but satisfactory interview with the redoubtable outlaw. He is in perfect health for one who has been wounded seventeen times. Shot three times in the mouth, there is a slight scar on the lower lip, which a long, fair mustache hides, and he is minus some eight or nine teeth. He is a little bald, but not from age, being now only thirty-eight. As has been always truly said of his great physical endurance, he can today, he says, ride further and faster, and do with less food and sleep, than any other man in Missouri.

He is 5 feet 11 inches tall, of very slender build, and having a tired and care-worn look. He is soft spoken, very interesting and intelligent in conversation, a good listener, quite deferential, cool and calm as a statue, and the quickest and deadliest man in a personal encounter between the two oceans.

While in conversation with Governor Crittenden, Frank unbuckled his belt, containing a Remington revolver, caliber 44, and 42 cartridges, handed them all to Governor Crittenden and remarked: "Governor, for the first time in 21 years I now permit another man to take my pistol. It is the happiest moment of my life. I feel freer, and braver, and better today than I have ever felt before since 1861. If you will, I would like for you to keep this pistol and belt as a gift from me. Each has a history. One day, if I am spared, I will give it to you so truthfully as I can recall it. That belt was captured in open fight at Centralia. That pistol after its owner had shot me through and through, was taken from him before I fell. I am now unarmed and your prisoner. I have trusted you as I have never yet trusted any man. Do with me what you please."

Governor Crittenden was evidently touched by the brave, simple faith of this notorious outlaw – a man who probably in all his life never knew the meaning of the word fear and who, as a soldier or otherwise, was capable of the most desperate deeds of daring known to human fortitude and courage.

The Governor accepted the pistol and belt and said to James: "You shall have every protection afforded by the laws of your country, and as fair a trial as though you were the son of a President."

Private Secretary Farr asked Frank why he carried a Remington revolver instead of a Smith and Wesson or a Colt's.

"Because," said Frank, "the Remington carries exactly the same cartridge that a Winchester rifle does. My armament was two Remingtons and a Winchester rifle. The cartridges of one filled the chambers of the other. You can now see why I prefer the Remington. There is no confusion of ammunition here. When a man gets into a close, hot fight with a dozen men shooting at him all at once, he must have his ammunition all of the same kind."

Governor Crittenden sent Frank James that night at midnight to Independence, Missouri, in the charge of his private secretary, F.C. Farr. The Governor also telegraphed Prosecuting Attorney Wallace, of Jackson County to meet the party at Independence the next morning. Secretary Farr went with Frank to turn him over to civil authorities.

Independence, October 6, 1882 – The end has come at last, and Frank James is in jail in this town, awaiting a preliminary hearing before Judge H.P. White, of the Criminal Court. That probably will not be for several days.

James' trip to Independence was probably one of the most remarkable trips ever witnessed. At every stopping place along the road great crowds had congregated to see the famous outlaw. Men, women and children crowded into the aisles to look at him, while hundreds of others stood on the outside at the *windows and devoured him with eager looks. Many rushed forward and grasped his hands, and many a hearty and heartfelt prayer went up for his acquittal. Only one man on the route knew him, Milton Wayman of Lafayette County, a brother of Matt and Luther Wayman, who were guerrillas with him. He called out to him, on a cheery voice, as the train was halted at Lee's Summit, "How are you, Frank? We are all friends up this way." Frank responded: "Tell George Maddox to come see me if I am alive."*

There were three indictments against Frank James in Jackson County. Colonel John F. Philips and Honorable Charles P. Johnson will defend him.

(Special to the Republican)

Gallatin, Missouri, September 6, 1883 – The jury in the Frank James case were given the case at 12:30 today and came into court after four hours deliberation and rendered a verdict of acquittal on all counts.

The Acquittal

Special Dispatch to the Globe-Democrat

Jefferson City, Missouri, September 6, 1883 – A few minutes after 4, the Court reconvened and it being announced that the jury had agreed, the defendant and jurors were sent for. After the usual questions, the foreman handed a verdict to the Court. It read:

"State of Missouri vs. Frank James – murder: We, the Jury, in the above-entitled cause find the defendant not guilty as charged in the indictment.

(Signed) William T. Richardson, Foreman."

Frank James stood trial at Gallatin, Missouri, and after a most noted legal contest, resulting in his acquittal; he settled down and became a law-abiding citizen of his Native State.

After Frank James was placed in Jail in Independence, Missouri a number of men went to visit him while he was there and the jailor, knowing how Frank liked shows about Shakespeare, took Frank out of jail, downtown to the theatre then took him back to jail.

CHAPTER FIVE

Ola asked Jesse if bob got the reward money for killing Bigelow and he said, "Bob got less than $500.00 of the reward. The rest trickled back into Governor Crittenden's pockets."

In 1884, after Frank was a free man and Jesse was back from South America, they went to Searcy County, Arkansas near the town of Marshall. As Ola recalled, their sister Susie and her husband Allen Parmer was living there at the time and Susie was teaching school. Allen Parmer, a native of Missouri, was also a member of Quantrell's outfit with Jesse and Frank.

Jesse and Ola were talking one time and he said, "In 1886, I was a Texas Ranger again and was sent to Killeen Texas to help straighten out a situation there. I was on the train with Sheriff White of Killeen. He met me at Copperas Cove, Texas and we rode on together to Killeen so he could brief me on the situation. When we got there and stepped off the train, Sheriff White was just ahead of me and just as he stepped down, he was shot right between the eyes by a man. The man ran behind a building nearby.

"There was a clearing between that building and another one close by and I knew that the man would make a break for that building in a little bit because it was the only way out for him. So, I watched and a few minutes later when he made a break for that building, I shot and killed him in the clearing before he reached the building.

"I didn't stay at Killeen long; about two or three months. By the time I left there, it was perfectly safe for people to walk down the streets without worry.

When I left Killeen, I went to Brownwood, Texas and stayed a short time with Colonel James Davis and his wife. They were living there then and of course I also went out to see Bloody Bill Anderson. He lived out in the country from Brownwood."

Ola asked him, "What name was you known as when you was a Texas Ranger there at Killeen?"

He said, "Well, I was Benjamin Franklin Johnson."

In 1887, and part of 1888, Jesse was in and out of Butcher Knife, Indian Territory a good bit. He was also in and out of Ardmore, Indian Territory and surrounding area which was the Chickasaw Nation. Butcher Knife was located on Mudd Creek, and was known as the home of the Outlaws at that time and it was mighty rough around there. (The name of the town was later changed to Atlee.)

In 1888, Jesse made the run for land during the opening of the Indian Territory. On October 5, 1888, James Anderson (Toby) Underwood, his wife Savannah and two children, Bertha (5) and Waco (3), stepped off the train in Ardmore, Indian Territory from Henry County, Tennessee near Cottage Grove. Ola's grandfather J.A. (Toby) Underwood was Jesse James' first cousin. Their mothers were sisters.

Toby took his family to a hotel there in Ardmore and then set out to find a job and a place for his family to live. He had raised tobacco in Tennessee but in the Indian Territory it was different. He did get a job, however, working for the Freeman brothers, taking care of their horses and moved his family out to Butcher Knife into one room in the Freeman home. They didn't stay there long enough, because Toby soon saw it was rough there for his family, which Jesse knew. So, with the help of some of his kin by the name of Akers, he moved them over in the Arbuckle Mountains not far from Woodford, Indian Territory, into a one-room log cabin with two oxen, he set about farming there. They were the 7th white family to settle in the Chickasaw Nation.

John Shevlin, former U.S. Marshal and one of the west's leading peace officers revealed some details to the *Police Gazette* about the deadly pay off of Ford. Frank James had publicly vowed, after Jesse's supposed slaying, to "get" Jesse's killer. But Shevlin saw Frank and Bob hobnobbing intimately in 1889 at Colorado City, Colorado seven years after Jesse's supposed death.

John and Mrs. Shevlin were in town in Colorado City and he pointed out two men to her. She said, "He told me they were Bob Ford and Frank James," and said, "that's a queer one all right. It makes me wonder." She said, "John told me that Jesse and Frank both had vowed that if either of them was slain, the other would avenge his death."

John said, "I can't imagine Frank consorting and hobnobbing with Ford. It just doesn't make sense."

In 1948, when Jesse came out with his true identity in Lawton, Oklahoma; John Shevlin came to Lawton to see him and Jesse confirmed to John while they were talking in Jesse's Motel room, that Frank and Bob were not only friendly but they were partners in the operation of the Grove Theatre in Colorado City, Colorado.

Aubrey and Ola were in the motel room visiting Jesse in Lawton when John Shevlin arrived from Chicago, Illinois.

CHAPTER SIX

(from a letter written to James O'Neal by Calamity Jane)

November 30, 1889

Dear Jim:

I now take my pen in hand to let you know your last letter came in due time. I am sorry you let Janey take that trip alone. You can't lie to me Jim; I know you are worried. Excuse this paper – ain't got any other.

I met up with Jesse James not long ago. He is quite a character – you know he was killed in '82. His mother swore that the body that was in the coffin was his but it was another man they called either Tracy or Lynch. He was a cousin of Wild Bill. You won't likely care about this but if Janey outlives you and me, she might be interested. He is passing under the name of Dalton but he couldn't fool me I know all the Dalton's and he sure ain't one of them. He told me he promised his gang and his mother that if he lived to be a hundred, he would confess – You and me won't be here then Jim. To make it strange, Jesse sang at his own funeral. Poor devil he can't cod me – not even with a long hair and a billy goat's wad of hair on his chin. I expect he will start preachin'. He is smart maybe he can do it. Beginning to snow and I have a roaring camp fire. I hope that Janey never has to live like I do. As long as you live Jim, she will always have a good life. She won't have to live beside camp fires with a saddle for a pillow and very little to eat.

Take care of yourself,

Regards –

from Jane

In a letter to Jesse, dated March 13, 1949, was the following:

"In southwestern Montana, five miles west of Melrose, is the ghost remains of a smelter town, Glendale, which flourished in the 1870s, 80s and 90s. It once had a population of 1800. There was a "Missouri Town" in Glendale where a number of families from Clay County Missouri lived. Two were the Tom Sappingtons and the Joe Sheppards. Now, the story goes that Jesse James came to Montana once upon a time and paid a visit to those former Missouri residents. Did you come to Montana to Glendale Mr. James?"

When Ola read the letter to Jesse, he said,

"Yes, I remember the Missouri Town in Glendale and I did go to Montana Territory and visit those families. I remember the Joe Sheppards and Tom Sappingtons well."

From the time of his official demise on April 3, 1882, and after his return from South America, Jesse James was on any frontier where there was excitement. He knew all the old cattle trails from Texas to Abilene, Kansas and changed his name as often as he changed his shirt.

He went to Dodge City, Kansas, where he served as a Marshal in that wild and wooly cattle town for a while following Bat Masterson, a famous gunman. Bat and Jesse were good friends for many years thereafter.

John Mark Bouyer, born at Talbaton, Georgia in 1844, was a Quantrell man. Him and Jesse met in west Texas years after Jesse was supposed to have been killed in Missouri.

In the late 1870s and 1880s, Jesse visited the home of Jake Johnson and family south of Austin, Texas. Jake Johnson and his family was originally from Clay County, Missouri and knew the James boys, their mother and step-father, Dr. Samuel in Missouri before moving to Texas and building a nice two-story rock home.

Old John Trammel said, "After Jesse James had been pronounced dead and buried, I saw him about twice a week for a long time in Texas."

On April 8, 1949, Jesse and Ola were talking and he said, "I went to Morgan City, Louisiana and visited John Dalton for a while, a cousin, you know.

"John was almost broke when he went to Morgan City. He finally bought a small boat and hired a few guys and got oysters and told sold them in jugs for 25 cents a jug. He paid the workers ten cents a jug to get them out and sold them for 25 cents a jug and done pretty good. I played the calliope on the Show Boat up and down the Mississippi River while I was there."

Ola said, "Why Jesse, I didn't know you could play a calliope!"

He said, "I can't. But they needed somebody to play it and I could make enough noise on it to attract the people and let them know that the Show Boat was coming so they could get down to the river."

Then he said, "John Dalton is in Morgan City now as far as I know and is running an oyster packing plant there."

John William Pierce who was born at Valley Falls, Kansas in 1854 was brought to Missouri when a child to Buchanan County. He and Jesse James first got acquainted back in the early sixties at New Market, Missouri, in Platt County. Pierce was 8 years of age and Jesse was about 15.

In the early 1870s, Jesse and Pierce were together in Excelsior Springs, Missouri. One of John's cousins, Charlie Pierce, was a member of the James gang. They called Jesse James, Jim Howard at the time. He went by the name of Thomas Howard a while.

Jesse and John were together in St. Joseph, Missouri quite a bit. They were together for a little while the night before Bigelow was shot and killed by Bob Ford on April 3, 1882. Jesse was known as Jim Howard or J.D. Howard.

Susan Lavenia (Susie) James, Jesse and Frank's sister was married to Allen Parmer, who was a Missourian and a Quantrell man with Jesse and Frank during the War Between the States. Susie and Allen owned a ranch in Archer County Texas and then in later years they moved into Wichita Falls, Texas. Jesse and Frank visited their sister from time to time, both on the ranch and in Wichita Falls.

Susie died in 1889 and Jesse and Frank were both at the funeral. Susie is buried in Wichita Falls.

In 1892 Jesse was in the Indian Territory. Going by the time of McDaniel. Allen McDaniel. He was there in the first opening of the Old Oklahoma. It wasn't the Oklahoma Strip; the Strip didn't open up for several years after Old Oklahoma opened. He was in the Run for Land when Old Oklahoma opened up and he got a homestead there. A farm located eight and a half miles southeast of Guthrie.

John W. Pierce got some land there too. His farm was a half-mile from Jesse's. Jesse, known as James I. McDaniels was a member of the legislature. The County of Territorial Legislature in Logan County. Guthrie was the capital at that time. Jesse owned that farm about eight years. He had been there quite a while before Pierce got his claim and moved in and he worked for Jesse seven years or better, putting up hay.

In 1893, while Jesse was still in the legislature, he went to Chicago, Illinois and visited for a week with his good friend Colonel William F. (Buffalo Bill) Cody who was there at the World's Fair with his Wild West Show and Pawnee Bill whose name was Gordon Lilley was there with his Far East Show.

It was on that visit to see Buffalo Bill that Jesse met a young man named Robert E. Lee, who was Buffalo Bill's bodyguard at the time. Jesse went to Buffalo Bill's private railroad car and was met at the door by Robert E. Lee, who didn't know him and wouldn't let him in until Buffalo Bill okayed it. Then, when Cody saw who it was, he was greatly surprised and pleased for him and Jesse had been friends for years. Jesse stayed there a week and visited with Cody and his bodyguard and then disappeared.

From Chicago in 1893, Jesse went to Frost, Texas in the vicinity of Waco to visit a close friend, John Sparks. John's sons ran a café there. John Sparks may have been a Quantrell man or a Marshal or Texas Ranger. Anyway, he and Jesse were friends.

When Jesse came out with his true identity in Lawton, Oklahoma in 1948, Robert E. Lee went from Louisiana to Lawton to see him. Lee stated that Jesse was the real Jesse James, just as he said he was. That he had listened to the conversations between him and Buffalo Bill Cody in Chicago in 1893, had seen Jesse James in Fort Worth, Dallas and Longview, Texas and had told people all over Louisiana, Texas and Oklahoma that Jesse James was not shot and killed in St. Joseph, Missouri in 1882. When Jesse's term was up in the Territorial Legislature in 1894, he went back to Fort Smith, Arkansas and he told Ola,

"From the fall of 1894 through the spring of 1896, I was a Deputy U.S. Marshal out of Fort Smith. Jake Yose was Chief Marshal at the time and Hanging Judge Parker was the Judge. I was assigned to what was then the Chickasaw Nation of the Indian Territory, in and around Ardmore, Fort White Bead, Woodford, Fort Arbuckle and surrounding area."

Ola asked him, "What name was you known as?"

He said, "Frank Dalton."

When Jesse was at home with the Everharts in 1950 at 1103 East First Street in Austin, Texas, he and Ola's mother used to talk about the old Indian Territory days when he was a Deputy U.S. Marshal in and around Ardmore. Ola's mother, Bertha G. Maddox was a young girl at that, growing up there in the Arbuckle Mountains near Woodford, 25 miles from Ardmore. Her mother said, "Jesse, Papa would always take us kids to get our clothes and shoes every fall, and I'll never forget when we'd all get in the wagon and go to Ardmore trading, as we called shopping then, and it just tickled us kids to death if we got to go to Ardmore on Indian Pay Day. As you know, the Indians got so much money a month to live on, and on their payday they'd all come to town by the wagonloads, and some on horseback. Ardmore was a busy town on their payday. I'll never forget how the Indians would do; the Indian women who had babies would bring their babies to town in bootjacks, stand the bootjacks up against the wall outside by the stores doors then go in the stores and do their trading."

Jesse said, "Yes, I've seen that many times too. You know the Indians, both men and women, loved firewater (whiskey) as much as anyone. And when they'd come to town and get their money, they always got them some. They never bothered anybody and the men never caused any trouble. They'd just sit down on the board sidewalks and drink until they passed out. I'd find them all slumped over, but I wouldn't arrest them and take them to the calaboose, I'd just drag them over to the side of a building there in town and prop them up against a building.

"According to the law, the Indians had to be out of town by 5 o'clock in the evening. So about four-thirty, I'd go around over town, find the women and tell them it was time for them to get their men-folks and children and head for home. Some of the women was so full of firewater too, I'd ask them, 'Are you able to drive the team?' They'd nod or say, 'Me drive.' They'd load their children in their wagons and then I'd help them get their men-folks in their wagons and tell the women, 'Now go on home.' Off they'd go toward home, but sometimes some of them would turn their wagons over on their way and would just lay there by their wagons until they sobered up, then they'd set their wagon up, climb in and go on home." Jesse grinned and said, "Lord, I've had as many as 8 or 10 drunk Indians propped up against the side of the building at one time."

Ola's mother said, "You know Jesse, I never heard an Indian baby cry in my life. They'd be there in those bootjacks propped up against some store and in the cold, the wind blowing or the sun shining on them, they never made a noise."

In 1895, Jesse went over to Paris, Texas for a few days. A black man had committed a crime and was taken out on the street there in Paris, tied to a stake and burned. Jesse and mother were talking about that and he said, "I made a record of the burning of that man at Paris in 1895, it was put on an Edison record. It was the type of machine that required earphones to hear the record. I had seven sets of earphones and charged twenty-five cents a person to put them on and listen to the record. I went many places and made a good bit of money with that record and those earphones."

Ola's mother had told her about the burning of that man and had told Ola why it was done. He had raped a white woman, so they burned him. Her mother also told her, "Papa went to Ardmore to visit with Jesse and while there, listened to that record. He came home and told Mama and us children what he'd heard. He said, "You could hear his flesh burn and hear him scream as it came out over the wires. It was awful! But that scoundrel deserved it for what he done."

That same year, 1895, a small-time outlaw known as Scarface Jim stole a fine heifer calf from a farmer out there in the mountains and brought it to Ola's grandfather's place and penned it in with their cows. Her grandpa was gone to the post office at the time so Scarface rode out in the field where her mother, her sisters and brother were working and said, "Children, I've pinned my heifer calf in with your cows because its give out. I'll be back later and get it." Then he rode off. When her grandpa got home, her mother, who was the oldest of the children, told him that the heifer calf penned with their cows belonged to "The Man" as they called Scarface. They knew him because he would come to the house sometimes real late at night and get a meal. The owner of the heifer calf was out looking for it and he found it with their cows so he went to Ardmore and notified Jesse, the Marshal.

The next morning, Jesse was on his way out to Ola's grandpa and grandma's place and her grandpa was on his way to the post office in Woodford. They met on the road and Jesse told her grandpa, "Well Toby, we caught Scarface Jim. So, you'll have to go to court."

Grandpa said, "Well I don't know anything. I wasn't there at home when he came to my place."

Jesse said, "But the calf was found with your cows. So, you'll have to go to court."

When Ola's grandpa went home and told the family about meeting the Marshal on the road and that he had to go to court in Ardmore, it scared them so bad and they all just cried and cried. They didn't know what court meant. They thought that court meant hanging.

The next morning, Ola's grandpa put a change of clothes in his saddlebag, got on his horse and headed for Ardmore. It took him a day to get there for it was 25 miles. He stayed a day and a night in Ardmore then it took a day to get back home. Ola didn't know where they held court, because there was no courthouse in Ardmore then. But when her grandpa got home, he told the family, "Well, they sent The Man off." So, Scarface Jim was sent to the pen.

Ola's mother and Jesse were talking one day when he was at home with them. They got on the subject of the old days in the Indian Territory and her mother said, "I was at my grandpa and grandma O'Daniel's house one time visiting on Indian payday. They lived in that big two-story home down by the railroad trussle there in Ardmore, you know. Late that evening a wagon load of Indians came by and just the other side of the railroad trussle there was a sharp turn in the road and just after this wagon load of Indians went under the trussle and hit that sharp turn, the wagon turned over and just poured the drunk Indians all over the road. Somebody called you. You came out, helped the Indians set the wagon up and get everybody in in, then told them to go on home."

In the fall of 1895, it got so when the farmers in the Arbuckle Mountains camped for the night at Rock Creek on their way home, they were always robbed. They always camped at Rock Creek on their way to town with their cotton and again on their way back home. They were never bothered on their way to town at Ardmore to sell their cotton, but were always robbed on their way home. They all wondered why.

Up in the mountains above Ola's grandparents place lived a farmer who was a friend of her grandpa's and he always spent the night at Ola's grandpa and grandma's place to and from town. One night when he and his little girl, who was 12 years old, stopped at for the night on their way home, he told them what had happened the night before at Rock Creek.

They had stopped at Rock Creek as usual on their way home after he had sold his cotton. While they were fixing their supper, a woman in a mother-Hubbard dress and bonnet came up and was dancing around a campfire. He told his little girl not to worry, that she was a crazy woman but she wouldn't hurt them. They ate their supper then went to bed in the wagon. The little girl was scared and was peeping over the end of the wagon watching the crazy woman dancing around the campfire when she suddenly said, "Daddy, that woman's got on boots!"

54

He knew then, that something was wrong. So, he just put on his Winchester by his side and told the little girl to just be still. When the crazy woman figured they were asleep, the man felt the wagon tongue give and knew she was coming up in the wagon. So, he just raised up and shot, then got out of the wagon and discovered he'd killed the crazy woman. He got on one of his horses, took his little girl and went back to Ardmore and told the Marshal, "You'd better come out to Rock Creek. I just killed a crazy woman. Marshal Jesse James took a couple of men with him and with the man and little girl went out to Rock Creek.

When Jesse pulled the crazy woman's bonnet off and her dress up, he said, "Why man, you didn't kill a crazy woman! This is a man! He's the president of the bank in Ardmore."

Jesse took the man and little girl back to Ardmore, gave the man some money, bought the little girl a new dress and then, patting the man on the back, said; "Just go on home and don't let this bother you. Man, you have done a good thing. People have been getting robbed out there for some time." No more poor farmers were robbed on their way home after selling their cotton.

A full blood Chickasaw Indian, the only full blood Chickasaw around there in the Arbuckle Mountains, lived not far from Ola's grandpa and grandma's place. He wore long hair, parted in the middle, a ring in each ear and a ring in his nose. He was married to a white woman and they had a little girl. They lived in the only big white house around there. Some white boys worked for the Indian and there was white bunk houses a ways from the main house.

The Indian began to think that his wife was interested in one of the white boys that worked there and got very jealous. So jealous, in fact, that one night he got up and with a knife in his hand, slipped out of the house, went down to the bunkhouse where the boy was sleeping, slipped in and cut the boy's head off then threw it in the hog pen and went back in the house. The squealing of the hogs woke the other boys who were sleeping in the bunkhouse. They jumped up, ran out to see about the hogs and saw the human head in the pen. They got the head out, ran back to the bunkhouse and found the boy's headless body on his bunk.

One of the boys got on his horse and rode as fast as he could to Woodford, where the only telegraph was, called the Marshal in Ardmore then rushed back. As soon as he got back, the other boy went to my grandparents as fast as he could and told them what had happened and he was scared half to death.

As soon as Jesse got the word, he and some other men came out to the Indian's place as quick as they could get there. The Indian and his white wife were in the house. Their little girl, about three years old, came outside and while Jesse was walking around out in the yard looking for the knife, the little girl, her hands behind her, walked beside him. She looked up at him and asked, "What are you lookin' for?"

Jesse replied, "Oh just looking around."

She said, "Well if you're lookin' for my daddy's clothes, you can't find them, 'cause they're hid under the back doorstep."

Jesse said, "All right."

He walked on until he got the child to the front yard then he went back, looked under the back doorstep and there was the Indian's blood-covered drawers and rolled up in them was the bloody knife.

The Indian was arrested, taken to Ardmore and placed in the calaboose. His wife and child left there. When the Indian was so sick and nearly dead, they let him be taken back home to die. His wife came back and attended the funeral and then she left there and never returned again.

When Ola's grandpa and grandma and the family lived out there in the Arbuckle Mountains and Jesse was the Deputy U.S. Marshal in and around Ardmore, he used to ride out to their farm and visit with Ola's grandpa. He could see that her grandma didn't like him, so he'd just ride by the house, speak to the family and ride on out to the barn where he and her grandpa would sit and visit for a good while at a time. Ola's Grandpa thought the world of him.

Why didn't Ola's grandma like Jesse? Well, she had heard her pa, as she called her father, say that in Jesse's young days, he had been an outlaw, even though he at the time was a law-abiding man. She never said a bad word about him. Fact is, she never said anything bad about anybody. She firmly believed, that there was something good about everybody. In some it was just a little harder to find, but it was there just the same. Jesse was Toby's folks and she never objected to them visiting, but not in her home.

Ola's Grandpa never mentioned his folks to her grandma. But when he and Ola's mother, the oldest child, were working in the woods or on the way to the mill, he would tell her about his folks and he'd let her look at his family bible which he kept locked in his small trunk. There were five generations listed on the family records in that bible. And there was a picture of his father, Henry Underwood, in the trunk who was with Quantrell during the War Between the States.

During the war while great-grandpa Henry was gone to war, great-grandma Sally and their three children were at home alone when she got word that the Yankees were coming. So, she took the two oldest children, James A. (Toby), age 8, and Eliza Ann, age 5, and hid them in the bushes not far from the house then holding the baby, William, in her arms and keeping out of sight but where she could see the house, she saw the Yankees come, ransack the house and then set fire to it. She died not long after that from exposure and grief.

A doctor Rainey in Cottage Grove, Tennessee took the children to raise. William died a short time later, but James A. and Eliza Ann lived to be elderly people. Ola's Grandpa always said, "A better man than Doctor Rainey never lived."

When Ola's mother would go visit grandpa's only sister, Eliza Ann, whom the family called Aunt Sis and married to James C. Alexander, Aunt Sis would talk to mother about her and her grandpa's folks. Then she'd get her album out and show mother pictures of the folks. She showed mother the pictures of the Dalton boys and said, "Now honey, that's the Dalton boys. They're your cousins." Sure, she knew that Bob, Emmett and Grat turned to outlawry, but she said, "Now honey they was mighty good boys. They was only trying to get justice." Aunt Sis and grandpa loved their folks.

Unfortunately, Ola's grandpa and grandma's house burned one Sunday when her mother was 16 while the family was gone to church and burned everything they had, which included her grandpa's trunk. So, the Bible and his father's picture was lost forever.

CHAPTER SEVEN

Let's go back to Bob Ford for a little bit. The family lived on Route 635 near Hume, Farquier County, Virginia on a farm called "The Dell" where J.T. Ford was a tenant farmer. It was there that Robert Newton (Bob) was born in 1862. In 1871, the family moved to Clay County, Missouri and then to Ray County, Missouri. Martha, the only girl, married a man named Bolton. After she was a widow, she, Charlie and Bob rented a farm near Richmond, Missouri. Then Charlie and Bob went to St. Joseph, Missouri and stayed for a while with Charley Bigelow under the names of Bob and Charlie Johnson.

On April 3, 1882 Bob shot and killed Charley Bigelow who was passed off as being Jesse James and after the boys were tried and sentenced, following the killing they were immediately pardoned by Governor Crittenden.

Jesse and Ola were talking one day and he said, "As I told you, me and Frank and Charlie and Bob Ford all stayed in the Blossom House Hotel across from the old Depot in Kansas City in adjoining rooms after the incident and excitement had subsided that occurred on April 3, 1882 there in St. Joseph, Missouri."

Then he said, "The Ford boys was first cousins. Bob and Charlie's mother and my mother was sisters."

Ola said, "Well, according to that, their mother was a Dalton before marriage."

He replied, "Yes, she was."

Ola said, "Then the Ford boys' mother was a sister of my great-grandmother and, they were my cousins too. Third cousins."

He said, "Yes, that is the way it is. So don't you forget that now."

Ola asked, "What happened to or about the reward money when Bigelow was killed?"

He said, "Well it wasn't like they tell. Bob only got between three and five hundred dollars. The rest found its way back into Governor Crittenden's pocket."

Then he said, "Charlie committed suicide on May 6, 1884 in a field near Richmond, Missouri. After Frank was acquitted, him and Bob went up to Colorado and went in business together. They owned and operated the Grove Theatre at Colorado City, Colorado. Then when they dissolved partnership, Frank went to Kentucky and Bob went to Creede, Colorado and opened up a Saloon and gambling place in a tent there.

In the April 7, 1882 issue of St. Joseph, Missouri Herald Newspaper under the heading:

A Paternal Visitor

The father of the Ford boys arrived in the city yesterday and spent several hours with them at the jail. The old gentleman had been very uneasy as to the safety of his sons but seemed well satisfied after observing the security of their surroundings.

Also, in that same issue of the St. Joseph Herald under the heading:

The Arrest of Cap Ford

Yesterday's Herald contained a brief mention of the arrest of Cap Ford. The particulars are that Mr. J.C. Morris, Constable of Richmond Township, Ray County, arrived here at 2:30 o'clock yesterday morning armed with a state warrant for the arrest of Cap Ford, for complicity in the murder, as accessory after the fact. In company with two policemen, the Constable went to the residence of Judge Belt, who recognized the warrant, whereupon the Constable and four policemen proceeded to the Bacon House, where it was found that Ford had retired in room 12. Mr. Bacon did not relish the idea of having his house invaded by officers of the law, but upon ascertaining the gravity of the crime with which his guest was charged he cheerfully escorted them to his room.

The arrest had to do with the murder and burial of Wood Hite, of which Cap Ford was not guilty. Wood Hite was a first cousin of Jesse James. Wood's mother was Reverend Robert James' sister. Cap Ford was a first cousin of Jesse. Cap's mother and Jesse's mother were sisters. Alias (Cap) Ford was Bob and Charlie Ford's brother.

After Bob went to Creede, Colorado and opened his Saloon he started drinking too much and talking too much. He was a heavy drinker and talking in his beer and had to be eliminated. The first man that was supposed to have done the eliminating got drunk and muffed the job. So, he was killed by a man named O'Kelly in April 1892 and is buried at Creede, Colorado. O'Kelly was given an 85-year sentence in the pen but was pardoned by Governor Waite in less than 30 days. Colorado was a populace state.

O'Kelly was killed by Joe Burnette in Pawhusky, Indian Territory. Then Duke Short killed the man that killed Burnette.

Mrs. Frances Tiller in Carthage, Texas wrote Ola about the death of Charlie Ford at Longview, Texas. Ola went out to the hospital and told Jesse about it and he said, "That Charlie Ford was Cap Ford's son. The Cap Ford was a brother of Bob and Charlie. Cap Ford ran a Saw Mill. And that Charlie Ford who died at Longview in 1950 was his son," Then he said, "Bob, Charlie and Cap's sister Mattie Ford (Bolton Cummings) died of blood poisoning from a rat bite in June of 1893.

CHAPTER EIGHT

Jesse and Ola were talking one day and he got to talking about when he was a Marshal. He said, "I was a Deputy U.S. Marshal at Paul's Valley and White Bead, Indian Territory for a while. Smith Paul run a store and blacksmith shop at Paul's Valley."

In 1897, Jesse was in and around Wichita Falls, Texas and surrounding area for a while visiting his brother-in-law Allen Parmer and friends there.

In 1898, he was back in the Indian Territory and was a Deputy U.S. Marshal at and around White Horse, Indian Territory for about three or four months under the name of J.D. Reed.

Then, the lure of adventure called him at the outbreak of the Spanish-American War, which began April 24, 1898. He was acquainted with Pancho Villa, the Mexican leader or bandit. So, he quit the Marshal force, went to Wagoner, Indian Territory and joined the Spanish-American War under the alias name of J.G. Hood or Frank Dalton. Ola couldn't recall just which. That war ended August 12, 1898.

Back from the war, Jesse went to Dallas, Texas and visited Frank James who was working at the time at Sanger Brothers Clothing Store and had been for some time. Fact is, Frank worked there for years as a floorwalker.

From Dallas, Jesse went to Brownwood, Texas and visited Colonel James Russell Davis and his wife and they all had dinner together in a restaurant in downtown Brownwood. Then while in Brownwood Jesse went out and visited Bloody Bill Anderson at his home in the country.

In 1899, Jesse was at Fort Sill, Indian Territory for a short time and while there, conversed with Colonel James R. Davis who had gone there on a subject that only four people knew anything about. They were Frank James, Sam Todd, Colonel Davis and Jesse James.

Then, Jesse went to Canada and the Boer War that began on October 11, 1899, found Jesse James fighting on the side of the British as an Army Colonel. Later, (date unknown) he went on another expedition to Africa where he engaged in hand-to-hand combat with the Hottentots. He told Aubrey and Ola, "That's the only assailants I ever fled from. Their methods of combat was not those of the white man."

Known as Colonel Dalton, Jesse returned to the United States and, with him, came a collection of shrunken heads. Treated by the headhunters until they were the size of apples. Some of them may be viewed today at the Smithsonian Institute in Washington, D.C. and at a Museum in Seattle, Washington.

In 1900, Jesse was in Texas and went down to Galveston. He told Ola, "I was in Galveston, Texas when the seawall was erected."

The fate that brought Jesse James in contact with Mr. John Shevlin, the St. Louis, Missouri detective and newspaperman is strange. Following his role as a witness to the pardoning of Cole Younger in 1901, the Missouri sleuth was employed as a detective to apprehend a flock of pickpockets who were following the Jesse James Show. Cole Younger and Frank James had some personal effects of Jesse James on display and was making money hand over fist. The peculiar twist to the show was that Jesse himself was selling tickets. But no one there but Frank and Cole knew. Even Mr. Shevlin who had observed the white-headed gentleman didn't suspect he was Jesse James. He assumed that Jesse was dead, as had been reported.

Before the year was out, Jesse left the show and went to Hot Springs, Arkansas. John Shevlin was sent to Hot Springs that same year and was Chief of the Government Reservation at Hot Springs, Arkansas. Jesse James was supposedly dead and had been for twenty years so nobody was looking for him. But there he was, the most publicized outlaw of the century, right under John Shevlin's nose for almost three years, running a shooting gallery, under the alias of Frank Dalton.

Before the end of 1904, Jesse was back with Frank James and Cole Younger's show. A good many old timers recalled in later years that they remembered a show of Jesse James' personal effects in 1904 and they also recalled that a white-haired gentleman was selling tickets there.

And, nearly fifty years later, in 1948 when Jesse came out with his true identity in Lawton, Oklahoma, Aubrey and Ola were in the motel room visiting with Jesse when John Shevlin arrived from Chicago, Illinois.

Shevlin had worn a mustache there in Hot Springs, Arkansas and when he walked into Jesse's motel room in Lawton and was clean shaven, Jesse looked at him and instead of saying hello, said, "Well John, you shaved your mustache off." Which was a big surprise to John, because Jesse, whom he'd known as Frank Dalton, was right. Then they started talking and Jesse was telling John the story of the greatest hoax ever perpetrated, Jesse James' supposed demise.

In 1905, Jesse was down on the Panama Canal and so was Colonel James R. Davis. Down on Culebra Cut, near a little place called Frijole. Or, to put it in American language, the little place was called *beans*.

In 1906, Jesse went to Portland, Oregon and visited Ruby Younger and the family. Ruby was the daughter of James (Jim) Younger, a full brother of the well-known Cole Younger. Ruby was fourteen years old at the time.

That same year of 1906 Frank and Jesse James was at the Dallas State Fairgrounds in Dallas, Texas. George Farris, who was eighteen years old at the time, his father and uncle all went to the Fair and when they stepped off the train, there was Frank James. The Farris and the James were by no means strangers. George's grandfather had grown up in Missouri, on a farm adjacent to the James family farm. Judge George Farris' father was a Deputy U.S. Marshal in the Indian Territory and as Jesse had been a Deputy U.S. Marshal there also, Judge Farris said, "I feel sure they knew each other there or rather were together from time to time during the time." Judge George Farris was born in 1888. Dr. George James, a cousin of Frank and Jesse's brought him into the world and helped him fight for his life for three days and nights.

Frank James accompanied the Farris party out to the fairgrounds and the entire group was about to enter an exhibit featuring boxer John L. Sullivan when George Farris noticed his uncle missing. He looked around and saw his uncle standing and talking with a man and the man had his arm on the uncle's shoulder while they were talking. When George Farris walked over to them the fellow wheeled and walked away. George Farris was certain that man was Jesse James.

Inside the exhibit, there was more excitement when Sullivan mistook George Farris' father for Bob Fitzsimmons, another famous boxer of that day. Denying he was Fitzsimmons; the elder Farris introduced the boxer to Frank James. Sullivan asked Frank, "Why don't you have a show? People'd pay more to see you than me since Jesse's dead." George Farris said Frank replied, "You give me $10,000 and give him a pardon and we might be able to show him up pretty quick."

Judge George Farris said, "Bob Ford was supposed to have killed Jesse, but they were seen together later," and said, "There is other evidence too. Dick Johnson, who had ridden with Jesse James in Quantrell's Raiders during the Civil War and who had belonged to the gang, later told George Farris' grandfather around Christmas of 1904 that he had seen Frank and Jesse together in Bonham, Texas." But George Farris didn't say when that sighting occurred.

Jesse and Frank were in Bonham, Texas for a short time. M.E. (Till) Baldwin who was born in Missouri in 1842 went to school with Jesse and Frank. Baldwin was a Baptist preacher there in Bonham. His wife was Rachael Gammon before marriage, a cousin of Jesse and Frank. M.E. (Till) Baldwin died January 12, 1912.

Jesse owned a ranch south of Denton in 1906. Frank James and Cole Younger were at Whitewright, Texas for a while. Exact date unknown, but thought to be 1906.

On a train in 1910, George Farris and his father met Doctor George James by chance. His father mentioned the Dallas encounter with Frank James four years before. The doctor asked if they had seen Jesse as well. George Farris' father said he didn't see him and the doctor said, "I'll be he was there. He lives south of Denton."

As mentioned earlier, the capital of the Indian Territory at Guthrie. Then steps were started for the Indian Territory to go into statehood and that was followed with lots of talk and trouble between the people in Guthrie fighting to keep the capital there and Oklahoma City wanting the capital there. Oklahoma City won the battle, the capital was built there and in November 1907, the Indian Territory went into Statehood and is now the State of Oklahoma.

That year, Jesse James went to White Horse, along the Washita River and lived a short while. Then he went to Adairsville, Kentucky and visited relatives and friends. The late John Thomas Shelton of Woodford County, Kentucky, son of Medley Shelton of Harrodsburg, Kentucky married Martha James, sister of Jesse's father, Reverend Robert James.

From Kentucky, Jesse went back to Oklahoma City and in that year of 1907, under the alias name of Jess Wilson was elected to the State Legislature.

In 1908, while Jesse was a legislature in Oklahoma, his stepfather, Dr. Reuben Samuel died in Kearney, Missouri. Jesse went back home to the funeral. Dr. Samuel was survived by his wife Zerelda, two daughters, Sarah Nicholson and Fannie Hall, one son, John Thomas Samuel, two stepsons, Frank and Jesse James and several grandchildren.

Jesse told Ola, "A better man than Dr. Samuel never lived."

In 1909, Jesse going by an alias name of Jesse Redman, was in Alexanderia, Louisiana with his race horses. In 1910, Jesse spent the night in the home of Mr. and Mrs. Arthur A. Beville who lived at the time, near Harrisburg, Oklahoma, about twenty miles east of Duncan, Oklahoma.

Mr. Beville remembered well that Jesse James, who introduced himself as Mr. Kelly, carried a Winchester rifle with no sight at the end of the barrel. When Mr. Beville called it to his attention, he merely announced that he could shoot just as good backwards as forward, and that he didn't need any sight.

The Beville's lived in Cache, Oklahoma in 1948 when jesse came out with his true identity and they went to Lawton, Oklahoma to see and talk with him. Yes, he was the Mr. Kelly who had spent the night in their home in 1910.

In 1910 Jesse went to Torreon, Mexico and lived for about two years. Torreon is in the northern part of Mexico, in the interior.

Jesse told Ola, "Me and Brushy Bill, who was the real Billy the Kid, was neighbors down there in Torreon. He lived across the street from my place and, down the street not far from us lived Luz Villa, one of Pancho Villa's wives or ex-wives. Bill was well liked there and could have run for office and won if he'd had any education, but he didn't and that held him back.

On July 1, 1948, Jesse was staying in the Ione Hotel in Guthrie, Oklahoma and had been for nine or ten days and on July 7, 1948 Brushy Bill Roberts, 88 years old, former scout and Indian fighter arrived in Guthrie to see Jesse. He said he'd known Jesse for 78 years. His father, Al "Wild Henry" Roberts was present to identify the body after Charley Bigelow, who was going under the name of Jesse Howard, who was shot and killed.

"He came home and told us all about it," said Brushy Bill and said of his father, "he identified Bigelow as Jesse James. He said Jesse's mother knew it wasn't her son, but claimed it was, to help Jesse get away."

Brushy Bill said he had visited with Jesse off and on ever since and, that he and his wife took care of him for several weeks in their home after had broken a leg in Gladewater, Texas.

In 1950 when Jesse was home with the Everharts at 1103 East First Street in Austin, Texas, they were talking one night and he said, "Back in my outlaw days, me and Frank was riding along in the Wichita Mountains not far from Fletcher, Indian Territory and we found several bars of Spanish Gold. We looked all around and didn't see anybody. We couldn't take it with us. Didn't want to. And didn't want to leave it there where we found it. So, we just took the bars over to another spot and buried them. Figured we'd come back later and get them, then we rode on. Time went by and we didn't get back to that area.

In 1910, Frank bought some land not far out of Fletcher and built him and Annie a home. He was close enough to the Wichita's so he could go over there, go up in the Mountains and find that gold we'd buried. He went up there in the Wichita Mountains where he thought was the place we'd buried it, but he couldn't find it. He went up there several times and looked for any signs that would lead him to where it was buried. But over the years the terrain had washed from rains and changed so much, that nothing looked the same and try as he might, he never could find it. Unless somebody has found it, which I don't think is very likely, it is still there."

According to an article in the Mexico, *Missouri Evening Ledger* Newspaper of October 11, 1948 –

In 1910 Jesse taught Bible classes and served the old Unity Church as Sunday school superintendent for a month and taught classes of little children in the open air. He was known as "Brother Johnson."

Jesse and Ola were talking one day and he was thinking back about the War Between the States and he said, "The Story goes that William Clarke Quantrell was killed in Kentucky during our siege through that state in 1865. He was also, according to stories, supposed to have gotten badly wounded in Kentucky in 1865, took a high fever because of the wounds he received and died there. That is not true. I was there and I know.

"During the siege on Lexington, Quantrell sent one of the men on his horse to a point of lookout. The boy was shot and killed and when the Yankees went to the boy and the horse, they found papers in the saddlebags that were Quantrell's, of course, so the word went out that they'd killed Quantrell.

"Quantrell's wife and little daughter were there in Kentucky. So, he went and got them and they headed for Texas. They settled in the little town of Osceola, Texas and once again he became the mild-mannered schoolteacher that he had been before the war. Was living under his own name, Charles Hart and was highly respected by all who knew him. None of the townspeople suspected that he was once the much-feared Quantrell, leader of Quantrell's guerrilla band. I visited him many times and so did Frank and other Quantrell men. He lived out his life there at Osceola, died there and is buried there."

James D. Fay, age 96 who lived at 5732 Willowcrest Avenue in North Hollywood, California was a bricklayer in his younger days. He laid the foundation of Columbia, Missouri and said he knew Quantrell in Brownwood, Texas.

Jesse said, "You know Ola, after I was shot in my right lung, they sent me home and it was some time before I was able to be up and around much. Robert E. Lee surrendered April 9, 1865 officially. But the truth is, the War Between the States is the only war ever fought that never ended. Never will. Some folks call it the Civil War, but there wasn't a damn thing civil about it. It was the War Between the States and war is hell.

"After the war closed, Quantrell's men scattered out. Some went to one place and some to another. Those that was left. But we pretty well kept up with each other and knew what names they was going by. Because we were all considered a bunch of cutthroats, after the war and had to change our names. Not Frank though, because after he surrendered himself to Governor Crittenden was tried and acquitted, he was free to use his right name."

On September 18, 1948 Jesse was staying for a short time in the Hermitage Hotel in Nashville, Tennessee and a 75-year-old Nashvillian went to the hotel to see him. Said he knew Jesse James and knew he was the real Jesse James. He knew Jesse and Frank. The Nashvillian, H.E. Umensetter of 1411 Kirkland Avenue, said he knew the James boys in Kirkland, Missouri and Ardmore, Oklahoma, many years ago. Umensetter said he knew the location of the James place on Fatherland Street in Nashville, Tennessee and once owned a building next door.

In 1880 and 1881, Jesse, using the alias name Elder Hopkins while posing as a preacher in Nashville, resided at 711 Fatherland Street. And, Mr. Umensetter said, "He looked like those pictures you see of old Quaker Preachers, the way he dressed in those days."

In 1911, Frank and Annie were living in their new house not far from Fletcher, Oklahoma and Zerelda, Jesse and Frank's mother went to visit them. Jesse was living in Torreon, Mexico but he came back to the U.S. and went to Frank and Annie's house so their mother had a chance to visit with both of her sons.

When her visit was over, she boarded the train and started back to Kearney, Missouri. Annie went with her to see her safely home. She was in a berth on the train and just before the train reached Oklahoma City, she got sick and died.

As soon as word reached Frank and Jesse, they got to Oklahoma City as fast as they could. They took their mother's body on to Kearney and she is buried beside Dr. Samuel. She died at age 86.

She was survived by two daughters, Sarah Nicholson and Fannie Hall. Three sons, Frank and Jesse James and John Thomas Samuel and several grandchildren.

After Jesse and Frank's mother was buried, Jesse went back to Torreon, Mexico. By 1912 the Mexican Revolution was getting pretty bad, so Jesse and Brushy Bill decided it was time they were leaving there and getting back across the Rio Grande and they headed for Texas. They left Torreon, Mexico, went down to Matamoros, Mexico and crossed over into Brownsville, Texas.

Back in Texas and using the alias name of Frank Dalton, Jesse served as a Peace Officer in many towns in the days of the first oil booms in Texas. He was a familiar figure in Burkburnette, Texas in 1914.

CHAPTER NINE

I'll turn back to the year of 1902. The following was written by Robertus Love:

THE HISTORIAN AT JESSE'S SECOND BURIAL

He wrote it himself, as a piece of staff correspondence from Kearney, Missouri, and wired it to his newspaper on Sunday night, June 29, 1902, which date the reader is to bear in mind:

> *Jesse James had a wife;*
> *She's a mourner all her life;*
> *His children, they were brave.*
> *Oh, the dirty little coward that shot Mr. Howard!*
> *And they laid Jesse James in his grave.*
>
> –From the old song.

"And they laid Jesse James in his grave," for the second and doubtless, the last time. Not as a bandit, but as a brother in arms, as a soldier, as a guerrilla rough rider of the border warfare, as a fighter in the lost cause, a squad of Quantrell's men who rode and shot with the boy Jesse James in the last two years of the Civil War, bore his bones this Sunday afternoon to his new grave between his new grave between those of his wife and his little half-brother.

"Not a sound was heard, not a funeral note," not a word was spoken at the grave during the twenty minutes required for carrying the coffin from the hearse, lowering it into the earth, shoveling in the clay and rounding off the mound.

"Yes, there was one sound – just a moment or two – the sobbing of Jesse's mother. It was a burial in silence. A preacher, in white necktie, stood in the crowd, but merely as a spectator. There was no religious ceremony, either at the farmhouse or at the cemetery. Frank James, who stood uncovered at the head of the grave beside his aged mother, Mrs. Zerelda Samuel, the young Jesse James, his nephew, turned away as the last spadeful of sod was tossed upon the mound, saying:

"Well, boys, that's all we can do."

"Then some flowers were brought from the yard of the old home and were planted on the mound by the comrades who bore the pall – and it was all over.

"Disinterment of the remains this morning revealed the fact that somebody – either the great State of Missouri or an undertaker – had deceived the James family at the first burial twenty years ago. It was represented at that time that the coffin in which the body was shipped from St. Joseph was an enduring metallic casket, costing $500, and that the body had been embalmed.

"When the old coffin was lifted out of the grave, it fell apart, and there was nothing inside but the skeleton in clothing. This was indeed a dreary day for a disinterment and reburial, from early morning until the noon rain poured. As a consequence, the crowd in attendance was small, many who had intended to come apparently believing that the burial would be postponed.

"But there was no thought of postponement. Jesse James, the bandit's son, came out last night from Kansas City and found his uncle, sick in bed, suffering from an attack of grip. There was a quiet talk between the two, and very early this morning young Jesse went to the home of John T. Samuel here in town, a half-brother of the James boys, and the two men drove through the rain out to the Samuel farm, three and a half miles northeast of the little town. With them went Zach Laffoon, the old gravedigger of Kearney, and his nephew an assistant, Zip Pollock. A handsome new coffin, covered in black, with a silver plate bearing the name "Jesse James" was taken out with the little party.

"The men reached the farmhouse shortly after 5 o'clock, and the two gravediggers set to work at once, in the heavy rain to open the grave. In a corner of the yard, toward the rear, under a gigantic coffee-bean tree, were the grave and the monument – a white marble shaft erected by the devoted mother of the dead man.

"Laffoon and Pollock, with pick and spade, dug away the hard earth whilst Jesse James and John Samuel stood by, partly sheltered from the rain by the spreading branches of the tree, and watched the work. The ground was very hard and dry beneath the first few inches. Every spadeful of earth turned to mud before it struck the ground. It was a job of digging that brought out the perspiration of the men, already drenched. Old Zach Laffoon said it was about the hardest job of the kind he ever attempted.

"Jesse James was buried deep. His mother, apprehensive lest the body might be stolen, had had the grave dug seven feet deep. Zip Pollock is a tall man, but when he stood in the bottom of the grave, his head was a foot below the surface of the ground.

"Nearly four hours work was required to reach the coffin. All this time the rain beat upon the men and into the grave. At last, the pick stuck against metal, boring through rotten plank, and the rusted top of the coffin was revealed. The men dug aside the earth near the foot and passed a plank underneath, raising the coffin slightly. Then they lifted that end of the coffin – and a startling thing happened.

"The top and sides of the metal casket came up, leaving the bottom to fall back into the grave, with the remains of Jesse James lying thereon. The men stepped down into the grave and lifted the bottom of the casket to the top. The foot came up first was mailed in a Kansas town and signed "Original Jesse James." The writer said:

"I will not be buried in Carny next Sunday. I am not dead. I was not shot by Bobie Ford. Tom Howard was shot by Bobie Ford, but I wasn't there, so you can't bury me."

"Laffoon and Pollock lifted the coffin bottom and carried it to the side of the new casket. They scraped the skeleton into the coffin. The hands were folded over the breast, just as they had been placed twenty years ago. The new coffin was closed and placed in the little parlor room of the house, to await the coming of the pallbearers later in the day, and James and Samuel returned to the town.

"Mrs. Samuel did not know that the body had been disinterred until young Jesse returned to the Burlington Hotel. She was there awaiting him, in the little parlor. She inquired immediately as to the condition of the body and appeared relieved when she learned that it undoubtedly was Jesse's.

"Meanwhile Frank James, in his bed upstairs, was receiving old comrades. Seven Quantrell troopers came in on the morning train from Kansas City. They went at once to Mr. James' room. The men are William H. Gregg of Kansas City, who was a Captain under Quantrell; his brother, Attorney J. Frank Gregg of Grain Valley, Missouri, a lieutenant in the same command; James Sim Whitsett, Lee's Summit, Missouri; Hiram J. George, Oak Grove, Missouri who was a Captain; Benjamin H Morrow, Lake City, Missouri; Warren W. Welch, Independence, Missouri, and J.C. Ervin, Marshall, Missouri. The first six served as pallbearers and Mr. Ervin followed to assist.

"Captain George brought his wife along. The Captain is called Hi by his comrades. In fact, all of these old men call each other by the names known to them when they were young fellows with Quantrell. Captain Gregg is Bill and Mr. Whitsett is Sim. The veterans gathered around the bed and told stories of the war days, in which Frank James joined with zest. Bill Gregg sat on the edge of the bed and remarked:

"Did I ever tell you, Frank, about the time I and some more of the boys caused our wives to eat dog? No? Well, our wives happened to be along with us that time, and we had been killing Indians all day."

"Possibly Captain Bill meant palefaces instead of Indians, but that doesn't matter; he was talking war. We had killed forty or fifty Indians, two at a time. They would come up and shoot at us, just two in a bunch and we would detail two men who would go out and kill them and ride back. We got pretty hungry, and we came to an Indian hut. Nobody was home, and we went inside. There was a stack of meat, in large slices, which looked like venison. We took some out and cooked it and our wives began to eat it. I smelt it and said to one of the boys that it didn't smell exactly like venison to me. We went back to the cabin and looked

74

for a fresh deer hide. There was none hanging outside, and we went into the little back room. There we found the hide of a big dog, freshly killed."

"All "the boys" laughed at this, and then came reminisces of narrow escapes in the war. Sim Whitsett told of his narrowest escape, Ben Morrow told of his, and Frank James related his. Then Hi George, who is the very man that enlisted Frank James and took him to fight under Quantrell, told his. Hi George is a humorist. It is marvelous that a man who could do serious work like that required in the Lawrence raid and the Centralia fight can be such a jolly old soul.

"The narrowest escape I ever had during the war," said Hi, "when I was kicked by a government mule and my nose was broken. They thought I was dead, and they didn't send for a doctor for two hours."

"Dr. Powell, Frank James' physician, came in and advised his patient not to venture out.

"I'm going, though," said the sick man. "I've got my winter clothes, a thick pair of overshoes and an overcoat, and I feel sure it won't hurt me to go."

Mrs. Samuel sent up advice for her son to stay in bed, but she was told he intended going to the burial.

"He'll go, then," was the mother's comment. "When Frank James says he'll do a thing, he does it."

"Dinner was served in the hotel dining room at 11:30 o'clock, and a few minutes after 12 the little procession started for the farm, the rain having subsided to a mere drizzle. Along winding country roads, deep in mud but fringed with green hedges, wild roses in full bloom, clover and cornfields, the hearse and the carriages wound.

"There is where little Jesse's sister lives," remarked my driver, pointing to a neat white farmhouse upon a hill, halfway out to the Samuel farm. Here in Kearney the son of Jesse James is called "little Jesse," though he weighs 190 pounds, 23 more than his father did, and is big enough to conduct a Kansas City pawnshop. His sister is Mrs. Mary Barr, wife of a prominent farmer. A little farther along, the driver pointed out the home of Mrs. Joseph Hall, one of the half-sisters of Frank and Jesse James. Mrs. William Nicholson, the other half-sister, also lives in the neighborhood. All these were present at the burial today.

"Crossing swollen and muddy creeks, one of which is called Muddy Fork, which fits its condition, and another of which is called Clear Creek, which is a misfit, our procession presently came in sight of the farmhouse where the new coffin awaited us.

"It may be noted in passing that Jesse James was baptized in Muddy Fork, in 1868, when he joined the Kearney Baptist Church. I talked today with Mr. Majors of Kearney, who witnessed the immersion.

"As the procession reached the farmhouse, the rain ceased entirely. The clouds broke into splotches and the sunlight shone out for a moment, just as the six veterans bore the coffin from the house to the hearse.

"Mrs. Samuel and Mrs. Frank James, with Mrs. Hi George, sat for a few minutes on the front porch before the remains were brought out. Frank James, during this time, pointed out to his friends the side window through which Pinkerton detectives in 1875 threw the bomb that killed eight-year-old Archie P. Samuel and tore off the right forearm of Mrs. Samuel. John, who as a boy was in the house at the time, told how the calamity occurred; and Frank James, who was far away that winter night, remarked with some sarcasm that a revolver was found in a field near the house next morning bearing the initials that showed it belonged to a Pinkerton.

"The State," said Frank James, "took the revolver as evidence, but I guess it never got any farther than that."

"At the side of the yard Frank James pointed out a whitewashed log cabin. Frank did not point out the portholes in the log house, nor the bullet holes in the fence and the stable. Some of "the boys" examined these.

"After the body was placed in the hearse, Mrs. Samuel, supported by young Jesse James and one of the women, walked back to the old grave under the coffee-bean tree. The wrecked coffin had been reburied there. She stood for a moment looking at the grave and then walked slowly to her carriage. Nature was kind on the trip back to town. It did not rain upon the cortege. A different route was taken on the wary back – a road over which Jesse James had ridden on horseback many and many a time, as boy and man.

"Hundreds of townspeople were gathered at the grave, where Zach Laffoon and Zip Pollock again performed the duties of sextons. Strangers read the inscription on the only tombstone in the family lot:

"Archie P., son of R. and Z. Samuel, killed Jan. 26, 1875, aged 8 years and 6 months. Our hearts in his grave are lying."

"The pretty little poem by Thomas Hood is carved upon the stone, the sexy pronouns being altered to suit:

Our very hopes belied our fears;
Our fears our hopes belied.
We thought him dying when he slept,
And sleeping when he died.
For when the sun came dim and sad
And chill with early showers,
His quiet eyelids closed – he had
Another morn than ours.

"Mr. Major, who told me of Jesse James' immersion in Muddy Fork, told also of his conversation and his joining the Baptist Church in Kearney. It is interesting to note that the Baptist Church of that day was located upon the spot, since turned into a cemetery, where Jesse James was buried today.

"He joined the church and was baptized in 1868," said Mr. Major. I noticed by the church records that he was 'excluded' the next year.

"I remember very distinctly the first funeral of Jesse James in April 1882. It was preached by the Reverend Mr. Martin, the minister, and there was a great crowd present. The body was brought here and placed in a hotel which stood where the Commercial Hotel now is. The coffin was opened and we looked at the face through the glass. The corpse wore a full beard and mustache. Everybody who had known him recognized him."

"The funeral services were held in the afternoon at the Kearney Baptist Church of which Jesse had been a member. In 1882.

"The pallbearers were five local men and a mysterious stranger. Nobody seemed to know this man who appeared to be somewhat in authority.

"It's Frank!" whispered a spectator, hoarsely. But it was a stout man, and Frank James was slender.

"Mr. and Mrs. Frank James and Mrs. Samuel accompanied the Quantrell veterans to the train this evening and bade them goodbye. Before boarding the train "the boys" began talking about horses.

"I can't ride a horse much," said Frank James. "I have a good saddle-horse here, but when I get on him I'm afraid he'll fall down with me."

"I can ride," said Hi George. "You ought to come out to my farm and see me gallop around, attending to my work."

"Precious little work you do these days, I reckon, Hi," remarked Sim Whitsett; "you're too old."

"I'm about sixty-six," replied Captain Hi, "but I get around pretty lively yet … Look out, there, Sim – the Feds are comin'," continued the humorist, and Lawyer Frank Gregg's mind harked back to the fight at Centralia, in which he took part with Frank and Jesse James.

"That was the only affair I was in with Jesse," he said, "but Frank James and I enlisted together."

"As the men boarded the train Ben Morrow called out:

"Better call the roll, Frank. Sim Whitsett is missing."

"Frank James boarded the coach and looked for Sim, who was sitting in another part of the car.

"Well, goodbye, boys, and good luck," called Frank James as the train pulled out.

CHAPTER TEN

Now that you have read of the 1902 reburial of the body of Charley Bigelow who was killed by Bob Ford in 1882 and buried as being the much-hunted Jesse James. Stop and think a little bit. If that had been the real Jesse Woodson James would his mother Zerelda Samuel have had her son's body dug up and moved from the farm to the Kearney cemetery? Absolutely not!

And, be assured, *if* the real Jesse James had been killed in 1882 as has been written for years, the killer would not have lived to tell about it. Frank James would have seen to that. Remember, Jesse and Frank had pledged to each other, that if one of them were ever killed, the remaining one would avenge his death.

Bob Ford certainly knew he didn't kill his cousin Jesse James. He knew the man he killed was Charley Bigelow, who looked enough like Jesse to be his twin and who had been doing things and claiming he was Jesse James.

Jesse told Ola, "Ola, Bigelow wanted to be Jesse James, so we just buried him as being Jesse James."

The killing of the real Jesse James was a hoax.

Now let's go forward to 1915. Frank and Annie James had rented or leased their place at Fletcher, Oklahoma and moved back to the farm near Kearney, Missouri. Frank, who was 72 had been failing in health since the fall of 1914. On February 18, 1915 at 3:40 o'clock in the afternoon he died. He had suffered a stroke of apoplexy earlier in the day and never regained consciousness. His wife and son Robert were at his bedside.

His desire was to be cremated so his funeral service was held there in the farm home and instead of having a religious service at his funeral; he made the arrangements with his friend Judge John Phillips to deliver an address for him. Phillips had also defended Frank when he was tried and acquitted in July 1883 in Gallatin, Missouri for the murder of Frank McMillan.

Pallbearers were Ben Morrow, who lived in eastern Jackson County, George Shepherd of Lee's Summit, Bill Gregg of Kansas City, Gabe Parr and John Workman of Independence. "All Quantrell men," and Thomas T. Crittenden of Kansas City.

When the service was over, Frank's body was taken to St. Louis to the crematory and after his ashes were placed in an urn, the urn was then placed in a vault and kept until 1944 when Annie Ralston James died in a Nursing Home at Kearney, at age 91. She too was cremated and after her ashes were placed in an urn, the urns of her and Frank were then taken to Independence, Missouri and buried side by side at Hill Park Cemetery.

Contrary to the belief of many people, Frank James never was convicted of train robbery, or any crimes connected therewith, and while he spent some time in jail awaiting trial, he never saw the inside of a penitentiary as a felon. He was acquitted at Gallatin, Missouri, where, after his surrender, he was charged with the murder of a stonemason named McMillan during the Winston, Missouri train robbery.

Not content with fighting in more wars than is common to the average man, when Britain became entangled, thus drawing Canada in to the conflict, Jesse volunteered for duty in the Canadian Army. Britain declared war August 14, to 1918. Because of his educational background he was quickly accepted as an officer.

He told Ola, "World War I was four years of hell. Part of the time, I served as an interpreter." During his lifetime he had become fluent in several languages. Among them were French, Spanish, Portuguese, German and the Indian Sign Language. Also, Sioux Indian language.

Jesse used to hold Ola's hand and sing love songs to her in Sioux Indian language.

J.R. Flynn in Waterloo, Iowa, stated in 1948:

"I ran across him (Jesse) in the Canadian Army at Camp Sewell in 1916. Not under that name, of course. I knew him under a different name. He was 68 years old at the time … and was awful handy with a pistol or rifle. A powerful man for that age. We knew, he had a past, but he was supposed to have had a parole from the Mounted Police."

Jesse told Ola, "I was in the Canadian Army for a while. In C Company – 126th Battalion – Heavy Artillery. Then I went to Winnipeg, Canada and joined the Royal Canadian Air Force R.A.F. in World War I. I went from Winnipeg, Canada to Halifax, Nova-Scotia then to Paris, France and Marseilles, France. Made Captain and flew a plane for twenty two months. I earned the title of Major and didn't want it. I left Paris on November 16, 1918 and arrived in Winnipeg, Canada in December 1918." Then he said, "Not long ago, the Canadian Government attempted to locate the old soldier to decorate him." Jesse was John Franklin in the Canadian military service as best I can recall.

In 1920, Jesse was in Ellensburg, Washington for a while and Mary Plina Norris, daughter of Frank James and her son Henry, went to Ellensburg and spent about a week visiting with her uncle. She was very fond of her Jesse James.

In 1922, Jesse was back in Texas and lived on a ranch for a while, twenty-five miles northwest from Mineral Wells, Texas, under the alias of Frank Dalton.

In 1924, in July or August, Jesse was in Wichita, Kansas for a short time, preaching at a big tent revival. He was 76 years of age at the time, but looked younger. He knew the Bible well and had a deep, rolling voice that carried well. A friend of the Everharts in Austin, Texas, Allen Mozingo, happened to be in Kansas and heard him preach. Allen said he had long, white hair and claimed to be the youngest member of the James gang. Large crowds gathered at the revival to hear him preach. Then when Allen saw and talked with Jesse in the hospital in Austin, he said that the man preaching in Kansas and the man in the hospital was one and the same person.

Jesse had told Aubrey and Ola that he had preached some mighty good sermons himself, a few years back.

The P.E. Pitman family owned and operated the Camp Cottages at Brighton, Colorado. It was a resort, really. There was a store, gas pumps out in front of the

81

store. Behind the store was a swimming pool. Back from the store a ways were cabins for rent and there was a trailer park. In the back of the store were the living quarters of the Pitman family. Two bedrooms, kitchen, sleeping porch and down in the cellar was a family room. There were two children in the P.E. and Oshie Pitman family and his father also.

Oshie told Ola, "We lived dangerous those days, there because we never knew when someone was going to pike a gun in our face. So, men and women knew how to handle a gun.

Well, it was to this Camp Cottages at Brighton, Colorado that Jesse James, using the alias of Jess Johnson came one day in 1926. He had long, white hair, was dressed in a nice dark suit, white shirt and necktie and wore a rather wide brim hat." He rented a small cabin there near the store and was no nice and kind but so alone, that the Pitman family, who called him "Old Timer," sort of took him under their wing. The children were very fond of Old Timer. He had quite a bit of money on him at the time and asked Oshie to put it in their secret safe, which she did. He wore his gun in a shoulder holster in the daytime and on Saturdays, he and Oshie would sit down at the kitchen table and clean their hand guns as they talked.

At night, P.E., Oshie and Old Timer would sit around the kitchen table and play penny-ante poker as a pastime. In the daytime, Old Timer was a wonderful babysitter to look after the children.

Oshie said, "One time while Old Timer was there at our place I was on my pony, it bolted, I fell off and right into a desert cactus plant and for two weeks I couldn't sit down, because my behind was so full of hairy stickers. Old Timer laughed so darn hard he nearly split his britches. But I darn sure never laughed. My behind was so sore, even my pride was hurt and that sandy ground wasn't a soft place to light."

Old Timer stayed ten weeks there and then said he had to go, that he was to meet some friends at the Depot in Denver. When he came out of his cabin with his suitcase, he also brought a jar of pennies that he'd won at our nightly penny poker games, set the jar on the table and said to Oshie, "Divide these between the children."

Oshie and P.E. took him to the Depot in Denver, walked over to the train with him and when she kissed him goodbye, he took a very unusual ring from his finger and said, "Here's something to remember me by," then walked off. She saw him meet the two men who were waiting for him but she didn't know them. They boarded the train and left and she never saw Old Timer again but has never forgotten him and how nice he was, how droopy and how interesting he was to talk with for he was so well versed he could talk on any subject. Jesse was 79 years old at the time.

Who is Oshie? Oh! Well, she is a Dalton.

On October 26, 1927, Allen Parmer, age 80, died at the home of Mr. and Mrs. J.A. Kemp in Wichita Falls, Texas. He drove his car from Alpine, Texas where he was living at the time, to Fort Worth, Texas due to the illness of a grandchild. His daughter was Mrs. B.A. Rose of that city. The child being improved, he drove on to Wichita Falls to visit friends.

Allen's first wife was Frank and Jesse James own sister Susan Lavenia (Susie) James Parmer who had died several years before and is buried in the Riverside Cemetery in Wichita Falls.

Allen Parmer was one of the last survivors of Quantrell's Band of Guerrillas in the War Between the States. He is buried in Wichita Falls near Susie. Mrs. Zelma Edwards of Alpine is a daughter of Allen and Susie.

I'll go back to Jesse's outlaw days for a little bit. The following was written by Alice Collins:

It is generally an accepted fact in Richland Parish Louisiana that the ill-famed Frank and Jesse James used to visit relatives there and hide out from the law. They were condoned by many people there, because their activities had been directed against some of the elements that had contributed to the misfortune of the Confederacy. The "relative's" house is still there in Delhi and is now known as the "Old Haney House". There is a hidden passageway and a hidden compartment where the outlaws may have kept their money. A holster belonging to them was found but has since been lost. There are houses all over the area with a lone pine tree in the front yard. E.B. Carson, Rayville, found out that they were planted as a sign that the people were friendly with the James boys. Therefore, any member of the gang could tell who could be trusted. People always kept quiet about the gang, though, because as Jesse said, "A dead man tells no tales."

A story told by Mrs. Earline Sarter, Alto, involved her grandfather, John Baker, who lived on a plantation near Delhi.

One day he met four men whom he'd known in Missouri and took them back to his home. Knowing them to be outlaws, he introduced them to his wife as "Brother Smith" and his three helpers in a missionary endeavor in that area.

During the visit, "Brother Smith" admired the Bakers' baby and took a walk with young Will Baker, whom he encouraged to always do what his parents said and do the right thing. Mrs. Baker later remarked, "Brother Smith was one of the most cultured, tender men I have ever met."

It was several months before she found out that "Brother Smith" was Jesse James and his helpers were brother Frank and two of the Younger brothers.

The following copied from an article in the St. Louis Missouri *Republican* Newspaper of October 6, 1882.

THE CRIMES CHARGED TO THEM

These raids became so notorious, daring and successful that they caused a great stir in the country, and rightly or wrongly, as one time and another, all the band of guerrillas who were known to be closely banded together were accused. The notoriety the James and Younger boys have attained is got to make people forget that there have been numerous others who were just as positively acquainted with following this class of industry. Tom Little and Andy McGuire were hanged by vigilantes for it. Oll Shepherd and Jim Reed were shot down by Sheriff posses while George Huckberd, Bill Greenwood, Bill Chiles, Ike Flannery,

Bud Pense, Jim White, Payne Jones, John Jarrette, Clell Miller, Artnar McCoy, Dick Burns, Jack Bishop, Red Moskus, and various others have at one time or another been almost as common names in print as the Jameses and Youngers, only they did not stay on the stage so long. It is probable that both Frank and Jesse are credited with crimes with which they had nothing to do. Though the public will never go so far as to believe nearly all that Mrs. James has said in defense of her husband since his death, or perhaps what her writers and publishers have made her say. The frequent occasions, however, as Mrs. Jesse James alleged with a show of reason, made it impossible for them to be anything but outlaws, and even after Frank had married the highly respectable Miss Underwood he would have, perhaps, found no little difficulty in reforming and settling down. – To honest citizenship. A glance at the robberies credited to him and his brother will show that if it required nerve and courage to remain in outlawry so long, it required no less of both qualities to surrender and face such accussions.

Yes, Frank James was married three times. They were Miss Welch, Miss Underwood and Miss Ralston.

While I'm back in Jesse's outlaw days –

A friend, Mrs. Corean Roberts in Texas, told Ola, –

"When us children were small, we were always happy when our Grandfather, Tom Martin came to visit. He loved to tell us stories of his growing up years.

"Tom Martin was an Irishman six feet two inches tall. He joined the Confederate Army when he was 15 years old. Lying about his age, and was wounded before he would have been legally old enough to join. But, after all, his two older brothers were fighting and he resented being left at home. Tom was a country veterinarian and his children learned many remedies from helping him.

"Tom Martin grew up in the community with Jesse James and his brother Frank. Tom told of helping the brothers to escape from the law after the Civil War.

"Once when they were hidden out in a bottom, Tom carried food to them Then one day he found a note on a stump that read: "Don't leave any food, today, Tom, we have a way out." Later on that day, a freight train came through and on a big grade, it slowed to a stop. A ramp was thrown down and several riders on horses boarded and the train rolled on.

"Tom Martin told of being on a train once that was robbed by the James boys and their gang. They took all the watches and billfolds, but when they came to Tom, one of them gave him a wink. After gathering the loot , they asked if there was any Confederate Veterans present and returned all of the items belonging to them. Tom told many such stories to his grandchildren."

The following is from a copy of a little bit of a book written by the mother of one of Ola's friends in Canada, K.M. Roberts:

"A big celebration at Kelwood was held for Andrew McCutcheon on his 101st birthday, who lived with his son George, daughter-in-law and grandchildren. After "Old Andy" danced a jig he returned to his favorite chair and watched the fun. His great-grandchildren crowded around him and directed his mind to the past.

"Grandpa, tell us about the time you rode with Jesse James," they asked. He didn't hear them very well at first so the children shouted a little louder. The old man smiled, nodded and his eyes misted up a bit.

"He said, 'When I was a young lad, I lived on my grandfather's farm near Mount Forrest in Ontario. The fellow came out of the bush one day. Said his name was Jesse James. We didn't know he was a holdup man. He stayed and worked at our place two or three weeks. Seemed like a good fellow. I was around 18 years then and he was four or five years older'n me. (22 or 23). Him and me went riding lots of times. Oh, that Jesse. Could he shoot! Could take three nicks out of a squirrels' tail as he run up a tree.' He told of Jesse's prowess with a gun – the wild pigeons they shot in the peafield, the bears and the coon they brought home. There was admiration in his voice, undimmed by the greater part of a century. It was with sadness and reluctance he tells the latter part of the story – of how his grandfather discovered that his new hired man was only using his farm as a hideout after a recent robbery in the States and had hidden his share of the loot in the loft of the barn.

"Shortly after this Jesse "borrowed" a horse and rode away. Down the trail he was joined by an accomplice. The two men headed for Mount Forrest where they committed a robbery and then disappeared. "Old Andy" shook his tousled white head. "That Jesse sure could shoot," he said."

Andrew McCutcheon was born near Arthur, Ontario, in 1852. His acquaintance with the notorious outlaw Jesse James may be a fact but there is no record that James or any member of his gang ever reached Canada. But there is a period of time around 1870 when his whereabouts were never definitely ascertained. Mr. McCutcheon may unknowingly hold the missing link to the James story. His reference to Jesse's age as compared to his own is correct as records show the outlaw was born in Missouri in 1847.

Research conducted by the Mount Forrest Historical Society revealed no written records to show definite proof that Jesse James was ever in the district but several residents were convinced of the fact because of stories which had been handed down to them from reliable sources.

Mr. McCutcheon accepted his longevity with apparent unconcern. He continued to enjoy above all three hearty meals a day, his pipe, the visits of his friends and memories of the days when he rode with Jesse James. Now, I'll come back to Jesse James after he was supposedly killed in 182 when Charley Bigelow was killed by Bob Ford and buried as being Jesse James.

In 1928, or around that time, Jesse James left the States and went to Canada. Using the alias of Frank Dalton, he went to Brighton, Ontario for a while then bought a ranch at Dryden, Ontario. There had had horses. Some fine Percheon or

Draft horses and some saddle stock. All fine horses. He owned that place about two years. Then sold it to the man he'd rented it to.

He tried mining but that didn't work out. So, him and couple of fellows went in together and bought the Minders Hotel, over at Purnell, British Columbia. After a while Jesse decided he didn't like the hotel business, he grew restless and sold his part in the hotel.

In 1930 and part of 1931, he was back in the States and him and DeWitt Travis went to Ardmore, Oklahoma for a while and while there, Jesse gave lectures in and around Ardmore and Wilson and went out and visited an old lady that Jones and Jesse knew real well as well as the Ingrams he'd known in Arkansas and Oklahoma.

In 1932, Jesse went to Shreveport, Louisiana and visited a Mr. E.E. Walsh who ran a repair shop there. Mr. Walsh was raised in Missouri. In the same Missouri county as Jesse. He was a little younger than Jesse. Nine years younger. Born in 1856.

Then Jesse went back to Texas and got in the oil game for a while. He was at Overton, Texas a while and several other towns. Kilgore, Longview, Carthage, Gregton, Hallsville, Jefferson, Daingerfield, Marshall and all around in those areas.

He loved to read and he told Ola, "Ola, the newspaper at Marshall, Texas is called *The Marshall Messenger*."

In 1933, Jesse was in Gladewater, Texas selling oil leases. Then he left there, went back to Canada and bought a ranch. His ranch was near Lea Park, Alberta, Canada. He had a mixed operation. Cattle, horses and growing wheat and oats. His home was beside the Vermillion River, made of logs. The Lea Park Rodeo grounds was about a quarter of a mile away from his place.

On Christmas Night, 1933, a young man named Mitchell Graves stopped at the log home of Jesse and when he knocked on the door, a white-haired man who appeared to be in his 80's came to the door. When Mitch asked if he could come in and get warm, the elderly 86-year-old man, who said his name was Frank

Dalton, replied, "You sure can. Go put your horse in the barn or stable and then get in here by the fire before you freeze to death." He did. It felt like it was about 60° below zero outside and Mitch was mighty glad to get inside where it was warm. They talked awhile and then went to bed. Jesse, or Frank Dalton as he was called, wanted the young man to stay there but Mitch explained that he couldn't, that he had to go on to his folks. Jesse said, "Well when you get through there, why don't you come on back here?"

So, on February 5, 1934, he went back to Jesse's place to work

In 1983, Ola got a letter from Mitchell Graves and in Canada and in that first letter, he said, "I worked for an old fellow at Lea Park, Alberta, Canada in 1934. His name was J. Frank Dalton. A known member of the old Jesse James gang used to live at Princeland, Saskatchewan, Canada. His name was Bob (Slim) Hendershire. He used to tell his neighbors that he was going to Lea Park to visit Jesse James. He used to call Mr. Dalton by the name Jesse. They both had very good horses, even at their ages. They were real horsemen.

"When Bob used to say he was going to visit Jesse James, the neighbors would laugh and say that Slim was living in the past again. I saw an article in the Police Gazette in 1950 about Jesse James being alive in 1950 with a picture of Mr. Dalton. It also had a good article which bears out what you have told in the World News article in December 27, 1983 by Dick Donovan. It was only then than I realized who Mr. Dalton was."

In another letter from Mitch, he said, "Getting back to the three men that used to visit Jesse, Slim Hendershire, Jim Sidner and Jack Walliver. They all claimed to have been members of Quantrell's Raiders. They talked a lot about Missouri. When they were all together at Lea Park, they would get their pistols and I would throw a can up in the air and they would blow it to pieces before it hit the ground. Any one of them could do it. The pistols that Jesse had were an old Frontier Model Smith and Wesson and a Colt. Both 45's. Quite long barrels and carried in holsters on each side under his coat. Cross arm draw.

"Rumor has it that Jim and Jack were chased by posses to the Canadian border. They were all very good horsemen and had good horses, Mr. Dalton (Jesse) was quite fond of Slim and Jack, but he did not have the same regard for Jim. The reason was that Jim was rustling cattle and horses, which did not set well with Mr. Dalton. When the three men would visit Jesse, they would talk a lot about Missouri and they told me things, but I did not make any connection until I saw the Police Gazette article.

"While I was working for Jesse there was another fellow that came quite often. He was a Boer War Veteran by the name of Albert Christopher. They had served in the Boer War together and were very friendly and used to visit a lot. When I worked for Mr. Dalton (Jesse), I did the general work one would do around a small ranch, such as looking after the livestock, cutting hay and putting it up. Also putting in grain crops in the spring and helping harvest them in the fall. I also rode the range some to keep tab on the cattle and horses. Jesse was a swell guy to work for. I was very fond of him and I think he was fond of me.

"Jesse was a person with a great sense of humor. He loved fun and got a big laugh out of telling some tall story. Like the following one: One night a fellow by the name of Roy Morris stopped over night at Jesse's ranch. He got to talking about how good a garden he could grow up at his place. Jesse asked him, 'Did you ever feed buttermilk to pumpkin vines.'

"Roy said, 'I never have, but I've heard of it being done.'

"Jesse said, 'I have tried it out in front of my house. I got the buttermilk from a creamery four miles away. The more buttermilk I hauled, the more the pumpkin vines wanted. It sure kept me busy. It vines took off down along the Vermillion River a mile and a half, then crossed the North Saskatchewan Rover three times and then ran 18 miles on the other side.'

"Roy Morris said, 'Wow! Some pumpkin vines.'

"Jesse said, 'I'll bet you can't guess how big the pumpkins were.'

"Roy said, They must have been some real old smackers.'

"Jesse said, 'No, the vines ran so fast, they wore the pumpkins out.'

Mitch said, 'Jesse liked to talk and while I was working for him, we would sit and talk a lot at night. He told me that he'd been down in the Argentine. But he didn't say how long he was there. He also told me that he was in the Canadian Army in 1915 – 1916 but was finally discharged because of his injured lung. On occasions, he would mention Belle Starr. He'd say, 'She was quite a woman. I had great respect for her.'

"One time when he mentioned Belle Starr he said, 'The James gang used to stay with her periodically. She was a good friend of Cole Younger.'

"Jesse told me about taking the preacher's watch. He said the James gang thought it was a big joke. Mitch said, 'As I told you, Jesse liked to talk and on cold nights we would set and talk for a good while. He told me that he owned land in Oklahoma, but I didn't think anything about it at the time. He told me that he lived at Dresdon, Ontario Canada a while then went back to Oklahoma and after a while came back to Canada and bought the ranch near Lea Park.

"Many of the things that he told me about the James gang, now makes sense. He could name them all, and I wondered how he knew so much about it. I used to sing the song about the dirty little coward that shot Mr. Howard and laid poor Jesse in his grave. Sometimes he would laugh like crazy and sometimes he would say, 'you young whipper-snapper, you don't know what you are singing about.'

"In the early part of March 1934, it was about 60 below zero, close to midnight I heard what sounded like someone crying outside. I went to the door and looked out. The sound seemed to be coming from the road. I thought someone must be freezing on the road. I woke Mr. Dalton and he said, 'I think it might be a Mountain Lion.'

"I said, 'I am going to find out.'

"He said, 'Take this with you and use it if it is a Mountain Lion,' handing me one of his pistols.

"I went out and when I passed the cutter, which is a light sleigh, the noise was behind me. I looked into the cutter and there was his dog with eight new pups. They were crying with the cold. I put the pups in my coat and took them and their mother in to the house and said, 'Your family has increased by eight.' You should have heard him laugh. When spring came, the pups were running around and followed him wherever he went.

"One day he came in from the bush that was around the yard, with the pups following him. He was fastening up his pants with a big smile on his face and said, 'A darn handy bunch of pups. You squat down to have a dump and get your hind end washed at the same time.'

"Jesse had trouble with his chest a good bit. He said it was caused by a bullet wound in his lung. Frank Dalton, as I called him, was a very fine man and well respected at Lea Park. Before he came to Lea Park he lived in or came from Oklahoma. But before that, he had lived at Dresdon, Ontario Canada. He owned a black stallion that I broke for him that he called Black Prince. He was a beautiful horse, jet-black, with four white feet and a white blaze on his face.

"The rodeo grounds was about a fourth of a mile from Jesse's house. A rodeo was going on and at that time there was a horse called Black Dynamite that was a real outlaw. The announcer called out over the loud speaker – "Frank Dalton from Lea Park on Black Dynamite." Everyone in the crowd was quite shocked, and saying that an old man like that would be killed if he came out on that outlaw horse.

"There were a lot of cowboys around the chute, so no one could see in it. Others were back behind the chute with clubs, hitting the rails to make it sound like a horse fighting. Some yelling. One old boy was in the chute with a buffalo blanket over him and he'd raise up so it looked like the horse's back. Jesse let everyone see him climb up the chute and got on the horse. The racket went on for about fifteen minutes, then the chute opened and Mr. Dalton rode out across the arena waving his hat. He was riding Black Prince, not the outlaw horse. He galloped around a bit and then rode out. Everyone really cheered."

Mitch said, 'Mr. Dalton was an expert with a pistol or rifle. One day he said, 'Well, I guess we better have some Prairie Chicken for dinner.' He picked up his gun, went out behind the house and in a little while came back in the house carrying two Prairie Chickens with their heads blown off.'

"One day I said to him, 'As good as you are with guns; you ought to go to the Turkey Shoot tomorrow. I heard about it down at the store when I went down there.' He said, 'Alright, we'll just both go.'

"'So the next day we both went. The shoot started and Jesse fired two shots and hit Bull's Eye both times. The men watching were amazed at such marksmanship by a man his age.' Jesse said, 'Well just move that target back about a hundred yards.' They did and he fired twice and again hit Bull's Eye both times again. They were so amazed at his skill and all talking about it that he decided to put on a little show for them and had me throw a can in the air and with a pistol in each hand he kept the can in the air until the guns were both empty. Then he said, 'Just give me a couple of turkeys.' They did and me and him started home.

"On our way we came to the home of an elderly couple. We stopped in, visited a little bit as we drank some coffee with them then Jesse gave them one of the turkeys. We went on toward home and in a house that nobody lived in, some people who had got caught in a storm had took shelter there. So, we stopped in and Jesse gave them the other turkey. They wanted to pay him for it but he said, 'No, that turkey didn't cost me anything.' So, we went on home empty handed to eat some more Prairie Chicken.

"Jesse began to laugh on the way and I asked, 'What's the joke?'

"Jesse said, 'This is a day they won't forget soon.'

"I said, 'I know I won't.'

"Jesse said, 'But didn't we have a good time.'

"I replied, 'I sure did.'

"In the fall of 1934, a fellow came there from the States and was staying there with us. He was called Bill Dalton – supposedly a brother of Frank Dalton. He was a much larger man than Frank. About six feet two inches tall and weighed about two hundred and thirty pounds and somewhat younger. He was a real nice fellow although he didn't resemble Frank (Jesse).

"In truth and fact, he was not Bill Dalton, nor was he Jesse's brother. He was DeWitt Travis whom Jesse had known all of his life and knew DeWitt's family."

Mitch said, 'In 1935, Jesse left the ranch and went back to the States. I left Lea Park in 1935 but Jesse and Bill Dalton was still at the ranch when I went back to my homestead. I was very fond of Mr. Dalton and I used to visit him after I went to my homestead whenever I was in Lea Park. I left for my homestead in 1935 before Jesse left for the States. I went back to Lea Park, stopped at the store and saw Bill Dalton. I said, 'Hello Bill. I'm going out to see Mr. Dalton.''

Bill said, 'He ain't there. He's gone back to the States and will be gone for a while. He's going to write some articles for a book. The one-time Governor of Missouri's son, is writing the memoirs of his father and he wants Frank to write the outlawry part for the book about the James boys.'

"I said, 'Well he couldn't have picked a better man. As much as he knows about Jesse James and his gang.'

"Bill Dalton replied, 'He ought to know because he is Jesse James.'

"Somewhat surprised, I said, 'Now wait a minute. Jesse James was killed years ago.'

"Bill Dalton said, 'That was another man that was killed and buried as Jesse James. His name was Charley Bigelow. He looked a lot like Jesse and claimed to be Jesse James when he'd pull a robbery.'

"I said, 'But Bill, Mr. Dalton is a good man. He reads the Bible a lot.'

"Bill replied, 'Yes, he reads the Bible a lot. He's got a Bible with him now and there's one up there in the safe. But, when you push a person like he was pushed and mistreated like he was mistreated, a person will do a lot of things.

"Jesse had told me one time, 'Bigelow got just what was coming to him. As once while he was impersonating Jesse James, he and a group of his cronies robbed a bank and on their way out of town, he shot a small boy on the lawn in front of the boy's home, killed him and the blame was put on Jesse James and Jesse was very angry about it.'

"Later in the year, Bill joined Frank in the States and it was in the spring of 1936, as best I can remember, that they came back to Lea Park."

Henry Houston Crittenden, son of former Governor Thomas T. Crittenden of Missouri, got in touch with Jesse, who was going by the alias of Frank Dalton and told him about the book he was compiling and asked for Jesse's help in writing the outlawry part of the book. So, in 1935 he left Canada and came back to the States. Then a short time later, DeWitt Travis left Canada where he'd been staying with Jesse and also returned to the States then he and Jesse got together and headed for Kansas City, Missouri. Hugh Crittenden operated an investment company in Kansas City at that time and Thomas T. Crittenden, Jr. was Mayor of Kansas City.

DeWitt Travis, who was a friend of ours, told Ola:

"When we got to Kansas City and went to the home of Hugh Crittenden, someone else let us in the door and when Hugh came walking in he said, 'Old Jess, I'll be damned, ain't you dead yet!' Then walking up to Jesse with a smile on his face, took hold of his hand and looking at him said, 'Well, old Jesse, my goodness alive, you don't look much older than you used to.'"

He greeted Frank Dalton as "Old Jesse". A bit unusual, isn't it?

DeWitt said, "He and Jesse put up at the Bray Hotel in Kansas City. Hugh came to the room and they talked a while then Hugh went and got a typewriter and brought it in for Jesse to use and Jesse went to work writing the articles. Hugh would come to the room and him and Jesse would talk. Sometimes they would talk until the wee hours of the morning. Hugh knew that Jesse had to write them in such a way as to keep his true identity covered. Jesse wrote the major part of the chapter "OUTLAWRY IN MISSOURI" and gave Hugh a lot of information. Hugh knew that the man called J. Frank Dalton was in truth, the real Jesse James. That's why he picked him to write the articles."

When the work there was all finished, Jesse and DeWitt went back to Canada. Got back to Jesse's ranch at Lea Park in the spring of 1936.

I'm going back for a little bit to the year 1928.

Jesse went out to California for a while. He did some work off and on at some of the movie studios but just which ones and kind of work he had done, I don't know. He didn't stay long, and then came back to Texas. One person he got to know while there and liked a lot was Judy Canova. He was 81 years old at that time.

In 1937, Mitch Graves went back to Lea Park and he told Ola, "I had been some time since I'd been back there. But when I told the man at the store that I was on my way out to see Mr. Dalton, the man said, 'Well he's not there. He's gone back to the States. So has his brother Bill.' The last time I saw Jesse was in the fall of 1936. He was a fine fellow to work for, had a wonderful sense of humor and I spent many pleasant evenings talking with him.

"I left Alberta and went to Ontario, Canada and did not get back to Lea Park again until 1976. The village had been done away with except the rodeo grounds was there. Still is, as there is still a rodeo there every year. Jesse's log house and barn is gone and that is something that should have been preserved. There is just a roadside park there now. Jesse sold his ranch in 1946 or 1947, I'm not sure which."

In the summer of 1936, Jesse and DeWitt were back in the States and was at Gladewater, Texas. On July 4th a pistol shoot was held for Peace Officers there in Gladewater. Chief Bob Goss was judge and at that time, State Pistol Champ. Jesse, who was almost 89 years old at that time, or Frank Dalton as he was called, was Master of Ceremonies of the shoot.

Jesse said, "They wouldn't let us shoot, we were too good for them. But we gave an exhibition of trick shooting. I took two six-shooters, had a can tossed into the air and kept it up until the six-shooters were both empty. If you miss once, you might as well let 'er come on down."

When asked, "Did you do it?" He replied, "Yep, the first time. I was a pretty good shot; I am now for that matter."

On May 12, 1937, while living there in Gladewater, Jesse, who was nearing 90 years of age at the time, slipped, fell and broke his leg. While in the hospital he wrote short stories about the War Between the States and paid his hospital bill with the money he received from them. When he got out of the hospital, he went and stayed with Brushy Bill Roberts and his wife while he was getting around on crutches and until he was able to get around again without them. Brushy Bill and Jesse had been close friends for many years.

Jesse told Ola, "Billy was a member of the Anti-Horse-Thief Association in part of 1883, 1884 and 1885 and he was with Pinkerton for a while too." He didn't saw what name or names Billy used at the time.

On July 7, 1948 in Guthrie, Oklahoma, Brushy Bill, former scout and Indian fighter who, although told them he was 82 but in truth and fact was 88 years old, was in town to visit Jesse who at that time, was in the Tone Hotel in Guthrie. Brushy told them that he had known Jesse for 78 years. That his father, Al, "Wild Henry" Roberts was present in St. Joseph, Missouri to identify the body after Charley Bigelow, who was going under the name of Jesse Howard, was shot and killed.

"He came home and told us all about it," said Brushy Bill, "and he identified Bigelow as Jesse James and he said Jesse's mother knew it wasn't her son, but claimed it was, to help Jesse get away." Brushy said, "I've visited with Jesse off and on ever since and me and my wife took care of Jesse for several weeks in our home after he had broken his leg in Gladewater, Texas."

In 1938, Jesse campaigned for Jerry Saddler for Railroad Commissioner and Pierce Brooks for Lieutenant Governorship. He made about twelve campaign speeches for the two candidates. Pierce Brooks was defeated by Coke Stevenson.

In 1939, Jesse went to Corpus Christi, Texas and lived a short while in a little old place eight miles from town. He was going by the name of Frank Dalton at the time and if I'm not mistaken, and I don't think I am, it was while Jesse was living there that he visited Indian Chief Red Fox and his son in Corpus Christi.

The following is copied from an article that was carried in the Corpus Christi *Times Newspaper* on Friday, June 30, 1939.

As you read this, keep in mind that Jesse James was still living undercover and therefore made some statements that are not correct.

LAST OF QUANTRELL'S NOW LIVING IN CORPUS CHRISTI, PLANS TO ENTER THE MOVIES. FRANK DALTON, 91 REVEALS INCIDENTS OF COLORFUL LIFE.

By Ron Buzbee

In one room of a two-room shot-gun house a half mile off the Old Dump Road eight miles south of town, the last of Quantrell's Raiders, that notorious band of Civil War fighters, is planning to enter the movies.

The only thing, so far, that has kept Frank Dalton, 91 from writing that script for the "Meter-Goldwyn people," as he calls Metro-Goldwyn-Mayer, noted Hollywood producers, has been a broken right leg, two broken ribs and a broken left wrist in the past two years.

Dalton is an uncle of three boys of the same surname, Grat, Emmett and Bob. But, back in 1892, on October 5, Frank recalls, with casual preciseness, that Emmett and Bob had trouble with a Coffeyville, Kansas bank, and were killed.

"GOOD BOYS – JUST DRUNK"

"They were good boys, just a little drunk," Frank admitted the other day. But they had none of the experiences that he has had, Frank said.

Dalton was born March 8, 1848, at Goliad, Texas. His father was a U.S. Army Colonel in the Mexican War and later became a U.S. Senator.

"I was an accidental Texan," Dalton said. He explained that he was born along the trail that led to the Mexican War.

He weighs 182 pounds and is proud, in his casual sort of way, of his 5 feet, ten- and one-half inches, and his mop of white hair that falls over his shoulders. The hair formerly dropped to his waist but when he broke his leg in 1937, it was cut off while he was in a Gladewater hospital.

Dalton joined William Quantrell's men when he was 15 when Quantrell was paving the way for such outlaws as Jesse James, Cole Younger and others. Dalton knew them all, but they were all on the same side then.

TELLS OF AMBUSH

What drove Quantrell's men to raiding, after they were formed as a militia during the war, was the refusal of the United States Government to grant amnesty to them, Dalton said:

"Everything we did during the war they considered as civil crimes, not military, and we had to be tried in state courts," Dalton explained.

He recalled once after the war when he, Jesse James, and 12 other Quantrell men sought to surrender at Higginsville, Mo., they were ambushed. Two were killed and Dalton and James were wounded before the 12 escaped on their horses.

William Quantrell was the name adopted by Charles Hart, of Hopkinsville, Ky., who later became a central Texas schoolteacher. "It was known that he was with Quantrell during the war but no one suspected the mild-mannered and gentle-speaking schoolteacher of being the fierce and terror inspiring leader of the fiercest and most ruthless band of raiders that the Civil War produced." Dalton said.

Since the Civil War, Dalton has been a U.S. Marshal, a U.S. soldier, a Texas Ranger and a Texas oil man, among other things, but always he has stayed along the frontier.

"I ain't as young as I used to be. I'm going to die someday," he said. "The doctor at Gladewater told me I had two months to live if I didn't get out of here."

WRITES SHORT STORIES

Which accounts for Dalton being in this vicinity. He draws an old age pension, but doesn't like to. That's why he is recuperating so that he can plug out his story for the "Meter-Goldwyn-people".

Dalton has written several short stories, made contributions to the Missouri Historical Society, especially since the film, "Jesse James" came out.

"They wanted me to give accurate accounts of the Battle of Centralia and other battles," he said.

Dalton has proof of all of his statements, too. But the way he talks leaves little room for doubt so exact is his information.

About Jesse James, Dalton scoffed at reports the desperado is still alive or was not killed April 3, 1882. Tom Crittenden, then Governor of Missouri, identified Jesse, his former schoolmate, Dalton said.

When he joined the U.S. Army on March 10, 1868, Dalton's first official act was to marry the regimental colonel's daughter. She died in 1928 and Dalton has been living under a handicap since. She wrote all his stories for newspapers, the pulp magazines and slick magazines. He has an offer now from Collier's, National Weekly Magazine. He has been unable to accept because no one has taken his wife's place.

WITH GENERAL CUSTER

As a member of Troop S, of the First Regiment, Fifth Cavalry, Dalton was with General Custer in the Sioux Campaign along the Big and Little Horn Rivers of Montana when the stage was set for "Custer's Massacre". But Dalton was not along with Custer on the General's last ride.

Nine years in the U.S. Army was followed by five years as a Texas Ranger and seven years as a U.S. Marshal out of Fort Smith, Ark. When Oklahoma Territory was opened up as a state, Dalton went to White Bead, Indian Territory, along the Washita River.

Years passed, and in 1931 found Dalton at Gladewater, Texas again as a Ranger. Then he decided on the oil game.

"It got me," he said. "Those oil filed fumes were hard on me and we didn't do so good, my partner and I. On May 12, 1937, I slipped on some steps and broke my leg.

"While I was in the hospital, I got to writing short stories about the Civil War. I sold enough to pay my hospital bill, but I fell and broke two ribs on those darn steps again."

CAMPAIGNED FOR SADDLER

Dalton still wasn't bothered until he broke his wrist and the doctor gave him two months to live in Gladewater.

I sold some stories to the editor of the Henderson Times and that got me out of the hospital and here. Here I am."

HE GOT HERE JUNE 22

Dalton was flat on his back on his single bed, in the one room which isn't much bigger than his bed. He doesn't look within 25 years of his age. He talks like a veteran of the lecture platform.

"Why, I campaigned for Saddler (Jerry Saddler, Railroad Commissioner) and Pierce Brooks (defeated by Coke Stevenson for Lieutenant-governorship) last year," Dalton remarked with a casual toss of his hand. He made about 12 campaign speeches for the two candidates.

Dalton wears glasses when he reads and has all of his teeth except some right jaw teeth which were knocked out in the Civil War by a gun butt.

"The Doc. told me at Gladewater I ought to have them pulled, but I said, 'What's the use of pulling them out as long as they're sound?'" He grinned to show them.

July 4, 1936, a pistol shoot was held for peace officers at Gladewater. Chief Bob Goss was judge and at that time State Pistol Champ. Dalton was Master of Ceremonies of the shoot. Both men were ruled out of the contest.

TOO GOOD TO SHOOT

"They wouldn't let us shoot. We were too good for them. But we gave an exhibition of trick shooting."

"What was one of your tricks?" Dalton was asked.

"I took two six-shooters, tossed a can in the air and kept it up until the six-shooters were unloaded. If you miss once you might as well let her come on down," he added.

"Did you do it?"

"Yep, the first time. I was a pretty good shot – am now for that matter."

Dalton has been so used to doing things that this lying in bed sick is more depressing on him than his injuries. Living eight and a half miles from town is not helping him either.

If I could get a little room in town where somebody could come and take dictation, I'd write that story for the Meter-Goldwyn people. I can't last always."

As I said at the beginning of the above article, Jesse was doing his best to stay under cover and therefore some of his statements are not correct. Such as the Dalton boys. They were his cousins, not nephews. His true birth date and place was September 5, 1847 at Centerville, Missouri, not March 8, 1848 at Goliad, Texas and his father was a Baptist Preacher not a Colonel. But Jesse was covering up the fact that he was Jesse James. Sure, he and Governor Crittenden knew each other and had met the night before the killing and was aware of the hoax that the dead man buried as being Jesse James was in truth and fact, Charley Bigelow. Yes, Jesse was covering up who he really was.

In 1939, Jesse was in Harrison, Tennessee for a short time and made a talk at the Princess Theatre there. Mr. Rowland O. Daughetee heard Jesse talk with Mr.

Bevel at the theatre. When Jesse was in Austin, Texas with Aubrey and Ola back in 1949, Rowland wrote to Jesse. When Ola read his letter to Jesse that he had heard him talk to Mr. Bevel at the Theatre in Harrison, Tennessee and that his grandfather, Andrew Jackson Daughetee, preacher and doctor, knew Jesse James back in Halls Gap, Kentucky, Jesse said, "You betcha I remember preacher Daughetee might well. He was a Baptist preacher. I've been to his house many times. He preached at a Baptist church on one side of town and I taught Sunday-school at another Baptist church across town there at Halls Gap, Kentucky."

Rowland also stated in his letter:

"I talked to Frank James in Missouri in 1915 not long before he died and Frank told me that Jesse was just as much alive then as he was in his boyhood."

Jesse got another letter from Rowland Daughetee and in it he stated that he worked for an Artificial Leg Company.

When Ola read the letter to Jesse he said, "Ola, I'm glad to hear from him so be sure and answer right away." Then grinning, he said, "Oh by the way, tell him I don't need any artificial leg right now, but I'll keep him in mind."

Jesse told me, "Ola, in the 1937, 1938 or 1938 issue of True Magazine is a story I wrote. In the September or October issue. The title of the story is *The Aftermath*. It's a pretty good story. You ought to try to get a copy and read it."

"What name did you use when you wrote it?" Ola asked and he said, "J. Frank Dalton."

Unfortunately, we have never been able to find a copy so we could read his story.

CHAPTER ELEVEN

DeWitt Travis of Longview, Texas who was 63 years of age at the time, told Ola that he'd known Jesse James all of his life. Said his mother always told him that she went to school with Dalton and knew that he was Jesse James.

In May 1948, Ola met a lady one day, a Mrs. Mannie Gault in Austin, Texas. Her husband, Mannie Gault, then deceased, was one of the three Texas Rangers who shot and killed the gangsters Clyde Barrow and Bonnie Parker, back in the 1930's.

Mrs. Gault told Ola, "I read in the paper about Jesse James still being alive."

Ola said, "Yes ma'am, he sure is."

She said, "My grandfather knew Jesse James very well. My grandfather is not living now, but his name was Jake Johnson. He was born and reared in Clay County, Missouri, about six miles from the James home. Jake had two brothers, Bill, a crippled boy, and Mose. Jake married Rebecca Gatalath of Missouri.

"Jake and Rebecca later moved to Austin, Texas. They bought some land about six miles south of town and about a mile from the Old San Antonio Highway and Jake built a rock home. It was a two-story home. Jesse James used to come there and see my grandfather and grandmother and stay for three and four weeks at a time."

She then said, "That of course, was many years ago, but the old house, the Jake Johnson home is still standing."

One day in March, 1949, Mrs. Gault called Ola and said, "I, my brother and his wife want to go out and see Jesse James. I called the hospital and they told me that he is allowed visitors but that he won't talk to people unless some of his folks are with him. I wonder if you'd go out there with us so we can talk to him?"

Ola said, "Yes ma'am. We'll come and get you and take you out there or we'll meet you out there."

She said, "Well we have a car so if you'll just meet us out there, we'll appreciate it."

A time was set and Aubrey and Ola went out to the hospital and met Mrs. Gault, her brother and sister-in-law and went up to room 251 to see Jesse. Aubrey and Ola introduced Mrs. Gault and Mr. and Mrs. Johnson to him and then stepped back and let them talk.

Mrs. Gault said, "Mr. James, my parents name was Johnson. Jake Johnson was my grandfather and my grandmother was Rebecca Gatalath, before her and my grandfather married. They used to live out there south of town, not far from Austin."

Jesse said, "Yes, I knew Jake Johnson well. I used to come and see him and stay there with Jake for weeks at a time. Jake and his family came here from Clay County, Missouri after the close of the War Between the States."

He described the grandparents to Mrs. Gault and then told her where their house was located there south of Austin. He told her that the house was a two-story house with an upstairs veranda and a wide gallery all across the front of the house and told her just which of the upstairs bedrooms he used to stay in while he was visiting.

He studied a little but as if he was looking back over those years and then said, "I sure did like old Jake. He was a good man and had a nice family. I can just see him now, with his long white beard, down nearly to his waist, walking around out in the yard with his hands behind him."

When Jesse brought it out about the beard, Mr. Johnson, the grandson of the Jakes who was listening from a chair nearby, jumped up and said, "Yes sir! That's right! I used to set on his knee and plat his long beard when I was a little boy." Mr. Johnson's eyes brightened up as if he was reliving those childhood days with his grandfather Jake.

Then Mrs. Gault said to Jesse, "One time when you started to leave my grandfather's place, you wanted to pay my grandfather for your room and board while you stayed with them. You'd stayed a good while and you tried to pay for your room and board, but my grandfather wouldn't take any money. There was a fence around the yard and so as you went out the gate, you put a roll of bills on the gate post, then got on your horse and rode off."

In a quiet tone of voice Jesse replied, "I don't remember."

Mrs. Gault said, "Well I know you did, because my grandfather and grandmother has told me many times about it. It was quite a bit of money all rolled up." Mrs. Gault and Mr. and Mrs. Johnson all seemed to really enjoy their visit with Jesse.

Aubrey walked out with them and down the hall when they left and after they'd all left the room, Jesse said to Ola, "I remember old Jake Johnson well and liked him." Then with a grin on his face he said, "I was ashamed to tell Mrs. Gault some of the things I remember about me being at Jake's house. But I'll tell you.

"One night after I'd left there, and I needed a fresh horse, I went back to Jake's place and stole one of his horses. I knew old Jake had two good ones out there in the lot and so I just stole one."

I said, "You mean you borrowed it, don't you?"

He said, "Hell no, I stole it!" Then after a minute or so, he said, "But he didn't lose anything on it. I left him plenty of money to pay more than the horse was worth. I took the horse because I needed it. But I paid for it and fixed it so he could get him another one. A damn sight better than the one I took. I knew all of the Johnsons and they were good people."

The next day, Mrs. Gault called Ola and said, "I just had to tell you. My brother and I were so happy to get to meet and talk with Jesse James. The man we'd heard about so much when we were young. And when my brother heard him tell about grandpa's beard and how he'd walk around out in the yard with his hands behind him, it just thrilled my brother so that we all set up until midnight and talked last night. We remembered so well, how grandpa walked around outside and always with his hands behind him. He thought lots of Jesse James. They'd been good friends for many years."

In the early 1940's Jesse, using the alias name of Frank Dalton, was back in Longview, Texas. He was with DeWitt Travis a good bit and frequently visited the Ford Grocery Store on Cotton Street. It was owned by Charles Coleman Ford and wife Lola Belle Foster Ford. He was the son of the late D.C. (Cap) Ford and wife Mary Owen Ford of Missouri, brother of Charlie and Robert Newton (Bob) Ford.

In 1942, Frank Dalton, as he was known, was still in Longview; he and DeWitt were together a lot and Jesse frequently visited with the L.L. Gamble's on Hudson Street. They knew he was, in truth and fact, Jesse James and that Frank Dalton was an alias name.

In part of 1943, Frank Dalton, as Jesse was known, was in Lampasas, Texas, Burnet and Marble Falls, Texas for a while. He lectured all fall. He made a talk at a school in Burnet and at the Baptist Church there on a Sunday night. The preacher turned things over to him and he talked for an hour and a half. The preacher didn't preach that night at all. He talked two Saturdays on the Courthouse Square, as well as the high school and the Church at Lampasas.

In a letter from a friend of Ola's, Mrs. Frances Tiller in Carthage, Texas was the following:

"I shall never forget my "visit" with an elderly white-haired, fine-looking man at the little country store of Charlie Ford, in Longview, Texas around 1944. His soft, wavy hair, shoulder length, and white, and his clean white shirt and blue or grey trousers, gave him the appearance of "stepping out of a picture!

"I had made the trip to Longview on the Santa Fe Passenger Train that day, and was to return to Carthage the next morning. My mother lived a short distance from the Ford Store. She was sick, and I had gone to the store to buy some groceries to make some soup for her. Mr. Ford was waiting on me, when he said someone was in the store and he wanted me to meet. I turned around, and saw that fine looking elderly man walking towards me from the back room. Mr. Ford said, "Mrs. Tiller, I want you to meet J. Frank Dalton." I said, "You mean THE Frank Dalton?"

"Mr. Ford said, "Yes!"

"I shook hands with him – I could hardly believe my eyes!

"I told him, "I thought you died, a long time ago!"

"He said, "No – I'm still living!" Then added, "And, if there are any questions you would like to ask me, I will be glad to answer them."

"I told him I would like to hear something about Belle Starr, that I knew she was the sweetheart of Jesse James.

"Well! He looked out the door, and up towards the sky, and said, "Belle Starr was a beautiful lady and was the smartest person I ever knew."

"I told them I would have to leave and prepare the soup for my sick mother. They followed me to the door, and Jesse James asked me if I could sit down and talk, for a few moments. So, I sat down on a step and they sat in cane-backed straight chairs. I asked Jesse James if all of the stories I had heard about the James and Dalton's were true. I thought I was talking to J. Frank Dalton you see.

"He said, "No!"

"After I had talked with J. Frank Dalton, I said to myself on my way to my mother's house – "Well, I sure found out something! Frank Dalton was in love with Jesse James' sweetheart."

"Imagine my surprise, while I was listening to the radio one night in May, 1948, I heard a man say he had a big surprise announcement to make! He turned the microphone over to his guest, which happened to be Jesse James! He said yes, he was still living and was born September 5, 1847. That the dead man who was buried in the yard of Jesse James' mother, was Charley Bigelow. Mrs. James knew that Jesse had not been killed. Jesse James lived until August 15, 1951."

In 1945 was the last time Jesse went to Brownwood, Texas to visit at the ranch of a very good, long-time friend of his, Bloody Bill Anderson. He had been there to visit a good many times over the years. Although Jesse was using the alias name of J. Frank Dalton, Bloody Bill knew he was Jesse James because he was the Captain Jesse had served under while with Quantrell during the War

Between the States. Bloody Bill went to Brownwood after the war, bought the ranch out from town and lived out his life there.

Jesse told Ola, "Some of Bill's grandchildren are living on that ranch, if I'm not mistaken."

While he and I were talking one day about the war. World War II that is. He said, "Honey the soldiers today don't know how well off they are compared to how it used to be. Us boys who served with Quantrell during the War Between the States got $14.00 a month and sometimes we didn't get a dime for three or four months at a time. Food at times was so scarce we had to eat horsemeat to keep from starving. Many didn't have many clothes to wear. We had a rough time.

"In World War I, the soldiers got $21.00 a month. But now the soldiers get pretty darn good money, good clothes, good food and medical care. I'm glad for them and I hope they will realize how much better off they are now than we were."

In 1946, he, 99 years of age at the time, left Longview, Texas and went to Palestine, Texas for a few days to talk with the principal of the high school there to get his help to get his Confederate Veterans pension.

In 1947 Jesse was living in Gladewater, Texas when he prepared to apply for his Confederate pension and decided he'd go to Austin, Texas to make the application in person. While there he stayed at Mrs. Danielson's home for two days because Sol Strickland was living there and Jesse stayed with him, for they had known each other for many years and they both applied for their Confederate pensions.

To qualify for the pension, Jesse, using the alias of J. Frank Dalton, produced an affidavit from Solomon Bedford (Sol) Strickland, known as the "Red Fox" Scout in the Charles Quantrell Guerrilla Division of the Confederate forces. This affidavit said that Dalton had served with Quantrell in Captain Anderson's Company in Missouri.

Solomon Bedford Strickland, called "Sol" and also known as "Red Fox" who was about five or six years older than Jesse. They were good friends and had been since the War Between the States.

Sol produced an affidavit from Jesse, or Dalton as he was called, as to Sol's age and service with Quantrell. Then after they finished making the applications for their Confederate pensions, Jesse left Austin and went back to Longview.

Before the year 1947 was over, he fell and broke his hip.

Ola asked him, "How did you break your hip?"

He said, "I was living in a hotel at Longview and I was walking on crutches then because I'd broke my leg not too long before, and I had to be careful. I went up town and was talking with some men. I was a big talker, when I could talk and before my throat started bothering me. I met a man that I knew pretty well and we got to talking and he wanted me to go home with him and eat supper. So, I did. And that night I got a taxi and went back to the hotel.

"Some men had been working on the front of the hotel and the light out in front of it had been changed and wasn't very bright like it had been. I couldn't see very good when I got out of the taxi. I took about two or three steps and my crutches gave way and I fell. A bunch of people ran out there and the men put coats down on the ground for me to lay on. I said, "The dickens, don't do that! Just call an ambulance. I'm broke all to pieces." So, some woman called an ambulance and I was taken to the hospital and they found that my hip was broken. This happened on the night of October 12, 1947." He was 100 years old at that time.

In early 1948 he was taken to a hospital in Dallas, Texas where he stayed for a while. He told them at the hospital that he would be 100 years old on March the 8th, so on that day they brought him a cake with a candle on it and Major Horace H. Shelton in Austin went to Dallas to see Frank Dalton, as Jesse was known. From Major Shelton, Jesse received a Confederate Service Commission. The promotion jumped him for the rank of a Private to that of General, Jesse said.

Jesse's actual birthdate was September 5, 1847, of course. But at the time and due to the fact that he was still living under cover, he gave March 8th as his birthdate. March 8th was the date in 1865 that he got out of Quantrell's outfit.

When he was released from the hospital, he went to Centerville, Texas. He was escorted from Dallas to Centerville by a man named Orvus Lee Howk. Jesse met him in about 1945. Jesse rented a corner room on the ground floor of a hotel. A real nice room and he used Howk, or as Jesse called him, "Old Hawk," as his flunky, to run errands and the like and to write some letters for him. Howk learned that Frank Dalton was an alias name, not his correct name which was Jesse James.

It was on a Sunday in the Austin newspaper that Ola read the article and saw the picture about Frank Dalton being in a hospital in Dallas who had just celebrated his 100th birthday. She made up her mind that she was going to go talk to him. She showed the newspaper article to her mother and asked her, "Could he be some of our kinfolks?"

Her mother said said, "Could be. If he is, he's mighty old now."

Ola grinned and said, "Well honey, he's a hundred years old and that ain't exactly young."

Then She said, "Well I'm gonna go talk to him."

Aubrey and Ola prepared to go to Dallas. Then it hit them that he may not be there by then. So, Ola told Aubrey to call the hospital in Dallas and find out if he was still there. Aubrey called and sure enough, Frank Dalton had been released from the hospital and was taken to Centerville, Texas by a friend. So, they got in the car and headed for Centerville.

When they reached there, they had no difficulty finding the hotel where he was. Aubrey went in, found out the room number, which was a corner room on the ground floor then he came back, got Ola and they went in.

Howk was there and answered the door and asked us in. Ola walked up to the foot of the bed where Mr. Dalton lay with a broken hip and said, "Mr. Dalton, I am the granddaughter of James Anderson Underwood and Savannah Elizabeth O'Daniel Underwood."

He smiled and replied, "Is that a fact. I knew them all. I knew them well." Pointing to a chair by the bed he said, "Sit down." Ola did and in a little bit, Aubrey and Orvus Lee Howk walked outside so Ola could talk with the elderly gentleman she had come to see. They had a nice talk about the kinfolks and she learned that she and he were related.

Ola and Aubrey were fixing to leave and Ola said, "We'd better head for home. Aubrey has got to be on the job in the morning so we can buy some more beans."

He said, "Well you come back next Sunday, you hear."

She said, "I will if a tree don't fall on me or something."

He said, "Well see that you do."

Ola caught hold of Aubrey's arm and as they walked to the door, she said, "Now you take care of yourself and we'll be back next Sunday."

He said, "I always take care of myself."

He repeated it and when they reached the door, Ola caught hold of the door facing, turned and looked at him and there he lay looking at me with a loaded 38 Special Revolver six-shooter in each hand, leveled down on me.

Ola said, "I see that you do take care of yourself."

She walked back to his bed, sat down beside it where she'd been sitting and said, "May I see one of your guns?"

Handing one to her, he said, "Be careful honey, it's loaded."

She said, "Yessir, I know that. It wouldn't be much benefit if it wasn't."

His guns were the type of 38 six-shooters that the Texas Rangers and U.S. Marshals carried. Which is understandable, because he had been a Texas Ranger more than once and a Deputy U.S. Marshal more than once.

She looked at his gun and said, "My this is a nice gun. I know you're proud of it. I love guns."

Ola handed it back to him and he put a gun on each side of him in the bed. They said goodbye, went out, got in the car and headed for home at 1212 Taylor Street in Austin, Texas. Ola couldn't hardly wait to get home and tell her mother about our trip to Centerville and what she'd learned.

They went back the next Sunday. Stopped at Buffalo and ate dinner then on to Centerville. Howk was there when they arrived but Aubrey and him went outside and talked so J. Frank Dalton and Ola could talk. He showed her some pictures of his. One was of him and Indian Chief Geronimo together, one of his mother at the James farm and one of her, him and Frank James together and other pictures. He gave Ola a picture of the three of them together and signed it J. Frank Dalton under the picture.

Ola asked him, "May I call you Uncle Frank?"

He said, "You sure can."

They went back the next Sunday and as usual, Howk was there in the room when they arrived at the hotel. After Aubrey and Howk went outside, Uncle Frank and Ola talked about the family and Geronimo, whom he knew personally.

Then he said, "You know Ola honey, my hair when I was young was just the color of yours. The natural color of my hair was auburn red just the color of yours."

Ola replied, "Well, I kinda thought you must have had auburn red hair when you were young because you have the complexion that goes with auburn red hair."

He said, "It was."

Then he said, "My half-brother, John Thomas Samuel looked a great deal like me and we both had auburn red hair and blue eyes."

The following Sunday when Aubrey and Ola went back to Centerville and while Aubrey and Howk was outside, Uncle Frank and Ola were talking and he said, "Ola I'm fixing to leave here in a few days. I promised my mother that I'd come out in the open with my true name when I got to be a hundred years old. I'm a hundred now so I'm going to keep my promise to my mother. It will shock a lot of people when they learn who I really am. Of course, there's a lot of people who already know. When I get where I'm going, I'll let you know where I am and when I do, you come to me, you hear."

Ola said, "Yessir, I will, if a tree don't fall on me or something."

He said, "Well you just see that it don't."

CHAPTER TWELVE

It was early May, 1948 when Howk and his wife Nadine took Uncle Frank to Lawton, Oklahoma. Frank O. Hall and Lindsay Whitten who worked for the *Lawton Constitution* Newspaper, went out to the motel cabin and talked with J. Frank Dalton, questioned him, then done a lot of checking and on May 19, 1948 Frank and Lindsay broke the big story with big headlines on the front page "JESSE JAMES ALIVE IN LAWTON". J. Frank Dalton was in truth and fact, the real Jesse James. The once noted outlaw that was supposedly killed in 1882. The Jesse Woodson James born September 5, 1847 at Centerville, near Kearney, Missouri. Son of Reverend Robert and Zerelda James and full brother of Frank James the bandit.

As Uncle Frank had told Ola he'd do, she got a card from him to tell her where he was. She called Aubrey at his office and told him, "We've got to go to Lawton, Oklahoma."

He said, "Well get ready and as soon as I get home, we'll hit the road."

Ola was ready when he got home and a little after five that evening, they were on their way. It was about five o'clock the next morning when they arrived in Lawton. They rented a motel room and cleaned up and then made their way across town to the motel where Jesse was. En route, they couldn't help but notice that people were gathering at the courthouse and many were already sitting on the steps waiting, because Jesse James was coming to town in the early afternoon and make a talk over a loud speaker.

When they arrived at the motel they had to wait outside until the nurse finished giving Jesse his bath and cleaning up his bed. His broken hip never did mend like it should so he was confined to his bed. When he heard that Ola and Aubrey were out there waiting, he told the nurse, "Hurry up! I want to see them."

When they walked in, Ola said, "Hello Jesse!"

She didn't have to call him Uncle Frank anymore because he had, as he told her in Centerville, Texas, come out with his real true name.

He smiled and said, "Damn I'm glad to see you!"

Ola walked over to the bed and he patted the bed and said, "Sit down."

She said, "Oh I don't want to wrinkle up your nice clean bed."

He replied, "Oh to hell with that! You don't weigh enough to wrinkle up the bed," and just pulled Ola down by him. They were talking and laughing and people outside would come up to the window, peep in and look at Jesse and Ola, then move on and another would come do the same thing. It seemed shocking to them that Ola, a small thin woman, was sitting on the bed of a former outlaw, namely Jesse James, talking and laughing with him. Ola had a deep voice like him and her hair was auburn red. The way they looked at her you'd have thought that they thought she was Belle Starr. It was funny to her.

After they talked a while, word was brought to Jesse that John Shevlin was there from Chicago. So, when he came in, Jesse didn't say hello to him, he looked at him and said, "Well John, you shaved your mustache off." Then Aubrey and Ola went outside so they could talk.

In a little while, up came the 1948 cream-color Cadillac convertible to take Jesse to town. But, before they took him out to the car, a psychiatrist went in to talk with him. Someone had arranged for that. Ola and Aubrey were standing near the door when he went in and was there when he came out. He stopped as he stepped out the door and waving his hands said, "My God! That man's mind is like a 35-year-old! There's nothing wrong with his mind. He's got a better mind than I have."

Paramount Studios had a man there and when they put Jesse in the back seat of the Cadillac convertible, old Howk had some woman get in beside him. Aubrey and Ola were right behind the Cadillac in their car as everybody started to town but they couldn't stay behind him or get very close to where he was because the sound truck needed to follow him because thirty thousand people had gathered in town to see and hear him. They parked their car and walked as close as they could so we could hear him talk.

When he finished his talk, in which he made it very plain to the people that he was the real Jesse James who was supposedly killed back in 1882, they wanted to take him to the hospital for a check-up and rest, but he said, "Hell no! I'm not goin' to no damn hospital! Just take me back to that motel room." They did as he wanted and then Ola and Aubrey went back to the motel, they talked to him a little bit before telling him goodbye and headeding for home in Austin, Texas. As they left, the grounds at the motel was covered with people.

They kept in touch with where and how Jesse was as best they could in the days that followed but they didn't see him again until he came to their house at 1212 Taylor Street in Austin, Texas in 1949, mighty sick with pneumonia.

On Sunday, May 23, 1948, Mrs. Emma Hardy Norman, 72, went to Lawton, from Atoka, Oklahoma to visit the man she knew when she was only 15. She said it was Jesse James and his brother, Frank who came to her home in Greenbriar, Arkansas to visit her father, John C. Hardy. They remained two days.

Upon mentioning the visit to Mr. James who was also known as Mr. Dalton, she was amazed that he recalled the incident vividly. He recalled many things that she had forgotten. Mrs. Norman said she did not learn until later that the two men who visited her father actually were Jesse and Frank James. Her father described them to her at the time as "two rich young gentlemen."

Jesse was 44 in 1891 which was the year him and Frank visited John C. Hardy. Another couple visited Jesse James, who was also known as Colonel Dalton, after his public appearance in Lawton, Oklahoma in May 1948 was Mr. and Mrs. Leslie Jump of Fort Cobb, Oklahoma. They left the bedside of him declaring they were positive that he was Jesse James.

"We knew Frank James well. He often told us that Jesse was still alive and could be reached in a matter of 24 to 48 hours," Mrs. Jump said.

In May, 1948, the following was carried in the Austin newspaper:

Frank Dalton who at 100 years of age Thursday claimed he was "The" Jesse James, could be James, but he isn't Dalton, according to research of Major Horace H. Shelton, Commander of the Texas Division, Sons of Confederate Veterans.

Major Shelton dug up a report of Captain Harrison Trow, one of Quantrell's Raiders in which Trow claimed to have identified the body of Jesse James. Major Shelton pointed out that the so-called Dalton in Oklahoma possibly could have been the legendary Jesse James, so far as age is concerned. Research showed that James was described in 1863 as being "scarcely 13 years of age." No Dalton with Quantrell. I knew Major Shelton. He was a fine man, and excellent attorney and a good friend.

In June 1948, Howk and his wife Nadine took Jesse and left Lawton, Oklahoma. They went to Pueblo, Colorado, then to Rye, Colorado. On July 2, 1948, Jesse and the Howks were in San Francisco, California. They went to California to attend a July 4th celebration at San Leandro, California.

On July 9, 1948 Jesse was taken to Tulsa, Oklahoma by Howk for Jesse to make a personal appearance at a theatre there, so Howk could make some money off him, for that's why he took the poor old soul from place to place. But at Tulsa, Howk was warned of threats of violence to Jesse James if he entered the theatre. So that appearance was cancelled and the Howks and Jesse got out of town.

On July 31, 1948, Howk had Jesse in Chicago, Illinois for a short time and Jesse was in a room at the Hermitage Hotel, as Ola recalled. On September 20, 1948, Jesse James was interviewed for the radio program "THE BIG STORY" which was broadcast from Chicago, Illinois. Jesse, Frank O. Hall and Lindsay Whitten all went to Chicago but Jesse himself was not on the radio program. Some man that was an actor played the part of Jesse. He had a high silly voice. Jesse had a loud deep voice, not a squeaky one.

I have the records of that program, The Big Story.

On October 27, 1948 Jesse and the Howks was in New Orleans, Louisiana and Jesse said, "Shortly after the killing in 1882, I saddled up and headed for Kansas City, Missouri, then to Memphis, Tennessee and down to New Orleans. I was here only a couple of days," he explained, "before I caught a boat for Buenos Aires. But I remember the Audubon Bird Park. Is it still here?"

On November 20, 1948 Jesse and the Howks were in Van Nuys, California. He talked with James D. Fay, 96, who lived at 5732 Willowcrest Avenue in North Hollywood, California. Fay knew Jesse in Missouri when Fay was a bricklayer in Columbia, Missouri. He laid the foundation of Columbia and he knew Quantrell in Brownwood, Texas.

On December 12, 1948 Jesse and the Howks were in New Orleans, Louisiana again and while there that time, Jesse asked, "Is that Daily Picayune Newspaper still going here?"

When assured it was, he said, "I used to write articles for it. Used the names 'Frank Dalton' and 'John Franklin' when I wrote stories about the West for the old New Orleans Picayune."

In 1948, H.E. Umensetter, age 75, of 4111 Kirkland Avenue, in Nashville, Tennessee knew the James boys in Kirkland, Missouri and Ardmore, Oklahoma. He talked to Frank James during World War I in Kansas City in a hotel and Frank told him that his brother Jesse was not dead.

On February 5, 1949, Jesse was brought to Aubrey and Ola's house at 1212 Taylor Street in Austin, Texas by Reverend R.E. Highley, Mrs. Highley and Ira Mann, from California. The Highley's of Pasadena and Mann of Santa Anna had brought Jesse away from old Howk because he was being so badly neglected. Lack of food and care. Jesse had known preacher Highley for some time and he told Ola, "He's not much of a preacher. Fact of the matter, I've preached better sermons myself."

Poor Jesse was a mighty sick man when he arrived at the Everhart house shortly after noon. Ola had a hospital bed ready for him but he had pneumonia and by 4 p.m. or near that, he was taken by ambulance to the hospital and put under an oxygen muzzle immediately.

It was Saturday when the Highley's and Mann arrived bringing poor sick Jesse and Cole James came to our house too from down near Kennard, Texas when the others came. When the ambulance took Jesse to the hospital, the Highley's and Mann left and went somewhere. Cole spent the night with us and went home by bus the next day. Ola couldn't go in the ambulance with Jesse to the hospital due to her handicap. She can't get around without some help, but as soon as Aubrey got home from work she and he rushed to the hospital as quick as they could. Poor Jesse was in a ward with several other patients, a very sick man, and they had an oxygen muzzle on him.

Ola walked up to the bedside, leaned over and said, "Now you look here, Jesse, you've just gotta get well. You're the only Jesse I've got and you've just gotta get well."

He said, "Well honey I'm trying."

She said, "Yessir I know you are and you've just gotta keep on trying."

He said, "Well I'll tell you one thing! If they don't do something and do it damn quick! People are gonna be walking by me, looking down, saying, oh my, don't he look natural."

Ola said, "Why Jesse!"

He said, "Well, now you just stop and think. Ain't that what they always say when they look at a dead person?"

She replied, "Yessir, you're right."

He was right. But Ola was a bit surprised when he came up with that. He was so old and so sick yet he could still come up with something like that. Jesse was a mighty man and Ola loved him.

The next morning, Sunday, preacher Highley, Mrs. Highley and Mann came back to our house. Preacher Highley rubbed his hands together and said, "Where's a Baptist Church around here that a person can go pick up a few quick bucks?"

They told him we didn't know. Then he got to talking about the Jameses and said, "I guess you know that there's lots of bastards in the James clan and their kin."

That made Ola as mad as a wet hen and she replied as she looked at him straight and hard, "Well, let me ask you something? Can you prove, beyond all shadow of doubt, that you are not one?"

Looking a bit stunned, he said, "Well – no."

She said, "Well!"

They left Monday and went back to California.

That good old Baptist preaching man didn't tell Ola the truth. He told her they had come from Cole James house near Kennard, Texas to her house. What he didn't tell her was that from California he had taken poor sick Jesse to Sweetwater, Texas and had him lecturing twice at the City Auditorium and that the preacher got the money for the lectures. It's a good kind-hearted preacher that will take a sick man out to make lectures so he can get the money. A sick man over a hundred years old.

On Sunday afternoon Cole James had left, Aubrey and Ola went out to the hospital to see about Jesse and Ola told him, "Cole James went back home this morning. He seems like a good man."

He said, "That so."

Ola said, "Yessir."

Jesse said, "Well he don't know nothin'."

She said, "Well I don't know about that. All I know is he seemed like a good man from what little I was around him."

He said, "Oh well honey, they won't pay him to be good, so he has to be good for nothing."

Cole's mother knew Jesse James back when he was an outlaw. He spent the night at her parents' home when she was quite young. He was using the alias name of Red Buck and when he left the next morning, he left a bulletproof vest in the bedroom. When her mother looked it over, she found a card in a small inside pocket and on it was the name Jesse James.

By the next day, Monday, when Aubrey and Ola got out to the hospital, they had moved Jesse out of the ward into a semi-private room on another floor. His roommate was a Mexican man, and there were so many Mexicans in the room Ola couldn't hardly get to Jesse's bed. And, of course, they were all looking at Jesse and talking in their Mexican language. To Ola, it sounded like a bunch of geese and she couldn't understand a word

That night when Ola and Aubrey went back to see Jesse, he was in the room by himself.

Ola asked him, "What happened to your roommate? I see he's gone."

He replied, "Well I'll tell you. Him and some of the others got to talking about me in their language. I heard what they said and I didn't like it a damn bit. So, I just hauled off and cussed them out in their own language. They didn't know I understood them and could talk their language, but I can. So, they moved him out."

Ola said, "Don't you know those Mexicans were surprised." She had to laugh about that.

They had put Jesse under an oxygen tent, which was easier on him and what he needed.

On February 27, 1949, between two and four o'clock in the afternoon Aubrey, Bill Payne and Ola were in the room with Jesse at the hospital. An orderly, Paul N. Sassman, came in the room to put ice in the unit by the side of the bed that the oxygen tent was connected with. They were talking to Sassman and the state of California was mentioned while they were talking.

Jesse spoke up and told Orderly Sassman, "That's what's wrong with me now, and that's how come me to be here like this, because of that trip I made to California and back."

Then he told Aubrey and Ola, "I started feeling bad when we got to the Rockies and started back this way. And just kept getting worse.

It was early in March, 1949 and Jesse had been in the hospital since February 5th. He was still under the oxygen tent and was slowly getting better; thank the Lord. Ola was out to see him one afternoon as she did every day. She was standing by his bed talking with him and over the intercom they kept calling, "Orderly! Orderly! Orderly!"

Jesse said, "Ola, what is this? I can't understand what they're saying."

She said, "They are saying 'orderly'. Calling the orderlies over the intercom, Jesse."

He said, "Orderlies?"

Ola replied, "Yessir. That's these men that come in and sets up your oxygen tank over there and checks on your oxygen and does other things for you."

He said, "Orderlies hell! That's the most dis-orderly damn bunch I ever saw!"

Well, that was so funny to Ola. When she got home, she laughed and told her mother and when Aubrey got home from work she told him. When they went back to the hospital that night, Aubrey told Orderly Clifford Harris, who was a real nice person and full of fun. Harris got a bang out of what Jesse said. He told Orderly Sassman and after that they called them "the damn dis-orderlies". Everyone had lots of laughs about that.

As Ola always did, she went out to see Jesse in the afternoon. He and she were talking and she said, "Jesse, I think your white hair is so pretty."

He replied, "That so."

She said, "Yessir."

He said, "Well honey, let me tell you something. Always remember, white hair is pretty on the other fellow. Like I've told you before, when I was a young man, the natural color of my hair was red like yours, auburn red. My mother's hair was dark red and so was John's. Of course, my hair has been other colors too, down through the years. As I told you, the Indians taught me how to dye my hair. I dyed it different colors. Sometimes it was dyed dark, sometimes red, other times white. I always wore it real long and braided. Always kept it nice and neatly braided and wore the braids in different ways. Oh, sometimes I wore it short or like I've got it now, Buffalo Bill Cody style. I wore false mustache at times. Sometimes I wore my own mustache cut in different styles. Then sometimes I didn't wear a mustache at all."

Ola said, "Your eyes are just exactly like my grandpa Underwood's. His eyes were beautiful to me. They were piercing blue like yours. The kind that never miss anything. And like you, he didn't blink them much."

He said, "Well I do now, because I've got granulated eye lids. Have had for years and the older I get, the more they bother me."

Ola looked at the palms of his hands and said, "Gee whiz, Jesse, you're the first one of the kinfolks that I've seen that the palms of your hands are red like mine. I've often wondered about mine. But now seeing that yours are red too, I guess I inherited them from way back."

He looked at Ola's hands with her red palms and long slim fingers like his and said, "Well honey, I reckon it's just the Irish coming out in us."

She said, "I 'spect you're right. I hadn't thought about that."

It was early in March and Jesse was still under an oxygen tent but he was getting better. Ola was out to see about him from two to five times a day every day. One afternoon, she was standing by his bed talking with him and he said, "Ola, where is my neck tie that I had on when I got here?"

She said, "It's at home, Jesse. I took your clothes home, washed and ironed your white shirt and have it ready to wear. Your tie was dirty, so I washed and pressed it. Did you want me to bring them to you?"

He said, "No honey. But I was just thinking. No bigger than you are, you take that neck tie, make you a dress out of it, and then save the scraps left over for patches," he grinned.

She laughed and replied, "Alright, I'll do that."

Ola told Aubrey, "Bless his heart, as sick as he'd been and still was, he had his sense of humor. His wonderful sense of humor, quick thinking and ability to cope with any situation, kept him going, and had for many years."

One afternoon she was out at the hospital standing by Jesse's bed talking with him. They talked about current events for a while and then started talking about the kinfolks and Ola asked, "Jesse, how many sisters did your mother have?"

He said, "Well honey, my mother had five sisters."

She said, "So there was six of the little girls."

He said, "Yes. That's right."

Ola said, "Now one of them was Bob and Charlie's mother?"

He said, "That's right. Those Ford boys was my first cousins. Their mother and my mother were sisters, as I've told you before."

She said, "Any my grandpa Underwood's mother, my great-grandma Sarah was their sister?"

He said, "That's right. And don't you forget it! You hear?"

Ola replied, "Yessir. And I won't forget it."

Then she said, "There was only one boy in the family, wasn't there?"

He said, "Yes, that's right. His name was Louis. James Louis Dalton. He was the father of Bob, Emmett, Grat and the others. He married Sarah Adeline Lee Younger and they had 13 children."

Ola said, "Well, according to what you've told me, then the Ford boys and Dalton boys were my cousins too."

He said, "Yes, that's right, they was."

Old then asked, "The Ford boys' mother, your mother, and my great-grandmother were all sisters and Uncle Louis was their only brother. They were all Daltons. Correct?"

He said, "Yes. That is absolutely correct."

Ola said, "The alias name of Dalton you used was your mother's maiden name?"

He said, "Yes. That's right. The "J" was for my own first name. Frank for my brother Frank and Dalton was my mother's maiden name. J. Frank Dalton."

Ola said, "Well it's not illegal for a boy to go by his mother's maiden name."

He said, "No."

The next afternoon when Ola got out to the hospital he was all cleaned up, his white hair all clean and he was powdered with Johnson's baby powder. Ola said, "Oh my goodness how pretty and clean my Jesse is today."

He said, "Is that so?" Then grinning, said, "Well I ought to. Them damn disorderlies have been in here."

A day or so later, Ola was standing by the bed talking with Jesse. A man kept yelling, "Oh! Oh! Do something! Oh! I can't stand this."

Jesse said, "Ola, what is that hollerin' about?"

Ola said, "Well, that's a man two or three rooms from you who I understand got shot."

"What happened?" He asked.

She said, "Well, I hear tell that him and some man had some trouble and the man told him not to come to his house again. That if he did, he'd shoot him. But this man went to his house anyway, and the man shot him."

Jesse said, "Oh well, he asked for it, and got what he deserved. Somebody didn't tell that son-of-a-bitch what they ought to."

One Sunday afternoon in 1949 Aubrey and Ola was out at the hospital with Jesse and him and Aubrey got to talking about race horses. Jesse had owned several good racehorses over the years and Aubrey had both trained and rode thoroughbred racehorses in past years.

Aubrey asked, "Jesse, which horse was your best race horse? The one that made you the most money?"

Jesse studied a while and replied, "Well, it was a horse called Queen of Hearts. That was a really good horse." One strain of thoroughbred racehorses that Jesse liked was what he called the Kent thoroughbreds.

He said, "Kentucky thoroughbreds, the copper bottom strain of Palomino had such good feet. Excellent travelers. The steel-dust strain brought up to copper Tacalong."

One afternoon, Ola was out at the hospital visiting with Jesse. She was standing by the bed and they were talking and laughing.

He told her, "Ola, I don't like to see a woman all painted up."

She said, "I don't either. Some women wear so much paint they look like Indians on the War Path."

Then he said, "A little bit of powder, a little bit of paint, makes a woman look like something that she ain't."

One of the head nurses had come in the room and was standing listening to them talk. Ola turned to her and asked, "Did you want something?"

She said, "No. I just wanted to hear him talk. He won't talk like that unless you're here." Then she said, "My goodness, he's got all of his teeth!"

She replied, "Yes. All but four."

She stayed a little longer then walked out.

Ola happened to be in the room talking with Jesse one afternoon when a nurse came in the room to give him a shot. He said, "What a minute! Before you give me that shot I wanna know, what is it? What's it for?"

She said, "It's penicillin, Mr. James. It will help you."

She gave him the shot and when she left the room Ola said, "Jesse I've taken penicillin and it helped me a lot."

He said, "Is that so?"

She said, "Yessir. And I think it will help you too. So don't be afraid. Just take all of the penicillin they want to give you, because it will help you."

He said, "Well that's alright then. I just didn't know what it was and I wanted to know. A person's got to be careful."

She replied, "You're right. I agree with you. It's lots safer to be careful and ask questions about medicine."

One afternoon a few days later, she was, as always, out at the hospital visiting with Jesse. she was standing by the bed and they were talking when a woman came to the door.

Ola turned to her and said, "Hello! Won't you come in?"

In a tone of voice as if she was scared half to death, she said, "Oh no! He's an outlaw!"

Ola looked at her hard and in not a kind but very firm tone of voice said, "*Was* – an outlaw!*" So, she walked away.

One day while Ola was talking with Jesse, she asked him, "Did you know Kit Carson?"

He said, "Yes. I knew Kit Carson well. Kit was raised in Missouri 'til he was 12 years old and then he run off from home and began buffalo hunting, and then scouting later on. He married a Yaqui Squaw. He died in 1867 at Fort Lyon on the Arkansas River where picket wire empties in to the Arkansas River."

Aubrey and Ola were talking with Jesse one day and he told us, "I used to have a lot of fun out of some guys. I'd see several of them standing talking. I'd walk over, get to talking to them and said, 'Would any of y'all be interested in buying some nice wardrobes real cheap? I'm gonna have several to sell real cheap.'

They'd say, 'Yes-suh, we's interested. Where's they at so's we can see 'em?'

I'd say, 'Well they're not quite ready yet. I've got a little work on some of them before I sell them. You see, we're moving a cemetery and some of the bodies will have to be put in new coffins. So, I'm fixing the old coffins up and selling them because they'll make real nice wardrobes.'

They would look at me, wall their eyes, back off and say, 'Naw-suh, I don't want none of them. Not them!' And they was gone. I got a big laugh out of watching them when they heard that."

In 1949 and again later, Jesse told Ola, "Ola, after my supposed demise in St. Joe and I'd come back from South America, I was living in the Indian Territory and I was appointed to the Territorial Legislature, House of Representatives in 1893, before the Indian Territory went into Statehood and became Oklahoma."

Records show that he, known as James L. McDaniel (Populist), was a member of the Territorial Legislature in 1893 just as he told her. He was 46 years of age at the time he was in the Legislature.

A day or so later when she and Jesse were talking he told her, "Ola, as I've told you, I was in the Texas Rangers for a while. Fact of the matter, I was a Texas Ranger more than once."

"What name did you use?" Ola asked.

He said, "Well, one time, back in the 1870's I used the name Benjamin Franklin Johnson. In 1874 I was in Company E, Frontier Battalion." Records show he, known as B.F. Johnson was in Company E. Frontier Battalion from May 31, 1874 to June 6, 1875. Eleven months and twenty-five days service. He was 27 years of age at the time he joined and 28 when he got out.

While Jesse and Ola were talking one time in 1949, they got to talking about the Daltons and he said, "Well honey, originally, the name was O'Dalton. But when they crossed the pond, they drownded the 'O'."

Ola said, "Well then Dalton is Irish."

He said, "Yes, and when some of them first came to this country from Ireland, they mixed with the Indians. Cherokee's."

Ola said, "Well you know my great-grandfather O'Daniel was three-quarter Cherokee Indian and one quarter Irish."

He replied, "Yes, I know. I knew him well."

Ola said, "But my great-grandpa Underwood was English. He was with Quantrell during the War Between the States."

He said, "Yes, he was."

She said, "Him and grandma Sarah Dalton Underwood and their children was living in Tennessee when the war started. My grandpa James A. (Toby) was 8 years old at the time, Aunt Sis (Eliza Ann) was 6 and William was just a baby."

He said, "Yes I know."

Well – St. Patrick's Day, March 17, 1949, when Ola went out to the hospital that afternoon, she took Jesse a St. Patrick's Day pin and pinned it on his gown. The doctors and nurses got a kick out of him laying there in bed wearing the St. Pat's pin with the bright green ribbon at the bottom.

When Aubrey and Ola went out to see him that night and started home, he said, "Ola honey, you better take my Irish pin home now."

She said, "Alright sir." She took it home and kept it.

One afternoon, while she was out at the hospital visiting with him, she was standing by his bed talking with him and rubbing his hand as we talked and Ola said, "Jesse, you've got long slender fingers. I have too."

Looking at my fingers he said, "You have got long slim fingers."

She said, "Yessir."

Then he said, "You know honey, in my business, my long slim fingers come in mighty handy."

Ola replied with a grin, "I bet they did."

As Aubrey and Ola were leaving the hospital that night after visiting Jesse, they met Don and Rose Harris, some good and longtime friends. Rose was visiting her father. Don is from Missouri originally and Ola laughed and told him what Jesse had said about his long slim fingers. Don laughed so hard he almost fell and said, "As many banks and trains as he robbed, I can see how his long slim fingers did come in handy to gather up the money."

Not only did the orderlies or, dis-orderlies as he called them, like to hear Jesse talk, but there was a young intern there who did too. He was Dr. Smallwood, a nice looking, quiet, easy-going young man. One afternoon Aubrey and Ola went out to see Jesse and just before they got to the room they met Dr. Smallwood and he said to Ola, "Ask Mr. James if he was a two gun man?"

Ola said, "Alright. You just come on in his room and I'll ask him, then you can hear the answer from him." He followed them into the room and set down over in a window. After Ola had talked to Jesse a little bit, she said, "Jesse, I wanna ask you something."

He said, "Alright, what is it?"

She said, "Back in your outlaw days, was you a two gun man?"

He said, "Two gun?"

Ola replied, "Yessir."

He chuckled and replied, "Four or five if I could get 'em."

She said, "Well, I thought you was a two gun man."

He firmly, very firmly said, "I was!"

Ola looked over at Dr. Smallwood and he was so tickled he was bending over laughing.

Ola asked him, "Did you hear the answer?"

He said, "I sure did."

It was March, as I recall, 1949. Thank the Lord, Jesse was getting better daily. Ola was out to see him as she was every afternoon. She was standing by the bed and she and Jesse were talking when a little boy about ten or twelve years old, a pretty little fellow, came rolling into the room in a wheelchair.

Ola said, "Hello! What do you want son?"

He said, "Well, I heard that Jesse James was in here and I wasn't to meet him."

Ola said, "Well this is him honey."

She turned to Jesse and said, "Jesse, here's a young man that wants to meet you."

Ola heard a little boy roll up to the side of the bed as close as he could and say, "Mr. James, this is (and told him the little boy's name)."

Poor old Jesse almost fell off the bed reaching down to shake hands with the little boy. The little fellow sat there a little bit and then said, "You was an outlaw? The outlaw Jesse James?"

Jesse replied, "Yes, that's right. But listen son, I want to tell you something. That is a bad way to live. It's the wrong road to travel. I know how bad it is." Then he talked on so nice and kind and Ola thought as she listened, "I have never heard a preacher in a pulpit preach a better sermon to a congregation in a church than the way he was talking to that little boy." Then he added, "Now son, pay attention to your parents, live a law-abiding life, get a good education and you'll be a fine man when you get grown. I'm glad you came to see me."

The little boy said, "Thank you sir. I'm glad to meet you." Then he left. Ola never saw him again, but she thought many times about when he visited Jesse and how Jesse talked to him.

There was another incident that Ola had forgotten for sure when it happened, but she believed it was in 1949. As she did every afternoon, she went out to the hospital to see Jesse. Well, this particular day she had heard on the news about the Brinks robbery and when she got to Jesse's room, she told him about it. He always wanted to know what the latest news was.

Then, much to her surprise, in came a young man whom she learned was a reporter from the Austin newspaper. He wanted to talk with Jesse about, of all things, the Brinks robbery.

Ola stepped back and just listened and after thy had talked a little bit about trivial things, this young reporter said, "Mr. James, if you'd have pulled that robbery, where would you have gone afterwards?"

Jesse replied, "Well, if I had pulled that robbery, I wouldn't have run."

The reporter, somewhat surprised said, "You wouldn't?"

Jesse said, "No! I would have stayed right there and mixed and mingled with the people."

"Well, if you was looking for the robbers, where would you look?" The reporter asked.

"Well, I wouldn't go very far," Jesse replied. "I'd look first, right in the area where the robbery occurred. They're most likely around close somewhere I'd say." Then after a bit he said, "It's a damn good thing I'm here and as old as I am and Frank is dead or they'd say me and him pulled that robbery."

The reporter thanked Jesse for talking with him and left.

As best Old could recall, from what she read and heard on the news, the Brinks robbers were caught not far from where the robbery had taken place.

It was in 1949. Ola had been out to the hospital three or four times during the day to see about Jesse then rushed home each time to see about her mother who was ill at home and in bed part of the time. Aubrey and Ola had gone out that night as they always did, stayed a while and then came home a little on the tired side from a busy day.

Hardly had they gotten in the house when the phone rang. Ola answered and a man said, "Me and my wife are in Austin to see Jesse James and we were told at the hospital that we can't see him until tomorrow. But they gave us your phone number. I want to tell you something. My wife is related to Jesse James."

Ola replied, "Is that so? On which side?"

After some hesitation, he said, "On the James side – I think."

Ola said, "Really! That's fine. I'm related on the Dalton side."

He said, "We want to come out and talk to you."

Ola replied, "Sure. Be glad for you to. Come right on. Do you have our address, 1103 East First Street?"

He said they did and in a little bit, up they drove. Hardly had they gotten inside and sat down when the woman, whom Ola judged was in her early forties, opened her purse, pulled out a folded piece of paper, unfolded it and said, "Look! I've got a Will Jesse James made out to me."

Her husband, or so they said, who was about her age, said, "Yes, he willed everything to her."

Ola folded her arms, leaned back in her chair, looked at her and said, "My God! Have you got one of them things too? There's a dozen of them things floating around."

She looked as if Ola had just hit her in the face with a wet dish rag. She folded the little paper purported to be the said Will, stuck it back in her purse, looked at her husband and he looked at her then they both stood up and said, "Well we better go." And in short order, they were in their car and gone. If they told had told Ola and Aubrey their name, they couldn't remember it. But they never saw them since and they did not go to see Jesse…and they were supposed to be related to him. It got funny to the Everharts. They had a big laugh. So did Jesse, when they went to the hospital the next afternoon and told him. I guess Ola had busted their bubble of dreams of wealth through that supposed will.

Another afternoon, Ola went out to see Jesse as usual and when she walked into his room, the first thing she noticed was that the shade on the window by his bed was pulled all the way down to the bottom of the window.

Ola walked over to his bed and as always said, "Jesse."

He said, "Yeah!"

She said, "Howdy!"

He said, "Oh, hello Ola!"

They talked a bit about the present goings on, Ola told him what she'd been doing that morning and after a bit she asked, "Why is the window shade down?"

He said, "Well honey it pays to be careful, so I had it pulled down. You never can tell who might be peeping in the window."

She said, "I know you're right, but Jesse, the man that peeps in that window will have to be a tall son of a gun, because this is the second floor."

She walked over to the window, raised the shade then back to the side of his bed and said, "You don't have to worry about anybody peeping in or crawling in the window Jesse, because this is the second floor and they can't see in or get in."

He said, "Well honey, you can't be too careful, you know."

As they talked, she thought, "Bless his heart he's been through so much in his life and has always had to be so watchful and careful and he's aware that at present, he's totally helpless and also that he's unarmed. Something he never was without until now was his six-shooters." Ola felt very sorry for him. She could understand. He was laying there thinking back over his bygone days when being watchful meant the difference between surviving or getting killed.

He often talked to her about his bygone days; the troubles in his childhood and when the War Between the States closed and him and Frank turned to outlawry.

He said, "They brought the Pinkertons in to catch us boys. Me, Frank and our men. Of course, they never caught us. But we caught several of them. They didn't know what me and Frank looked like.

"Ola, when they went out to our home that night, sneaked up to the house and threw that homemade bomb in the house that injured my poor mother real bad, and killed my poor little half-brother, Archie, me and Frank wasn't at home at the time it happened but as soon as we heard about it, we went home as quick as we could and when we saw what had happened, me and Frank just went wild. We was really tore up about it. I made up my mind that I would kill that damn Allen Pinkerton for what the Pinkertons had done to my poor mother and little brother. But I was going to catch him out where I could tell him why I was going to kill him.

"I seen him several times and could have killed him easy. But that wasn't the way I wanted to kill him. I wanted the son-of-a-bitch to be where I could look straight at him, let him know who I was and why I was going to kill him and then kill him. "That's the one thing I didn't get to carry out as I planned. I always said that I knew the Good Lord would fix it so I could, but it didn't happen. But I wanted to and wish I could of."

Ola said, "Well Jesse, I can certainly understand you feeling that way. I know I would have felt the same way."

It was in the middle of March, 1949. Jesse was still under an oxygen tent due to his severe bout with pneumonia since February but was getting better day by day. One night Aubrey and Ola went out to the hospital to see him as always, and he said, "Oh say, Ola, I'll tell you what I want you to do."

She said, "Alright sir."

He said, "I want you to bring me some oatmeal and a pint of milk from home. Put some sugar and milk over the oatmeal and get it here hot, if you can."

She said, "I'll do it."

The next day, Ola bought a purse so big it almost looked like an overnight bag. It was suede, so it would hold the heat and had a wide shoulder strap. That night, off to the hospital she and Aubrey went and she told Aubrey as they walked down the hall to Jesse's room, "Oh my God, take it slow and easy so I won't fall because this purse on my shoulder is mighty heavy with this pint of milk and pint of oatmeal in a jar in it."

When we got in the room, Aubrey closed the door almost to and stood watch while she fed Jesse and then stuck the jar and milk bottle back in her purse. Ola said "Oh, it made Jesse happy to get that and he enjoyed it so good, bless his heart." Ola knew she was not supposed to do that, but catching is before hanging, you know, and she was going to see that he got it. She took oatmeal and milk to him every night until one night in early April when quite unexpectedly, in came a doctor.

He caught Ola feeding Jesse and said, "Don't you know you're not allowed to do that?"

Ola, looking shocked, replied, "Well I am sorry sir. I was not aware I was doing anything wrong."

The young doctor said, "Well you are not allowed to bring food in here. So don't do that again."

Ola replied, "No sir, I sure won't. I just didn't know."

Did She? Well, no, not oatmeal and milk, but she took cookies to him. The next night when they went out to the hospital, in her purse she had some cookies she'd bought on her way out there. She said, "Jesse, I brought you some nice cookies. I think you can eat them because they've got soft marshmallow tops."

He said, "I 'spect I can eat them honey. These teeth have served me pretty good for a long time."

Then it hit her and she said, "Oh Jesse! I feel so silly. You look so much like grandpa Underwood and he didn't have any teeth so we always had to buy soft cookies for him and I just simply completely forgot that you have most all of your teeth."

He said, "Yes honey, I've got all of my natural teeth but four. They're dark now, but they're sound."

Ola said, "Yessir I know. But I just forgot it."

They had a good laugh about her forgetfulness and after he'd eaten a couple of cookies, he said, "Yes I remember that Toby didn't have any teeth."

Ola said, "Mother told me that grandpa had scurvy when he was about twenty-nine or thirty years old and lost all of his teeth."

One Saturday in early April, 1949, Jesse had been in the hospital about six weeks. After Ola had seen that her little mother was taken care of at home. It being Saturday, Aubrey was off work and as always, they had some things to do that morning but with an early lunch they were soon at the hospital to see about Jesse.

Ola walked up to the bed and said, "Hello Jesse!"

He said, "Damn, I'm glad to see you! I'm as mad as hell!"

Ola asked, "What happened?"

With a look in his eyes that showed he was plenty mad, he replied, "Why some son-of-a-bitch stole my tobacco pouch when they cleaned up my bed this morning and I sure have been wanting a chew mighty bad."

He chewed Tennessee Twist tobacco and he got his from Tennessee. A "hand" at a time. A hand of tobacco is several leaves cut in such a way as to be able to tie them together in a bunch. Ola had bought Jesse a real nice tobacco pouch. Brown leather with an easy to work zipper at the top. Now it had been stolen. He wanted a chew and didn't have it. So, of course, he was as mad as the dickens.

Ola said, "Oh Jesse, I'm so sorry about that. But don't worry. You've got some tobacco at home. So, we'll go get some for you." Picking up her purse and patting him on the arm, Ola said, "We'll be back in a little bit."

Aubrey and Ola hurried out to the car, went to the drug store and bought him a tobacco pouch then hurried home. Ola's mother put some tobacco in the pouch then poured a little slightly sweetened warm water over it. Just enough to moisten the tobacco. Ola Zipped the pouch closed and they headed for the hospital.

Ola walked up to the bed and said, "Jesse, here's you a brand-new pouch and some fresh moistened tobacco. So, you're back in business."

He said, "My God I'm glad to get that!" He took some, put it in his mouth and then zipping the pouch closed and looking at it, said, "By golly they won't steal this one, I'll fix that." He reached under the sheet and put his new tobacco pouch under his hip so he could lay on it. It amused Ola, that he would think of hiding it there, but he did. Then looked at Ola and said, "I've been chewing tobacco since I was just a boy, and that's been some time." His temper simmered down and he relaxed when he got some tobacco in his mouth.

A few days later when the Everharts were out at the hospital talking with him, he told Aubrey, "I want a barber to come out here and trim my whiskers. They're getting too long."

So, Aubrey set about looking for a barber that would go to the hospital. It took some doing, but he finally located a Mr. Brown who agreed to if Aubrey would come get him and bring him back. Which of course, Aubrey gladly did. And, thinking it best, he told Mr. Brown who the man in the hospital was and that he'd have to be careful around Jesse's neck, that there was rope burn scars on his neck and how the scars came to be there.

Well, Mr. Brown worked slow and careful and of course, saw the rope burn scars as he was trimming the whiskers. When he did, he got as nervous as a scared cat and as quick as he could finish, he was ready to get out of that hospital room and on his way home.

The fact that the man had trimmed the whiskers of Jesse James; a man that had supposedly been killed many years before, a man that had once been a noted outlaw, but there he was, alive and living and one-hundred and one years old with a mind as clear as a bell and the pride of a young man. Land sakes that barber went home as nervous as a bowl of Jell-O and needless to say, he'd never do that again.

Jesse and Ola were talking one afternoon and Jesse said, "After Frank was pardoned and I had come back from South America, Frank took tickets and I sold tickets at the Strand Theatre in St. Louis, Missouri for a short time."

While they were talking one day about Billy the Kid, Jesse said, "Old man Roberts, Wild Henry, Billy's father was as mean as hell to poor Billy. Wild Henry lived between Hico and Hamilton, Texas and as I told you, Billy's real name is Roberts and he is the real Billy the Kid. And as I told you, when me and Bill lived in Torreon, Mexico we were neighbors, and one of Pancho Villa's wives lived down the street from us."

One Sunday afternoon, Aubrey and Ola were out at the hospital talking with Jesse. A man that Aubrey had known since boyhood brought his wife and came out to see Jesse. She was not only quite a bit older than him but she was painted up like a circus clown. Too much rouge, too much lipstick, she'd shaved her eyebrows off then had painted eyebrows on in a big half circle way above where her eyebrows was supposed to be and way down on each temple. Her hair was dyed red over dark brown and curled up so it looked like a windstorm had just hit it. But Jesse was well dressed and looked real nice.

Jesse looked her over and when they left, Aubrey walked out with them for a few minutes. When they got out of earshot, Jesse said, "Ola! Where in the god-damn hell did you find that?"

Ola said, "Wait a minute, Jesse! Don't blame that on me. Aubrey sort of grew up with that boy. They've known each other since they were young boys. He hasn't been married to that woman very long."

He said, "Now you listen to me Ola! Don't you be out anywhere with that woman! She's not the kind of woman for you to be out in public or anywhere with!"

Ola said, "I know that, Jesse. She's not my kind of people."

He said, "Hell no! So don't you fool with her!"

Ola said, "I don't."

He didn't like painted women. He liked for ladies to be ladies.

It was April 1949 and Jesse was feeling a lot better. Ola got a call from Mr. Ray Chitwood, manager of the Jesse James Hotel in St. Joseph, Missouri and he told her that they challenged Jesse to return to St. Joseph, Missouri and they would prove him to be a fake in two weeks time and that he would stay at the Jesse James Hotel while there.

CHAPTER THIRTEEN

Ola went out to the hospital as soon as she could after she got the call. After she and Jesse talked a little bit, she said, "Jesse, Mr. Chitwood, manager of the Jesse James Hotel in St. Joseph, Missouri called me this morning."

He said, "Is that so? What did he want?"

She replied, "Well, he said that they want you to know that they challenge you to come back to St. Joe. That they'll prove you to be a fake in two weeks."

He said, "Well honey, you just call him back and tell him that I will be glad to come back to St. Joe and let them prove me to be a fake, if they can. Providing of course, that I go by plane."

Ola said, "Well, you will stay at the Jesse James Hotel there. Is that alright with you?"

He said, "Yes. That will be fine with me."

Ola went back home, called Mr. Chitwood and told him what Jesse said. He told her, "Tell him to send me a letter stating that he will come back to St. Joe. Signed by him."

Aubrey and Ola went out to the hospital that night and Jesse told Aubrey what to put in the letter and then bring it out for him to sign. The next day, Aubrey typed out the letter while he was at the office and while he was doing that, Ola called Frank Hall in Lawton, Oklahoma and he arranged for a private plane to take Jesse to St. Joe and for his wife Fern to go along as an escort for Jesse.

The next night, Aubrey and Ola had some friends; Mr. and Mrs. Hughes meet them at the hospital and taking the young ex-Marine, Walter O. Dyer who lived with them, they went to the hospital. Aubrey read the letter to Jesse and he found it all right and signed his name to it. Then, Mr. and Mrs. Hughes and Walter Dyer all signed as witnesses to Jesse's signature. In the State of Texas, three witnesses to a signature is equal to a Notary seal.

The next day, Ola arranged with the hospital to have a professional photographer come out to the hospital and take some pictures of Jesse before he left. That night, Ola got a call from Frank Hall telling me that Fern Hall would be at the hospital the next morning and the plane would be there before noon to take her and Jesse to St. Joe.

The next morning, Ola got dressed and Walter Dyer took her out to the hospital. Sam Campbell who was a police reporter for the Lawton, OK *Constitution* newspaper brought Fern Hall to Austin and they were already at the hospital with Jesse when Walter and she arrived. Fern had been trying to get Jesse to let her comb his hair but he wouldn't let her. Ola walked up to the bed and said, "Jesse."

He, laying there with his eyes closed, said, "Yeah."

Ola said, "Howdy!"

He opened his eyes and said, "Oh, hello Ola honey. Damn, I'm glad to see you!"

She said, "Well I'm here." They talked a little bit and then she said, "You know what? I've got a woman coming out here in a little bit and me and you are gonna have our pictures tookin' as Uncle Josh used to say."

He smiled and replied, "Alright, that's fine."

Fern called Ola over to her and said, "Ola, see if he'll let you comb and brush his hair. He damn sure won't let me touch it."

She said, "Well, let me see what I can do."

Ola walked over to the bed and said, "Jesse, do you mind if I comb and brush your hair and fix it pretty before the picture woman gets here and we have our pictures taken?"

He said, "Honey you just comb and fix my hair all you want to."

Fern stomped her foot and went out in the hall cussing a blue streak because Ola could fix his hair and he wouldn't let her touch it.

Fern was running around calling him Uncle Frank. Ola called him Jesse because his true name was Jesse. A nurse came in the room and in a few minutes asked, "Why do one of you call him Jesse and the other calls him Uncle Frank?"

Jesse spoke up and said, "By God I'm damn particular who calls me Jesse!"

Elinora Douglas, the photographer came out and took some pictures. One of Jesse alone on the bed and another of he and Ola together where she was standing by his bed. Shortly before noon on April 12, 1949 the pictures had been taken and the photographer had gone to develop them and get them back as quick as she could because Jesse was leaving the hospital the next morning. Sam, Fern, Walter and Ola went home, ate lunch and visited a while before going back out to the hospital to see Jesse.

About eight o'clock that night, Elinora Douglas brought the pictures out to the Everhart home. The next morning after breakfast, Aubrey went to work, Fern and Ola got cleaned up and then Sam and Fern got in his car, Walter and Ola got in Walter's car and they all went to the hospital to see about Jesse. The private plane had not gotten there as first planned, but that morning in a little bit after they'd gotten to the hospital, Fern got a call from the airport that the private plane was there. So, the next step was to sign Jesse out of the hospital and then an ambulance was called to take him to the airport.

When the ambulance arrived, he was put in it, then with Sam and Fern in the lead and Walter and Ola following the ambulance, they went to the airport and Ola watched Jesse as he was put aboard the plane. Fern then got in and the plane started and took to the air. They were on their way to St. Joseph, Missouri before noon.

Arriving at St. Joe, Jesse and Fern were taken from the airport to the Jesse James Hotel, located at Jules on Third. Ola waited all afternoon for Mr. Chitwood to call and tell Ola they had arrived. He said he would but by late afternoon he hadn't so Ola called him. She called the hotel, asked for him and when he got to the phone he was in a frenzy of excitement. He said, "Yes they are here and, oh my God, this hotel is in such an uproar I can't even think." Ola heard all the noise and people talking and there seemed to be lots of excitement.

On April 14, 1949, former representative William C. Cole and Thomas F. Ryan went to see Jesse there in the hotel and he told them about the killing of Bigelow and that Bigelow's wife claimed the body and that his wife wasn't even in the state when that took place. She was in Nashville, Tennessee.

Well, the two weeks that Jesse was supposed to stay in St. Joe and during which they said they would prove him to be a fake, had gone by and although Ola called the hotel to see about him and had talked to Mr. Chitwood, she could not get any information from them as to him being the real Jesse James. They would not say he was. Nor would they say he wasn't. They just wouldn't say.

About six weeks went by then Rudy Turilli went to see Jesse and got him to go out to the Meramec Cavern at Stanton, Missouri on Route 66. Rudy was the manager of the cavern but his father-in-law, Lester B. Dill, was the owner. Rudy hired an ambulance to take Jesse from the Jesse James Hotel in St. Joe, out to the Meramec Cavern at Stanton. They had a nice cabin fixed for him and a nurse hired to take care of him due to his bad hip that had been broken before he came out with his true identity. Lots of people went there to see him and talk with him, including some reporters.

The following is copied from an article that was carried in the Veedersburg, Indiana newspaper on Friday, August 19, 1949.

Ozark Jack Berlin returned to Veedersburg and says there is no doubt in his mind that this man is the real Jesse James now 102 years old. Charges were closed on James when he was believed killed in 1882 and a reward collected for his body.

Bob Ford, a semi-bad man and distant relative of Jesse James, shot a man by the name of Bigelow who looked much like Jesse.

Following this episode Jesse James retired to Arizona where he owned a ranch under the name of Jesse Williams. He led a quiet life until the Boer War, at

*which time he joined the Canadian Army. He rose to the rank of Colonel and was
known under the name of Dalton.*

*Ozark says he and Jesse talked of mutual acquaintances and of episodes
which only Jesse could have known about. Ozark Jack was then convinced that
the real Jesse James was still alive.*

On September 5, 1949, Jesse celebrated his 102 birthday there at Meramec
Cavern. A big party was given in his honor. A large birthday cake was baked at a
bakery in St. Louis, Missouri for the party and some of those attending was
Colonel James R. Davis of Nashville, Tennessee, age 109 who had known Jesse
since he was a boy. Brushy Bill Roberts of Hico, Texas, 89 years of age who had
known Jesse since Jesse's outlaw days. Brushy Bill's father, Wild Henry Roberts
was with Quantrell during the War Between the States, Frank James daughter,
Mary Plina James Norris of Claremore, Oklahoma who knew that her Jesse was
never killed and was still alive, DeWitt Travis of Longview, Texas, who was in
his 60's and had known Jesse all of his life. His mother went to school with Jesse
in Missouri. Old John Trammell of Guthrie, Oklahoma, age 110 who had been
with Jesse and his men back in Jesse's outlaw days as their cook, handy man and
looked after their horses.

John Trammell had seen Jesse many times after his supposed death. Ozark
Jack Berlin of Veedersburg, Indiana who was in his 80's and had known Jesse for
many years. Henry J. Walker of Iowa who was in the process of compiling a book
about Jesse and Frank James, and Morrey Davidson of New York City and of
course some reporters. Aubrey and Ola couldn't go because Ola was needed at
home to take care of her aged mother who was not well at the time. It was a big
birthday party.

On November 26, 1949 a reporter for the St. Louis *Post Dispatch* newspaper
went to the Meramec Cavern and talked with Jesse. He asked Jesse, "Was there a
plan, as is claimed, to murder the man named Bigelow and say it was Jesse?"

"There's a lot to that," said Jesse, "that I ain't a-gonna tell. They buried a man named Bigelow." Then he also said, "But I will say this, my disappearance was not my own idea. Other people were in on it. The Governor of Missouri, for one, and the Sheriff, for another."

Morrey Davidson was working at the time at a radio and television station in New York City, and after Jesse's birthday party he thought about how nice it would be to have Jesse James appear on the, then, very popular program called "WE THE PEOPLE." So, he talked to Jesse about it and then started making arrangements for his appearance on it. It was arranged and agreed between Morrey and Rudy Turilli that Rudy would take Jesse to New York City when the time was set. So, in January 1950, Rudy put Jesse on a plane and off to New York City they went.

On Wednesday morning, January 11, 1950, at 9:35 a.m. the phone rang at the Everhart residence. It was a Mrs. Beck at the State Capitol in Austin, Texas and she said, "I am trying to locate a Mrs. Olga or Ola Everhart."

Ola said, "I am Ola Everhart."

She asked, "Are you crippled?"

Ola replied, "Yes I am."

She then asked, "In both legs?"

Ola replied, "Yes I am."

Then she said, "Well Jesse James is calling you from New York City."

Ola said, "Alright. I've been expecting him to call."

So, they put the call through and Rudy Turilli said, "Hello Ola! Do you know who I've got up here in the room with me?"

She said, "Jesse!"

Rudy said, "Yes, I have that damned old Rebel here."

Then he put Jesse on the phone.

Ola said, "Hello Jesse! This is Ola."

He said, "Yeah, I know who it is. I know who I'm talking to."

She asked him, "How are you?"

He replied, "Oh, I guess I'm alright. I'm laying on a bed up here in a hotel in New York." Then he asked me, "Oh say, Ola, have you still got those pictures of me?"

She replied, "Yessir, I have."

He asked, "Have you still got the one of me taken at Long Branch, Kentucky?"

She said, "You bet I have."

He said, "That's what I told them."

Then he asked, "What picture have you got of Frank?"

She said, "I've got a picture of him when he worked at Sangers in Dallas."

He asked, "How is your mother?"

She said, "She's doing pretty good."

He said, "Say, Ola, what is your husband's first name? I can't remember it."

Ola said, "His first name is Aubrey."

He said, "Well, I just couldn't remember it."

Then he said, "Oh, say Ola, I'm going to be on the radio and television program *We The People* Friday night, so be sure and listen."

Ola said, "Oh that's wonderful! You bet we'll listen." Then she said, "Jesse I'm so happy to talk to you. You take real good care of yourself and good luck on the program. I'll be listening."

He said, "Alright. Goodbye Ola."

They had spoken for about 25 or 30 minutes.

He was on the program Friday night, January 13, 1950. His being on that program was made possible by his good friend Morrey Davidson and was there at the station and present when the men looked at Jesse's bullet scarred body that proved he was the real Jesse James the former outlaw, before he went on the air.

CHAPTER FOURTEEN

The following was sent to Ola from a friend in Toledo, Ohio.

TO WHOM IT MAY CONCERN:

On January 13, 1950 Jesse James was interviewed on the radio program, "WE THE PEOPLE. Jesse told how the hoax in St. Joseph, Mo. occurred in response to a series of questions by the interviewer.

Charles Bigelow, alias Thomas Howard, was an undercover agent for the Pinkerton Detective Agency and was out to get him in order to collect a bounty of $10,000. Jesse was going under the name of Jim Crowe. Jesse decided to get Bigelow and enlisted the help of the Ford brothers who were his first cousins. Bigelow visited Jesse's home at various times and they would go horseback riding. Jesse would always ride a little behind Bigelow for self-protection.

On Saturday, April 2, 1882 Jesse and Bigelow went for a ride near dusk so as to be less likely to be noticed. When they returned to the barn out back of the house, Jesse said that he would take care of the horses and told Bigelow to go into the house through the back door.

When Bigelow went through the door he was shot in the back of the head by Bob Ford. The victim fell forward causing a flesh wound over the left eye. Mrs. James (Bigelow) had purposely taken the children to visit a neighbor. She returned after dark and the children, ages 5 and 7, were put to bed.

The next morning about 9 a.m. Bob Ford shot a hole in the wall, Mrs. James (Bigelow) hurried from the kitchen to the front room, put the head of the victim in her lap and poured chicken blood on her dress. The children were allowed momentarily to see Mrs. James (Mrs. Bigelow) with the head of the victim on her lap. Mrs. James (Bigelow) then hurried to a neighbor's house and reported that her husband had just been killed.

Mrs. Samuel was not aware of the plot and at first said that the victim was not Jesse. Later in the day, after meeting privately with Mrs. James (Bigelow), she reversed her statement and put on a crying act.

In response to another question Jesse told how that the bank vault at Neosho, Mo. was opened. When he had finished, the interviewer said, "You are right." Apparently, the vault was different from most vaults. In response to another question, Jesse denied that there was any plan to rob the Platte City, Mo. bank nor any other bank.

In exchange the following took place:

Interviewer: Did you ever meet any historical person who knew who you were?

Jesse: No.

I: Now I want you to think real hard and try to remember some historical person who knew who you were.

J: (after a pause) I met Calamity Jane.

I: Did she know you as Jesse James?

J: Yes.

I: Did she ever tell anybody?

J: No.

At the end of the program, the interviewer said that N.B.C. investigators had concluded that Dalton was the Real Jesse James.

So far as I know the above information has never appeared in print. It is unfortunate that N.B.C. did not keep a recording of this particular program so that the only evidence is in the memory of the listener.

At the time of the murder investigation, rumors spread far and wide that the victim was not Jesse James for the following reasons based on circumstantial evidence which appeared in the St. Joseph, Mo. newspapers for April 4 and 5, 1882, but it was never reprinted in any other newspapers. This was probably because Jesse had many friends in the news media who were willing to participate in the cover-up.

1. *The victim had been dead for at least 12 hours.*

2. *The blood on Mrs. James (Mrs. Bigelow's) dress was not human.*

3. *The bullet that killed the victim was not the bullet that made the hole in the wall.*

4. *Mrs. James (Mrs. Bigelow) said that there was nothing wrong with the victim's hands even though the tip of a finger was missing.*

5. *To begin with Mrs. Samuel denied that the victim was Jesse.*

6. *The Governor ordered the coroner to turn the body over to Mrs. Samuel, thereby preventing the request of the St. Joseph and Kansas City Police to examine the victim.*

7. *Mrs. Samuel had the body buried in her yard 2 feet deeper than usual and hired guards for a while to watch over the grave. This suggested that she feared that the plot would be revealed.*

I read these articles in 1929 but they disappeared from the St. Joseph, Mo. Public Library and the Missouri State Historical Society at Columbia, Missouri about 1950 before the papers were put on file. Apparently, somebody didn't want any evidence around that would support the claims of Jesse.

Apparently, the Ford brothers made up the story about the Platte City Bank in an effort to win public support for their act. Also, the Ford brothers apparently made up the story about the hole in the wall as a cover-up for the flesh wound over the left eye.

Since bodies could not be kept very long in ice, the coroner used a maneuver by recommending to the jury that they accept the victim as Jesse James so that the Ford brothers could be brought to a quick trial and they and Mrs. James (Mrs. Bigelow) questioned by the prosecutor about the characteristics of the body and the circumstances of the murder.

The maneuver failed when the Ford brothers pled guilty and received a quick pardon from the Governor to keep them from talking. The coroner refused to sign a death certificate for Jesse.

It is ironic that a letter by Calamity Jane telling about her meeting with Jesse was made public the same year that Jesse died without his ever knowing about it.

Jesse was said to have died with a broken heart in 1951 near the age of 104 when Hollywood refused to make a movie of his true story.

E.T. Huff

Following the killing of Bigelow – supposedly Jesse James, the following article was carried in the St Joseph, MO *Daily Herald* on April 6, 1882:

There was another story that upon examination, they found that the wound over the left eye was not made by the exit of the bullet, which according to rumor was found to have lodged against the frontal bone about a half-inch to the right of the wound over the left eye, and the rumor went on to relate that the doctor's cut this bone and extracted the bullet.

Dr. W.I. Heddens, the coroner's father stated yesterday that the wound over the eye was a flesh wound and was not made by the passage of the bullet. It will be remembered that during the examination before the jury all of the witnesses were asked if any blows were struck before or after the shooting. The questions all having been answered in the negative, the doctor's theory is that in falling, Jesse's head came in contact with some hard substance. This however, would seem impossible, since the witness testified that he fell backward off the chair to the carpeted floor. There is a strong suspicion that if the ball did not pass out through that opening, Jesse James was struck with a pistol.

It was found that the bullet had entered the lower portion of the occipital bone on the right side of the median line, and had taken a course slightly upward and to the left. The ball did not pass through the head, as at first stated, as it was found partially embedded in the bone, the scalp bot being punctured at all.

The ball was lodged at the junction of the sutures or seams dividing the occipital, parietal, and temporal bones on the left side. The occipital bone was very much shattered, whole continuity of the cranium being broken up. The cerebellum was found crushed and mangled terribly, large pieces of bone having been carried into the brain by the bullet in its progress.

The wound over the eye was not made by the bullet, and was probably made by the fall from the chair. The outlaw was a man of fine physique and was evidently possessed of unlimited powers and endurance.

St Joseph, MO *Herald* April 7, 1882:

In a rambling talk of half an hour the Ford boys asserted positively that the ball which brought Jesse James down, passed through his skull, came out over the left eye and entered the wall. Robert says he distinctly saw the plastering break.

It has been intimated in the Herald heretofore that an autopsy of the head of Jesse James was made on Monday night. The suspicion that this had been done was occasioned by the fact that Dr. J.W. Heddens, the coroner, Dr. Jacob Gieger, professor of operative surgery in the College of Physicians and Surgeons, F.C. Hoyt, demonstrator of anatomy in the same institution, and Dr. George C. Catlett, Superintendent of the State Insane Asylum No. 2 had been seen entering the room where the corpse lay, and where they remained several hours, no one else being admitted during the time. The fact that they carried in with them several cases of instruments strengthened the theory that a surgical examination was made. When questioned the doctors gave evasive replies, but made no direct denial. It was leaked out that a most thorough examination was made.

After examining the general contour of his head, the skill cap was removed and the brain exposed. It was found that the brain was above average, both in weight and appearance, showing conclusively that the possessor was a man of more than ordinary intellect.

The St Joseph, MO *Gazette* April 9, 1882:

Reporter: Will you state how many shots you heard at the time your husband was killed.

Mrs. James (Mrs. Bigelow): I heard only one shot, but I afterward saw a bullet hole in the wall I had never before seen.

Reporter: The object I had in asking the question was to accound for the presence of the bullet hole in the wall and the fact that the fatal ball was recovered embedded in the skull of your husband. The Ford brothers claim that the bullet came out over the left eye and lodged in the wall.

Mrs. James (Bigelow): I cannot explain it. Although half a dozen queries were submitted, she excused herself from answering them and the reporters left.

In the St Joseph, MO *Gazette* was the following on April 12, 1882:

JESSE'S RUSE
HE USED HAIR DYE TO PREVENT IDENTIFICATION
– A PERFECT DISGUISE

One of the most successful means of concealing identity by the famous freebooter Jesse James was accidentally discovered yesterday. A Gazette Reporter learned the facts from headquarters and can vouch for their authenticity.

It has been handed down through all the fables regarding Jesse that he was of a light complexion, that his beard and hair were rather light and of a reddish hue. This statement has been corroborated by parties claiming to know him, and with bluish-grey eyes, a lighter color of hair and beard might have been expected than existed at the time of his death. Yesterday a gentleman was sitting in the room where Mrs. James was at work packing a valise preparatory to departure. As she bent over at her work, a small vial dropped to the floor and broke; the gentleman picked it up, and naturally enough asked what the substance might be.

Mrs. James seemed embarrassed, and at first did not know what to say. She finally, however, said that it was a kind of dye needed by her husband for the purpose of coloring his hair and beard.

She stated that his beard was colored at the time of his death, and had been ever since his residence in St. Joseph. Mrs. James had endeavored to conceal this ruse of her husband to protect identification and requested that nothing be said about the matter. This little fact will explain away the doubts of skeptics regarding the identity of the murdered man

The above article should show the readers that the real Jesse James was right when he stated that nobody except kinfolks and close friends actually knew how he looked. He was also right when he stated that him and Bigelow looked enough alike to be twins. Both had light complexion, blue eyes, light hair and beard of a reddish hue. And, he was right when he said that Bigelow's wife claimed the body after the killing. So, it *was* Bigelow that was killed and *not* Jesse James. Just as Jesse James, alias J. Frank Dalton, said.

The *Police Gazette* files of 1882 produced conclusive evidence in 1950 that the famous Outlaw Jesse James was never killed.

Jesse James' "Identification Marks."
1. Rope burns on neck
2. Evidence of severe burns on feet
3. Bullet hole through left shoulder
4. Bullet hole in lower belly
5. Bullet scar under left knee
6. Bullet scar under right eye
7. Bullet hole along hairline of forehead
8. End of index finger "chewed" off

All of the above identification marks were found on Jesse James alias J. Frank Dalton before he went on the air in New York City. Jesse stated in 1950. "Bigelow's wife claimed his body. My wife at the time was in Nashville, Tennessee and didn't come near there. I rented the house on Lafayette Street in St. Joe but I never lived there. I told the Bigelow family they could live there. I was in Excelsior Springs, Missouri most of the time and didn't need the house, just the stables."

After the program was over in New York, Rudy Turilli put Jesse on a plane and took him back to his cabin at Meramec Cavern.

April 1, 1950. An old man 84 years old at Republic, Indiana told a reporter, Dale Freeman, "Jesse James never got shot by Bob Ford or anybody else! It was a feller named Bigelow."

The following is copied from a clipping sent to Ola from Ozark Jack Berlin in Veedersburg, Indiana in 1950:

The group included Mr. and Mrs. Max Grady, Miss Bette Francis and Austin Baker, this city, (Veedersburg, Indiana) and Miss Helen Swisher, Danville, Illinois.

Arriving at Meramec Caverns, Miss Bette Francis introduced herself as granddaughter of Ozark Jack Berlin, a friend of Jesse James for many years. When she asked to visit Jesse James she was told that he no longer saw visitors because he is confined to his bed with paralysis.

Upon learning the presence of the Veedersburg group, the aged man asked that he see them, and he talked freely to them, of a trip he made last year by plan to New York to appear on a radio program. He related a few interesting experiences off his early life.

When asked his reason for making himself known after the world had believed him dead for 66 years, he stated that he did so to clarify some of the false stories that had been told about him.

His last words to Miss Better Francis were, "Tell Ozark Jack Berlin, my friend, to visit me soon. I am lonesome."

The local man plans to visit him in the future.

While Jesse was there at Meramec Cavern after the appearance on the *We the People* program, Rudy Turilli hit upon the idea to take him into court and petition for his true name to be restored. When he called and told Ola about it, she told him that she muchly disapproved of it and thought it unnecessary, for Jesse had done his best to prove who he was. But, on March 10, 1950 Rudy took Jesse into court in the Franklin County courthouse at Union, Missouri and the trial began to restore Jesse's name from J. Frank Dalton back to Jesse Woodson James. The truth of the matter was, the name J. Frank Dalton was an alias name. His true and correct name was, and always had been, Jesse Woodson James. Judge Ransom Bruer was the presiding Judge.

Witnesses for Jesse were Colonel James Russell Davis of Nashville, Tennessee, John Trammell of Guthrie, Oklahoma, Robert E. Lee of Louisiana, who was once a bodyguard for Buffalo Bill Cody and had known Jesse James for many years. William Pierce of Ray County, Missouri and Henry M. Priest of St. Louis, Missouri formerly of Nashville, Tennessee.

Witnesses against were William Stafford of St. Joseph, Missouri, John Roach of St. Joseph. Mrs. Quantrell Sallee Steifers of St. Joe, daughter of William Sallee who took Jesse and Frank's father Robert to California and Jonathon D. Roberts of Cameron, Missouri. The courtroom was full of people to hear the trial.

When Jesse was on the witness stand, he was asked who he saw that knew him and knew who he was when he came back from South America?

He studied a little bit and replied, "I saw and talked with Calamity Jane. She knew who I was."

The following will substantiate what he said, in a letter written to James O'Neil by Calamity Jane, on November 30, 1889 she stated:

"I met up with Jesse James not long ago. He is quite a character — you know he was killed in '82. His mother swore that the body that was in the coffin was

his, but it was another man they called Tracy or Lynch. He was a cousin of Wild Bill.

He is passing under the name of Dalton, but he couldn't fool me. I knew all the Daltons and he sure ain't one of them. He told me promised his gang and his mother that if he lived to be a hundred, he would confess – To make it strange, Jesse sang at his own funeral. Poor devil he can't cod me- not even with long hair and billy goat's hair on his chin. I expect he will start preachin'. He is smart maybe he can do it. -Jane"

Calamity Jane was born May 1, 1852 in Princeton, Missouri. In her diary, she reveals that she married Wild Bill Hickok September 1, 1870 and that a daughter was born to them in 1873. James Butler (Wild Bill) Hickok was born in 1837 in Troy Grove, Illinois and was killed in 1876. Calamity Jane died August 1, 1903 and at her own request, was buried in the plot next to Wild Bill. In 1890 or early 1891 she married Charley Burke.

When the trial was finished, Judge Ransom Bruer stated his conclusion. He stated, "I cannot restore a name that has never been legally changed. If you was ever Jesse James, then you are still Jesse James."

Morrey Davidson was at the trial and after it was over, he went in the Judges chamber and talked privately with the Judge. He asked the Judge if he did not believe that the petitioner was the real Jesse James the former outlaw?

The Judge replied, "Hell yes, that's him! But I ruled the only way I could." Then said, "I ruled the only way I could, under the circumstances."

In September 1950, shortly after Jesse's 103 birthday, Rudy Turilli and a friend brought Jesse back to the Everhart house at 1103 East First Street in Austin, Texas from Meramec Cavern in Missouri. As he was bed-ridden due to his hip that had been broken and had not knitted back as it should, plus his being 103 years old, he was brought back by ambulance. Rudy and his friend brought him in and got him settled in bed. They all visited a little while and then Rudy said, "Well, we've got to head on back to Missouri."

He walked over the bed, took Jesse's hand and said, "Well, goodbye you damned old Rebel."

Jesse replied, "Goodbye, you damn Yankee."

They both smiled. That was their parting words and they never saw each other again because Rudy was real busy from early to late.

The next morning after breakfast, Jesse said, "Ola, where is my purse?"

Ola said, "It's in the top dresser drawer over there, Jesse." She got it, took it to him and he said, "Honey, I haven't got but $15.00 left, but I brought it to you."

Jesse never knew that Ola had already used all of it and more, hiring women to come in and clean him and his bed up every morning. She had to hire a different woman every morning, because when they found out who he was and saw the scars on his body, they wouldn't come back again.

While they were talking, he said, "Ola, that set up at St. Joe sure was a mess."

He liked an egg, a couple of sausage patties, a cup of coffee and two slices of light toast for breakfast. Ola's mother would cook it and Ola would feed him. Then, at night, he wanted a cup of milk and two doughnuts put on a stand by his bed to eat during the night.

The next morning after breakfast, Jesse told Aubrey to go get him a pint of whiskey. Aubrey did and when he got back, Jesse told him to pour half of it into another bottle. Ola didn't recall where he got another bottle but he did and poured half of the whiskey in it.

Then Jesse said to Ola's mother, "Bertha, if you don't mind, will you boil some tea and when it gets done and cool, pour it in the two bottles of whiskey so they'll be half whiskey and half tea so I can take a swallow every once in a while to clear my throat. It helps me."

Ola's mother said, "I sure will." So she went in the kitchen, made the tea and in a little while she came in and brought a bottle and said, "Now Jesse, here's your bottle fixed just like you said, half whiskey and half tea."

"By golly I really appreciate it," as he took the bottle.

One morning after he'd finished his breakfast, he said, "Ola, how much is eggs now?"

"Well, they're 50 cents a dozen now," she replied.

He said, "Land sakes! Eggs used to sell for 10 and 15 cents a dozen and I ate a good many of them, but when they went up to 25 cents a dozen, I quit eating them. Chewing that much money hurt my teeth."

Another morning, Ola was feeding him his breakfast and, being a person who likes to talk, she was talking while she was feeding him when suddenly he stuck his finger up and said very sternly, "Don't talk to me while I'm eating!"

Boy! She clammed up but quick! Then she silently finished feeding him. After he'd finished eating, in a soft, kind tone, he asked, "Now honey, what was you saying?"

She said, "Well first, I want to tell you that I'm sorry for talking to you while you were eating. I knew better. I just forgot and didn't do better. I was raised to know better."

He said, "Well honey I don't want anybody to talk to me while I'm eating."

She said, "I understand. Grandpa Underwood was like that too." You can bet your last dollar she remembered her raising after that. She didn't tell him, but she could have. If you started talking while eating at Ola's grandpa Underwood's table, he would just very quickly and firmly tell you, "Now if that's the best you can do, just leave the table, right now!"

One day after dinner Ola took a book she had, went in Jesse's room, sat down by his bed and said, "Jesse, I thought I'd come in here and read some to you from this book I've got."

He asked, "What's it about?"

She grinned and replied, "Oh, it's about those awful James boys. I thought since you hailed from Missouri, you might have known them."

He said, "Well I went to see them several times. But every time I went, they was always gone."

They had a big laugh and then Ola said, "The book is about Harrison Trow. He gave the information to the writer about himself and the men with Quantrell."

He said, "Oh yes I remember him well. He was a big liar but he was one of the men who identified old Bigelow as being me. Yes, he was a Quantrell man. He's alright."

Jesse had a very pretty pocket watch. It was a Helbros make, thin model about two inches in diameter. Seven jewel, white gold with yellow gold numbers, hands and second hand with a closed link square watch chain of yellow gold. On his watch chain was a watch charm that was the emblem of the K.P. Lodge and the letters F.C.B. When someone would ask him what the F.C.B. stood for, he'd reply, "That stands for Fresh Country Butter." Other times when asked what they stood for, he'd say, "They stand for Fools Can't Belong."

He told Ola, "Ola hone that stands for Friendship, Courage, and Benevolence. I am a member of the Knights of Pythias Lodge."

When he came back to the Everhart house at 1103 East First Street in Austin, Texas in 1950 he didn't have the Fresh Country Butter watch charm. Instead, he had a facsimile of a twenty-dollar gold coin. As I said earlier, he had come back home from Meramec Caverns where he'd been for some time.

The Meramec Cavern had been known as the old Salt Peter Cave when it was Jesse James' hideout. The coin on his watch chain was a facsimile of gold coins discovered February 4, 1941 in the Jesse James section of Meramec Cavern. Gold coins were part of the loot from the train robbery that Jesse and his men pulled at Gads Hill, Missouri January 31, 1874. Lester Dill, owner of Meramec Cavern and Rudy Turilli had the facsimile of the twenty-dollar gold coin made into a watch charm for Jesse.

In September, 1950, Jesse had come back to the Everhart house at 1103 East First Street in Austin from Meramec Cavern. Ola had fed him his breakfast. He'd finished eating and she and he were talking.

He asked me, "Ola, do you think I've got money?"

She said, "No sir."

He said, "You don't?"

She said, "No sir, I don't."

He said, "Well why don't you? Everybody else does."

Ola said, "Well Jesse, you've got a lot of years on your head and my common sense tells me that what money you had, you had to use it to live on over the years because you had to live."

He said, "Well honey, you're right. But you'd be surprised how many people never think of that."

Ola said, "Well Jesse, the way I see it, when you were younger and in your outlaw days, what money you got wasn't all yours. It was equally divided between you and your men. So that mean that none of you got much at a time after it was divided."

He said, "Honey you're right."

Then she said, "As you told me, it took more money for you and your men to live on than just ordinary people."

He said, "That's right too. For when we were out on the road and people were nice enough to give us food or took us in for the night and give us shelter, we always seen that they were well paid for their kindness when we left."

Ola said, "I can understand."

Then he said, "Ola, I wish you could have been there for my 102 birthday celebration. Colonel Davis was there, Brushy Bill, DeWitt, Old John Trammel, Morrey Davidson and a lot of others. I can't remember who all. Oh yes, Frank's girl Mary was there too. Rudy had a birthday cake made that weighed a hundred pounds. I wish you could have seen it. It was quite a birthday celebration for me. I got five-hundred dollars for my birthday. But there was a young woman there at Meramec who took care of me and cleaned up my cabin every day, and one morning right after my birthday, she came in and we got to talking and she said, 'I don't want to be a nurse.'

"I asked her, 'Whatta you wanna be?'

"She said, 'I want to be a beauty operator.'

"I said, 'Well, why don't you?'

"She said, 'I haven't got the money.'

"I asked her, 'How much does it cost?' She told me. So, I just pulled my purse out from under my pillow, got the money out that she needed, handed it to her and said, 'Now, get out of here and go be a beauty operator.' So, she took the money and left. Then they had to hire another nurse for me. The forty-five dollars I brought to you is all I've got left. It ain't much but it's all I've got and it's for you."

One day when Jesse was at home with the Everharts in 1950, he and Ola were talking about different members of the family and Ola asked, "Where is Frank's boy? He had a boy about the age of your boy I understand."

He said, "Well honey, I'll tell you about little Frank. His name was, or is, Alexander Frank Jr. of course, but I always call him Little Frank."

Ola asked, "Where is he? Is he still living?"

Jesse said, "Well honey, Little Frank is in a Mental Hospital near Los Angeles, California. Or was the last I heard."

Ola asked, "What about Frank's boy Robert, who lives in Missouri on the James home place?"

Jesse said, "That boy Robert James in Missouri is an adopted son. But Little Frank is Frank's own son."

Ola said, "You had one son, Jesse Edwards. Where is he?"

He said, "Well honey, young Jess is in the T.B. Hospital out in Los Angeles, California and is in a very serious condition. Or at least that's where he was the last I knew of him."

Then Ola asked, "Jesse, was there ever a Jesse James Junior?"

He said, "No! There was never a Jesse James, Jr. My boy was named Jesse Edwards, just as I've told you. That Jesse James, Jr. you hear about is, in truth, Bigelow's boy. Not mine. Never was."

Then he said, "My boy, young Jess Edwards, was County Attorney of Wyandotte County, Missouri for a while. As best I know, the name of the county has been changed over the years."

Ola asked Ozark Jack if he ever saw Frank's son and he said, "I only saw Young Frank one time. Me and Frank was on the old Gray Eagle Steam Boat going north out of St. Louis, Missouri on the Mississippi River and Frank had Little Frank with him."

CHAPTER FIFTEEN

Now we'll go back for a little bit.

Jesse told Ola, "In 1877, using the name Benjamin Franklin Johnson, I joined the Texas Rangers and was stationed at Fort Concho at San Angelo, Texas. I was in Company C. Border Battalion."

Ola's mother, Bertha Underwood Maddox told her what happened one day back in 1895 when her grandparents were living on a farm in the Arbuckle mountains there in the Indian Territory not far from Woodford.

She said, "Scarface Jim, an outlaw, had been coming to our place late at night and getting a meal. We never turned anybody away. Us kids didn't know that Scarface was bad, but we knew one thing for sure, and that was not to be talking and telling anything.

"One day Papa went to Woodford to the Post Office while me and my sisters, Annie and Lee was out in the field chopping cotton. He hadn't been gone long when Jesse, who was a Deputy U.S. Marshal, came riding out in the field and said, 'Did you children see a man?' and he described Scarface Jim.

"Me, being the oldest, I done the talking for all of us and replied, 'No sir, we ain't seen nobody! We've been working!'

"Jesse smiled, said, 'Alright. Thank you.' Tipped his hat and rode off. I watched him ride off and thought, what a pretty man he was. He always wore a nice dark suit, white shirt, tie and a fairly wide-brim black hat and right in front on his hat was a pretty Marshal emblem."

In 1950, Jesse was there at home with them at 1103 East First Street in Austin, Texas. One afternoon he and Ola's mother were talking about the early days back in the Indian Territory when he was a Deputy U.S. Marshal there and mother said, "I well remember the day you rode out in the field where us kids was chopping cotton and asked if we'd seen Scarface Jim."

Jesse grinned as he said, "Toby sure had you children trained. I seen that."

Ola's mother laughed and said, "Land sakes, papa would have skinned us alive if we'd have told anything. He gave us strict orders, 'Now don't be talking your heads off! You hear me?' You bed we heard and we knew what he meant."

"Then," mother said, "when I got to be a good big girl and me and papa was gone to the mill or was working in the woods, he told me that the Marshal was his first cousin and who you were, but gave me strict orders to keep my mouth shut and not tell a soul."

Jesse said, "Toby was a good man."

This, Ola said she would never forget. The year was 1950. Jesse had come back home from a lengthy stay in Missouri. Jesse was wanting his morning back and as they had been doing, Aubrey and Ola went and hired a woman to come give him a bath and clean up his bed. He didn't want anybody to see him until he'd had his bath and a clean white shirt and necktie on.

The particular morning, the woman didn't want to be in the room alone with him, so Ola stayed in there with them. She finished her work, Aubrey and Ola took her home and Ola asked her if she would work for them the next morning. She said, "Yes ma'am."

The next morning, they went after her. She came slowly out to the car and Ola said, "Are you ready to go?"

She replied, "No."

Ola asked, "What's the trouble? Didn't I pay you enough yesterday?"

She replied, "Yes ma'am."

Ola said, "Well, what's the trouble?"

She dropped her head a minute or so, raised it and looking at Ola as if she was wondering what she would do, said, "Well I just tells ya. When I got home yesterday, I got to thinkin' 'bout who that man is and I didn't sleep a wink all night long. And I just tells ya, I just don't wants that job, at no price."

So, Ola had to go and hire another woman. A new one every day. Jesse's deep voice, piercing blue eyes, and particularly the bullet scars on his body, scarred neck and bad feet combined with his name Jesse James, no working woman would come back a second time.

When Jesse was at home with the Everharts on East First Street, every time their little Chihuahua dog, Dolly, got a chance, she'd run like the dickens to his room and jump up on the bed with him. Ola was so afraid she might hurt him or bother him. Ola would go get her, give her a spanking and run her out of his room. But the first chance she got; she was back in there. So, she told Jesse, "I'll tie her so she can't bother you." She picked her up off his bed and he said, "Wait a minute, Ola." He reached out and caught her front leg. He was blind by then, but he run his hand up, patted her head and said, "Why she's a little-bitty thing!"

Ola said, "Yessir. She's a midget Chihuahua."

He said, "Well honey, that's the best kind of dog to have. A little one. They have sharper hearing than most big dogs. Another thing, by her being little, you can keep her in the house and if anybody tried to break in the house, she can show you where they are. Because she can see them and they can't see her."

Ola put a harness on Dolly and a leash and tied her to the piano leg to keep her off Jesse's bed. One day a friend, Mabel, came over. She had heard that Jesse had come back to the Everhart place from Meramec Cavern and she wanted to see and meet him. They went to his room and Ola said, "Mr. James, this is a friend, Mabel."

He said, "Glad to meet you ma'am. My apologies for my appearance just now. I hate for ladies to see me with my necktie on."

"Oh, that's alright, Mr. James," she replied.

Ola said, "Jesse, she and I have known each other for years."

As he and Ola talked, she stood by, looked and listened. Then in a little bit she said, "Well, I've got to go."

They walked back to the living room and she said, "My God Ola! You can tell y'all are kin. You and him favor a lot and you talk a lot alike. Your voices are both deep. My God I wouldn't stay all night in this house for a thousand dollars! I would be scared to death!"

Ola asked her, "Why?"

She said, "Why he's been an outlaw and I know you, you ain't no softie. Lord! I'd be scared to death here."

She left and Ola told mother, "I thought she was different to that." It was several years before she came back to their house. She was what Ola called a coward. How silly of her.

Three weeks after Jesse got back home, his hip began to bother him so much that he wanted to go to the hospital. So, Ola called a doctor out and then called an ambulance and he was taken to the hospital. As before, Ola was out to see him from two to five times a day. One day she went out to see him, the weather was very changeable and when she got in his room Ola said, "Gee whiz, Jesse, the weather outside is so darn changeable a fellow don't know what to wear when they leave home."

He said, "Well honey, always wear a light dress, carry a heavy coat and an umbrella and then you're prepared for any kind of weather."

She said, "By golly I hadn't thought of that. That's a good idea."

Ola went out to see him one afternoon as she did every afternoon and after they'd talked a while, she said, "Jesse, I won't be out tonight, because there's a movie on that I want to go see, so I can come tell you about it."

"What's it about?" he asked.

She said, "Oh it's about the James boys."

She stayed with him as long as she could then went home and as soon as she and Aubrey had eaten supper and Ola had gotten someone to stay with her mother, they went to the show. Oh, what a mess it was, as Ola figured it would be, of course, and the next afternoon when Ola got to Jesse's room, she told him, "That show was a mess! It showed you and Frank turning to outlawry because of the railroad!"

He said, "That's all wrong."

Ola said, "Then they showed Jesse James, Bob and Charlie Ford all in a room, Jesse pulled off his guns and put them on the bed then stepped upon a chair to dust a picture. I've seen some shows where the picture showed a house and the words Home Sweet Home, but this time it was a picture of a horse."

He said, "That's wrong, all wrong about me pulling off my guns. I never done that. Not me. Not Jesse James. And as I told you, I don't know if there was a picture on the wall in that house because I never lived there."

Ola said, "Jesse, I think it's awful for them to make those kind of shows about you and Frank. It makes me mad!"

He very calmly said, "Now listen honey, let me tell you. Always remember, movie people have to eat too. And when they need money, there's no better way to make a quick buck than to make a movie about the James boys. Don't make a damn about the truth. Facts don't matter. Just write something and make money."

Ola said, "I know you're right, but I still think those shows are awful!"

"Well honey, just simmer your temper down now and remember, movie makers have to eat too." He said.

Mr. Bob Jackson of Austin, Texas who was in his late 70's or mid 80's in age, went out to the hospital and talked with Jesse. They talked about this and that for a little while and then got around to talking about a swimming hole toward Bee Cave, not far from Austin where both of them had gone in swimming at the same time.

Jesse told him, "I left here right after that." Neither of them said what year that was, but Bob Jackson told Aubrey and Ola, "His name wasn't Dalton or James then. I know him as Fred Mayo. I saw two places on his back where he'd been shot, when he got out of the swimming hole."

On October 10, 1950, Ola was out at the hospital to see about Jesse. Standing by the bed and they were talking. They got to talking about the kinfolks and Ola said, "I know you've told me before but I want to ask you again so I can get it straight in my mind."

He said, "Alright. What is it?"

"Now you and Bob and Charlie were cousins."

He said, "Yes, by golly, we were first cousins."

"And how does that fit in? On which side of the family?" Ola asked.

He said, "Well as I told you. Charlie and Bob's mother an my mother were sisters."

Ola said, "Well then their mother was a Dalton before her marriage."

He said, "Yes. She was."

Ola said, "So the Ford boys mother was a sister to my great-grandmother?"

He said, "Yes. She was."

Ola replied, "Well I wanted to get that straight in my mind."

He said, "Well honey that's the way it is, so don't you forget it."

Ola continued, "I read the article in Crittenden's Memoirs book that you and Frank, Bob and Charlie all stayed at the same hotel in Kansas City one night after Bigelow was killed and buried."

He said, "Yes. I wrote that article myself, that's in that book."

She said, "Yes, I saw your name under the article, or the alias you were using at the time."

He said, "Yes we did stay in the hotel together. That was the Blossom House Hotel in Kansas City, across from the old depot. Me and Frank was in one room and Bob and Charlie was in the other next to ours."

While they were talking, he said, "Me and Zee had four children. Jesse Edwards, Mary and a pair of twins. As I told you, there never was a real Jesse James Junior. My boy was named Jesse for me and Edwards for Major John N. Edwards of General Shelby's outfit, who was a mighty good friend of mine."

Ola asked him about Mary and he said, "She married a man by the name of Barr there in Missouri. He was a pretty successful farmer and they owned a nice home. But the twins only lived a few days."

On October 16, 1950 Aubrey and Ola were out at the hospital talking with Jesse and he said, "I am related to one of the signers of the Declaration of Independence. Stephen Hopkins married my father's aunt. Stephen Hopkins was one of the two signers of the Declaration of Independence who was from Rhode Island. Of all of the signers, only two of them was from Rhode Island. Stephen Hopkins was one and William Ellert was the other. Ezekiel Hopkins, a cousin of Stephen Hopkins, was First Commander of the American Navy. That was the First American Navy. In the days when the boats were all old wooden boats and the ships were wooden ships."

One afternoon, Ola was out at the hospital talking with Jesse and she said, "Grandpa Underwood used to love to go hunting. He'd take his gun and go hunting real early in the morning, when they lived out there in the Arbuckle Mountains in the Indian Territory.

"One morning he got up real early, got his gun and went hunting and when he came home at breakfast time he said to grandma, 'Vanner, I saw something this morning that looked pretty bad.'

"'Well, Toby what in the world was it?' She asked.

"He said, 'I saw three men, all hanging in one tree. I thought that was kinda bad.'

"She said, 'Land sakes Toby, that's awful!'"

When Ola finished telling him, Jesse looked at her, smiled and said, "Lord, honey, I've seen as many as four and five men hanging in one tree at one time."

Ola said, "I'll bet you have."

In November of 1950, Mr. and Mrs. Everette Samuel of Clay Country, Missouri came to Austin and went out to the hospital to visit Jesse. It was most unusual that Jesse would talk to anybody unless Aubrey or Ola were out there with him. But when he learned the visitor's names were Samuel, he agreed to talk with them.

Mr. Everette Samuel's great-grandfather was a brother of Reuben Samuel who was Jesse's stepfather. Jesse really appreciated their visit. Ola was sorry she didn't get to meet them.

Back when Al Jennings was young, Jesse went out to the C Dot E Ranch in west Texas and visited with Al. They had known each other since way back when

Al was a young lawyer back in the Indian Territory, now Oklahoma, before Al became an outlaw. While they were together out on that ranch, they had a shooting match for pastime and Al won. Which really pleased him.

On July 3, 1948, Jesse was in Oakland, California. Al lived at Tarzana, California and he came over and visited with Jesse for they had been good friends for years. Al Jennings, famed Oklahoma bad man, was well remembered by many Lawton, Oklahoma old-timers, because he one-time owned property in Comanche County, had made his home in Lawton and practiced law there.

One afternoon Ola was out at the hospital talking with Jesse and they started talking about his longtime friend, Al Jennings and he said, "Al Jennings is from Bascoce, Indian Territory. Now Oklahoma of course. He run for Governor once and nearly got it. He was County Attorney once in Oklahoma. Al had two brothers and all the boys and their father was lawyers."

Ola asked, "What made him turn into outlawry, Jesse?"

"Well, I'll tell you," He replied. "There was a trial in Woodward, Indian Territory. Al's father and a brother was the lawyers on one side and Temple (Tempie) Houston was on the other side. Tempie was Sam Houston's son. After the trial, they all met in a Saloon and got in a quarrel about the outcome of the trial and Tempie Houston shot and killed Al's father and brother.

"After that, Al turned outlaw. But Al was a mighty good man, a good lawyer and as smart as a whip. Still is." Then he said, "John O'Mallie and Morris O'Mallie were caught in Al's gang and served four years in the Federal Pen and died there. Their father was foreman of the Murray Ranch there in Oklahoma. John Polk killed Frank Murray on the Washita River.

"Al was caught, served a term in the pen then lived a straight life after he got out. He lived in Lawton, Oklahoma for a while but lives in California now. He run for Governor of Oklahoma after he got out of the pen and almost won. Him and his wife Maud are mighty good people."

Ola said, "Mother has told me many times about how she used to read about Al Jennings in the old St. Louis *Republican* newspaper and the old *Ardmorite* newspaper when she was a girl there in the Arbuckle Mountains. Al was an outlaw at the time."

Ola wrote to Al for Jesse when he was with her and then, after Jesse passed away, she kept up with Al and Maud until they died. Al wrote Ola and said, "Old Howk was worse than any damn pick-pocket I ever knew while I was in the pen."

Back in 1949, when Jesse was in the hospital in Austin, Texas where he'd been for some time due to pneumonia and before he went back to St. Joseph, Missouri on that challenge where they thought they would prove him to be a fake in two weeks – which they didn't prove because he was not a fake, Ola was at the hospital standing by the bed talking with Jesse one day when a man came into the room. She learned that his name was R.E. James and that he and his wife had come from Oklahoma. Hardly had he come in and gave his name until he turned to Ola and in a not very courteous manner, said to her, "You leave the room because I want to talk to Jesse alone."

Ola looked at him and thought, "You rude so and so." She walked out of the room but stood against the wall just outside the door so she could hear what he said to Jesse. She quickly learned that he didn't come to see how Jesse was doing. He made that trip to question Jesse about the location of some James buried treasure that Howk had ribbed him up about.

Well, he'd ask Jesse questions and Jesse would answer. As to his question about the location, Jesse said, "Well you know where that rock wall is? A ways back from that wall there's a big old tree and on that tree is a limb sticking straight out from the tree. Just start at the tree and go out in the direction that the limb is pointing for about (so many) feet and that's where it's buried. Just dig there."

R.E. left as happy as a lark. He had found out where the treasure was buried and could now go dig it up. After he was gone, Ola went back in the room and said, "Jesse, I heard what you told R.E. Boy! You sure told him a lot of malarkey. That was quite a line you handed him."

He said, "Oh well, hell! He don't give a damn about how I'm doing. All he wants to know about is buried treasure. So, just let him go ahead and dig his damn fool head off. He ain't gonna find a damn thing. Him and old Hawk, that son-of-a-bitch, thinks me and Frank didn't have a damn thing to do back in our outlaw days but rob trains and banks and then bury the money, so people like the two of them could come along later and dig it up. So, just let them go on and dig their damn fool heads off, they ain't gonna find anything because there ain't nothing to find."

He really sent R.E. on a wild goose chase. It was funny to Ola and Jesse and they had a big laugh about it.

In 1950, after Jesse had come back from Missouri, he had to go to the hospital due to his broken hip bothering him so badly. One morning after he'd finished his breakfast, a hired woman had been in, given him a bath, cleaned up his bed and put his white shirt and tie on him which was a must with him because he didn't like for people to come in and see him without his white shirt and a tie on.

Ola was sitting by the bed, we were talking and she said, "Jesse, I wanna ask you something."

He said, "Alright. What is it?"

"Why is it that when your name is mentioned, people immediately think of you having money buried from by gone days?"

He said, "Oh people say and imagine a lot of things and don't know what they're talking about."

Ola said, "Old Howk, R.E. James and others are always talking about the Jesse James buried treasure, looking for it and digging for it."

He gave the same reply he had given that day in the hospital, which was, "Hell yes, they think me and Frank didn't have a damn thing to do but go rob banks and trains and bury the money so some of them could come along later and dig it up. Hell! Just let them go on and dig their damn fool heads off. They ain't gonna find a damn thing. Because there ain't nothing to find."

Ola never ceased to be amazed at the number of people who thought that Jesse James had lots of money because he'd been an outlaw for a number of years. She had letters that were written to him in Austin, Texas wanting him to send them money. Then, there was those who thought he had money buried at various places. Some of them came to see him and wanted to know where to dig. There was none, of course, but many thought there was and old Howk was worse than any of them.

As Jesse was laying there in the hospital, he got to thinking about the way old Howk had treated him and the more he thought about it the madder he got. So, he told Aubrey, "I'll tell you what I want you to do. I want you to go get me a 38 revolver." And then explained just what powder load of shells to get for it.

Aubrey said, "Well I'll see what I can do."

The next day when Aubrey and Ola got to the hospital, Jesse asked Aubrey, "Did you find what I was telling you to get for me?"

"Not yet." Aubrey replied.

He said, "Well, I need it."

Aubrey and Ola both knew that he couldn't have a gun in the hospital. They also knew that if he had one and old Howk came in the room, Jesse would eliminate him quick and that would get all of them in a peck of trouble. For several days he kept after Aubrey to bring him a six-shooter and shells and Aubrey had to keep telling him different excuses. As much as they knew how he felt about how Howk had drug him around, made money off him, had hounded him about buried treasure that wasn't there and told tall stories about him, they both knew that they could not take him a gun.

When poor Jesse came back to their home from Missouri, he had lost his eyesight. Something that he had feared for a long time, and they felt so sorry for him.

As Christmas neared, Ola wanted to do something to cheer him up. So, she went to the store and bought a little Christmas tree about eight or ten inches tall, a little Santa in a sleigh, took them out to the hospital and said, "Jesse, I brought you a little Christmas tree and a Santa to put on your bedside stand."

He said, "Honey, I think that's mighty nice of you, but I can't see them."

She said, "Oh but you can see this one." She held the little tree in her hand and he ran his fingers all around it. Then, she held the little Santa in her hand and as he run his fingers all over it, he said, "Why he's in a sled!"

She said, "You bet!" Then she said, "See, you could see them. I have a good friend who's blind and she sees how things look with her fingers."

The next afternoon when she went out to see him and while she was standing by the bed talking with him, a Mrs. Davis, who was a beauty operator there in Austin, Texas came in to see him. She brought him a little China dog and I set it by the little Christmas tree on the stand by his bed.

In a little bit, she said, "Mr. James, your niece Ola sure does look pretty today."

She thought Ola was his niece because she called him Uncle and that was not the place to explain to her that he was a third cousin but being raised by the "old school" she called him Uncle, due to his advanced age.

In answer to her statement, Jesse said, "That so?"

She said, "Yes, it is."

"Well, I never seen her any other way," he replied, "so I hadn't thought anything about it."

Ola appreciated the compliment, and said, "Thank you." Then stood aside and listened to them visit. She was a very nice, kind lady and it was sweet of her to come out to see him. Jesse got a lot of Christmas cards. All of which Ola would not only read to him but she held each one so he could run his fingers over the fronts of them as she described each one and the colors on them. She also bought a box of cards for him, addressed them, signed his name on them and mailed them.

Come Christmas Eve night, she was standing by his bed as the lights were dimmed and the nurses, two-by-two came marching down the halls holding a candle in one hand and songs in the other as they walked slowly along singing Christmas carols.

When Jesse heard them coming, he started singing with them and continued to sing with them as long as he could hear them. That was a Christmas Ola said she would never forget…and it was his last Christmas. 1950.

Ola kept that little Christmas tree, Santa and little China dog until the day she died.

One Saturday morning in early 1951, Aubrey and Ola walked over to the grocery store, two doors from their house at 1103 East First Street there in Austin. After they'd got their groceries, they had been checked out and put in two sacks, Ola told Aubrey, "You'd better not try to carry both sacks at once because they're pretty heavy."

He replied, "Oh, I can carry both of them."

She said, "Well, my mama didn't raise a dummy," picked up a loaf of bread and they started home. Before they got half way, Aubrey's hands went up and the sacks went down and scattered the groceries.

Ola said, "What the hell are you doing, taking flying lessons?"

He said, "My ankle turned. I sprained it!"

A boy at the store saw what happened and came running with some sacks. And a nephew of Ola's drove in the driveway just then, saw what happened, came running and gathered up the groceries and took them home. Aubrey's ankle was paining him pretty bad and was swelling, so right after lunch Ola got him off to the doctor and a while later, they went out to the hospital to see about Jesse.

Ola walked up to the bed and Aubrey sat down in a chair. After a bit of talk as to how he was doing, Ola said, "Jesse, you know what you do to a horse when he breaks his leg, don't you?"

He said, "Uh huh, you shoot him!"

Ola said, "Yes, that's right. Well, I ain't so sure I ain't gonna have to do that to Aubrey."

He asked, "What happened?"

She told him about Aubrey spraining his ankle and how she thought he was taking flying lessons the way his hands went up when it happened. Then we went on talking about other things. The next afternoon when Ola got out to the hospital and walked up to his bed, Jesse said, "Oh hello Ola! By golly, I'm glad to see you. I've been anxious for you to get here."

She said, "Well I'm here."

"Oh, say Ola, what did you do about Aubrey? Did you have to shoot him?" He asked.

She said, "Well I'll tell you, he makes such darn good cheese sandwiches, I decided to keep him around. So, I took him to the doctor."

"I 'spect that's the best," he replied. They had a good laugh then he said, "I hope his ankle get alright soon."

One day in February, 1951 while Ola was there at her home, a Mr. Fred Nolan with Dunn and Bradstreet's office in the Littlefield Building in Austin, Texas called her and asked, "Where is Mr. Dalton? I am making a personal survey about him."

Ola said, "Well, his real name is Jesse James and at present he's in the hospital."

"What is his age?" He asked.

"He's 103." Ola replied.

He asked, "How long has he been here in Austin?"

She told him and he asked, "Did he have any money or own any property?"

She replied, "No!"

"How did he earn his living?" He asked.

Ola said, "My God! He's over a hundred years old and is a Confederate Veteran. What do you want to know all this for?"

He replied, "I don't know. All I know is that I was told to call you and ask you the questions."

Ola wondered then and wondered until she died why was he nosing around and who was behind him. She never did find out.

One night Aubrey and Ola were out at the hospital talking with Jesse and he got to talking about when him and old Howk were going to fairs. He said, "I took in $32,832.00 from three State Fairs when I was with old hawk, as he called Howk. One of the fairs was at Nashville, Tennessee, one at Pensacola, Florida and I can't remember where the other one was. What town and state it was. But I only got $14.00 total cash from old Hawk out of all that was made. Old Hawk got all the rest. I got itemized statements of the amount of money took in from each fair. Old Hawk was a sorry son-of-a-bitch. His actual name was not Howk. Some people by the name of Howk raised him. His actual name was Barnhill. It never was Howk. And as I told you, Ola, he was no kin to me whatsoever."

Ola read in the Austin paper one morning that Jesse James, Jr. of California, a 75-year-old Kansas City lawyer, died March 26, 1951 at his home at 4124 West Slauson Avenue in Los Angeles, California. He was survived by his widow and daughter, Mrs. Ross. He also left three other daughters, Mrs. Lucille Lewis, Mrs. Estelle Braumel and Mrs. Ethel Rose Owens. When she went out to the hospital and read the article to Jesse he said, "Well, well."

He lay there thinking for a little bit and then said, 'Ola, as I told you, Bigelow's boy was about the same size and age of my boy. There never was a Jesse James, Jr. My boy was Jesse Edwards. Bigelow's boy wanted to be a lawyer. So, I made it my business to see that he got to be a lawyer. I helped him and Governor Crittenden helped him too. He was a lawyer in Kansas City a good while, and from what I heard, had a good practice there."

Rudy Turilli told Ola, "Ola, I went to Los Angeles, California to this Jesse James, Jr.'s home and look him right in the eye and told him, "You are not Jesse James' son. You are Bigelow's son. He never replied. He just looked at me as if he was stunned. But never denied what I said."

So – Jesse was right. He *was* Bigelow's son, *not* Jesse's.

One Saturday afternoon when Aubrey and Ola walked in Jesse's room at the hospital, a woman was in there and she said, "I'm sure glad to see you."

Ola asked, "What's the trouble?"

She said, "I can't get Mr. James to eat. Maybe you can."

Ola said, "Just leave the tray there on the table and I'll see what I can do."

She left the tray there and walked out. Ola walked over to the bed and said, "Jesse."

He said, "Yeah."

Ola said, "Howdy!"

He said, "Oh hello Ola! Damn I'm glad to see you!"

She said, "Well I'm here." We talked a little bit and then I said, "Gosh! I should've come out here and eat dinner with you. I looked on your tray over there an you've got better food to eat than I had at home."

He said, "Is that so?"

She said, "Yes sir, and it looks darn good."

We talked a little more and then he said, "Oh say Ola, what all is on the tray? I might want some of it."

Ola had Aubrey move the tray over by the bed and put it on the stand. Ola called off everything on the tray and then started feeding him and he ate most everything on the tray. Ola was glad, because he needed the food. But he just didn't want to let the worker feed him.

Ola wrote that she would never forget the message she I had to take to Jesse shortly after Christmas in 1950. As I have stated before, Brushy Bill Roberts, who in truth and fact was the real Billy the Kid, was a very close friend of Jesse James and had been since Billy was a young boy. One time when he was without work and a place to live, he went to Belle Starr's house near Briartown, Indian Territory and stayed for a while. He was always welcome at her place.

Brushy Bill wrote to Jesse there in Austin and also wrote to Ola. He and his wife lived in Hico, Texas and were preparing to come spend the weekend with the Everharts. Them and DeWitt Travis of Longview, Texas who had known Brushy Bill many years and we were looking forward to their visit.

But on December 28, 1950, Brushy Bill who was a rather small man that was quick spoken and moved about quickly, was walking to the post office to mail a letter and on his way, he had a heart attack and was dead in a little bit. Had he lived until the last day of December, he would have been 91 years old.

It fell to Ola to go tell Jesse. So, she went out to the hospital, talked to him a little bit and then said, "Jesse, I've got to tell you something. Something I wish I didn't have to tell you."

He said, "What is it?"

She said, "Well, Brushy Bill died this morning. He had a heart attack on the street in Hico on his way to the post office."

He said, "Well, well, I've lost a mighty good friend." He broke down and cried as Ola stood by patting his arm, it was heartbreaking to her to see the tears roll down his face. With tear-filled eyes and a choking voice he said, "Poor little Billy. He was a good boy. He had a mighty hard time growing up. I've lost a mighty good friend. It hurts me mighty bad. I'm sure sorry he's gone."

Ola said, "I'm sorry too Jesse and I feel like I've lost a good friend." Ola never forgot that day. Brushy Bill and Jesse used to meet at Las Vegas, New Mexico years back when Las Vegas had a very prominent hotel where Jesse found some interesting poker games. And he loved to play poker. Ozark Jack Berlin was a good and longtime friend of Jesse's and Brushy Bill's. He told Ola what happened at Old Tascosa, Texas.

Ozark Jack, Brushy Bill and Al Jennings and his gang was in the Old Blue Goose Saloon and there was several other men inside. Some man came in and pulling his six-shooter from the holster, started shooting up the place. Brushy Bill fell down on the floor and played dead, Al and his gang rushed out the side door and Ozark ran for the front door and was shot as he ran, but he made it on outside before he fell.

When the shooting stopped and the man left, Brushy Bill jumped up, ran outside and found Ozark Jack, who was laying on the ground bleeding and begging for water. Brushy Bill ran to the windmill a short distance away, got some water in his hat and ran back to Ozark Jack, gave him a drink then got him to a doctor.

Old Tascosa was a wild and wooly town back in the old days. Frank and Jesse James, Brushy Bill, Ozark Jack and Al Jennings were all there from time to time back in the old days.

Ola wrote to Brushy Bill, Ozark Jack and Al Jennings until they died. Then she wrote to Al Jennings and Lizzie Roberts, Brushy Bill's wife, until they died.

One Sunday afternoon in 1951, Aubrey and Ola were out at the hospital talking with Jesse and he said to Aubrey, "If I was back ten years younger, I'd kidnap Ola and run off with her and hold her for ransom."

Aubrey said, "Reckon you could get fifty dollars for her?"

Jesse laughed and replied, "Why hell! If I couldn't get a thousand dollars, I wouldn't take her!"

They had a big laugh about Ola's worth.

Jesse came out with his ture identity on May 19, 1948. In Lawton, Oklahoma and since that time, Carl Breihan has spent a lot of time, trying to prove him to be a fake. Breihan claims he knows that Jesse James was killed by Bob Ford in 1882.

My question is, how does he know? There was no adult pictures of Jesse James in 1882 when Charley Bigelow was killed by Bob Ford and buried as being Jesse James. None of the laws and the Pinkerton Detectives knew how Jesse James looked. Only close friends and relatives knew. Strange that Carl Breihan is so positive that the outlaw Jesse James was killed. How does he know that that the man who was using the alias of Frank Dalton, J. Frank Dalton was not the real Jesse James?

If he knew that the man killed was Jesse James then why did he write Ola back in 1949 and say, "If you believe that Frank Dalton is Jesse James, don't answer. But if you don't, write me?"

That, to me, was plain that he was fishing for information. He was not sure. So, he was fishing for information. In other words, it could be the real Jesse James, he wasn't sure. Well needless to say, Ola did not answer his letter.

In the March 1951 *National Police Gazette* was the following:

There is another mysterious item in Breihan's purported proofs to disprove Jesse James. When the historian applied to the General Services Administration of the National Archives and Records Services in Washington, D.C. He was advised:

"The data and information contained in Mr. Dalton's file is deemed privileged and confidential and may not be disclosed."

Jesse was back in the hospital on St. Patrick's Day 1951 and Ola was out to see him every day and every night. She took him another St. Pat's pin but it was different. It was a three-leaf clover pin with a little white, Irish top hat fastened to the three-leaf clover. After he'd worn it through the afternoon and evening, when Ola started home that night, he told her to take it home.

One afternoon while Jesse and Ola were talking, he said, "Ola, Mrs. Shevlin's got a picture of mine of Cole Younger and one of my mother and I want them back. So, you write to her and tell her to send them back to me."

Ola wrote to her but she never sent them back. Ola read his mail to him every day then took the letters home and answered them for him.

CHAPTER SIXTEEN

In March, 1951, just like a Black Cat or the bad luck of Friday the 13th, old Howk came to town. He called the Everhart house and asked where Aubrey was. Not thinking that he would call Aubrey's office, Ola told him that Aubrey was at work. In a few minutes Aubrey called home and told Ola that Howk had called him and for her to be careful, and not let him come in their house.

Well next, old trouble-maker Howk went out to the hospital and Ola didn't know what all he said to Jesse, but it must have been pretty bad, because when Ola and Aubrey went out to see Jesse that night, they could tell he was greatly disturbed. After a little bit he told Ola, "Ola, I'm fixing to leave here in the morning with old Howk."

Ola said, "Jesse, I wish you wouldn't, because you're not able to be drug around by him like you have been. I wish you'd stay here where you can get good care because we love you."

He said, "Well honey, if I go, it will save your life. Because old Howk has got it in for you so bad that you are in danger. Ola, Hawk, the son-of-a-bitch, is just crazy enough to be dangerous and I don't want anything to happen to you. So, I'm going with him."

The next morning just at daylight, Aubrey and Ola went to the hospital with Jesse's clothes and hat but he was already in an ambulance and they didn't get to tell him goodbye. Old Hawk, Jake Wilson and a man named Woodell were all out at the ambulance. Howk and Jake were wearing handguns so they'd look tough. Jesse always called Howk, "Old Hawk the son-of-a-bitch." In my opinion, he wasn't a hawk. He was a buzzard.

Aubrey took Jesse's clothes and hat over and gave them to Howk. He put them in the ambulance and at 5:50 on Saturday morning March 24, 1951 and they drove off in the ambulance. The license number of that ambulance was J-J 3133. Of course, Ola and Aubrey worried about poor old Jesse. Howk didn't have a place to take him and take care of him. He just started dragging the poor old fellow from place to place, making money off him like he was a sideshow freak. By night on March 24th, they were in Galveston, Texas then on to Gilchrest, Texas. Howk didn't care Jesse's physical condition, food, clothes and shelter. His mind was on the James buried treasure, that wasn't there and never was. He also wanted the money he could make by charging the people to see and talk with the real Jesse James. Ola had never heard of Howk working.

By August poor Jesse's health was failing fast due to lack of care and old Howk got in touch with a Mrs. Burk at Granbury, Texas and asked her to go from Granbury to Gilchrest and help him get Jesse to Granbury to her father's old home place there. This was where Jesse wanted to go when he left Austin because her father, Sam Rash and him had been good friends for years before Sam Rash died. Jesse told Ola, "I would like to go back to Granbury and see the old Rash home again before I die. Me and Sam were good friends for many years. I've been to his home many times. He was a good man."

Old Howk told Golda Burk that Jesse James was his grandfather, but he sure wasn't. Howk was no kin whatsoever to Jesse James. At first, he was just an acquaintance. Then he was just a friend who ran errands for Jesse when he needed help after he fell and broke his hip. Next Howk graduated himself to a cousin but after Jesse was too old and feeble to fight back, Howk started telling people that he was a grandson.

Well, on August 15, 1951 Jesse died there in the old Rash home in Granbury, Texas. He was born on September 5, 1847 and died August 15, 1951. Therefore, he was 103 years and 21 days old when he died. His body was taken to the Estes Funeral Home. As soon as Ola and Aubrey heard on the TV news about his death, they began making preparations to go to Granbury and their phone rang ever little bit from people telling them that they'd heard about his death.

There was a lot to do there at home before they could go, including getting someone to come stay with Ola's little mother while she was gone and, before they got things ready to go, she got a letter from old Howk in which he made a threat on Ola's life if she came to the funeral.

Ola said, "Well, I'm going to Jesse's funeral, you can bet on that! That's not going to stop me!"

Aubrey's brother's wife had come in, had read the letter and said, "But Howk has threatened your life and if you go, he may kill you!"

Ola replied, "Oh well, you don't die but once!"

So, early the next morning Aubrey and Ola got in their old 1941 Packard straight eight sedan and headed for Granbury. When they got to the funeral home, they were absolutely horrified when they walked in and saw pictures of poor Jesse all over the funeral home. Even in death, old Howk was displaying the poor old fellow like a freak of nature. It made them very mad but they were at a funeral home and that is no place to say anything, so they kept quiet.

DeWitt Travis came in from Longview, Texas shortly after they arrived and they were glad to see him. They were expecting trouble from Howk any minute for he kept walking by and giving them some looks that made them know he'd love to kill them. Ola thought about what Jesse had told her the last time they had talked, that old Howk was just crazy enough to be dangerous.

Ola walked over, sat down by DeWitt and said, "Gosh I'm glad to see you!" Then in a low voice said, "My God, I was 20 miles from home when I realized I'd forgot my gun, have you got yours?"

He just pulled up his trouser leg a little and patted his boot in which was his gun. So, Ola said, "Well stay close by me. I don't trust old Howk." And that he did. While Jesse's body was being prepared for burial, scars from what were 28 bullet wounds were found on his body. The scars were counted by DeWitt Travis, Sheriff Oran C. Baker and undertaker Ben Estes. Aubrey and Ola were there in the funeral home and she was sitting by the door that led into the room where they were looking over the body and she could hear them talking.

Of course, those scars they counted were not all of them. The others didn't show, but they were there just the same, like the injury to his right lung. He was shot in the right lung and under the right lung at the close of the War Between the States when he and some other Quantrell men were riding in to surrender, with Jesse James in the lead carrying the white flag of surrender.

Now I have read that old Carl Breihan of Missouri said that old J. Frank Dalton would not allow an x-ray made of his lungs because that would prove him to be a fake. That the real Jesse James had an injured lung. Yes, Jesse did have a badly injured lung but Carl Breihan wrote a big fib when he said that old J. Frank Dalton, as he called Jesse James, would not allow an x-ray made of his lungs. There was a photocopy made of his injured right lung.

When the Pinkertons were looking for the James boys, back before April 3, 1882, they didn't know how they looked and there were no adult pictures of them. When Bigelow was killed by Bob Ford, those who knew the dead man was *not* Jesse James kept their mouths shut. Those who didn't accepted the dead man as being Jesse James.

When Governor Thomas T. Crittenden's son Henry H. Crittenden wrote the memoirs of his father in 1935, he contacted Frank Dalton and had him come to Missouri and write the outlawry part of the book about his father. Isn't it unusual that the son would pick Frank Dalton to write the outlawry part of that book? But who would know better than Jesse James about those outlaw days? So, the son must not have considered him a fake.

Yes, old J. Frank Dalton, as Breihan calls Jesse James, had the bullet scars and could tell of his robberies when he was travelling the outlaw trail. Which only the real Jesse James could do and yes, he did have the badly injured lung. So, Carl Breihan made a misstatement of the facts.

Two women in their mid-fifties or early sixties came to the funeral from Louisville, Kentucky and said they were kin to Jesse James. They, too, were only interested in the James buried treasure, for they kept on making so much noise about the buried treasure of Jesse's. Jesse's oil wells and the like until DeWitt heard all he could stand and when one of them followed him outside and was asking him about Jesse's buried treasure and his oil wells, DeWitt turned to her and said, "Up to now, I have considered you a lady and treated you as such. Please don't do or say anything to force me to think otherwise." So, she shut up and walked away from him.

Another of old Howks stupid doings came to light at the funeral home. He had a woman come to the funeral home and pose as being Jesse's daughter. Her name was Harriet Redding and no kin whatsoever to him. Ola said she would never forget how she acted, her and her husband, daughter and son-in-law were all there and Harriet and her daughter would just twist around in the funeral home talking as if it was a picnic gathering or something, saying, "Jesse" this and "Jesse" that. Never: 'my father'. It was sickening to Ola and Aubrey and, in their opinion, very disrespectful to the dead.

Sheriff Baker who was a very nice person, came out to the desk in the front where Ola was sitting and Harriet was standing nearby. He tried to talk to her about her "supposed to be" father and she talked so off handed and twisted up to such extent that he just looked at her. He started to leave and she said, "Well, if you want to know more, just came back and I'll tell you."

He replied, "No, I've heard enough."

He turned to Ola and asked, "Are you related to Jesse James?"

Ola replied, "Yessir."

He asked, "How are you related?"

She replied, "My great-grandmother and Jesse James' mother were sisters. He's my third cousin."

He said, "I see. Thank you." Then he left.

That night several people were gathered around in the funeral home talking about where they'd spent the night. Aubrey and Ola and DeWitt Travis were standing talking to Ben Estes the undertaker about where they'd stay that night. Harriet's daughter was standing nearby listening and she said to Ola, "You folks sure do talk funny."

Ola asked, "Whaddya mean?"

She said, "Well when someone comes to see us, we say, when they leave, 'we are sure glad you folks came and do come back.'"

Ola looked at her right straight and replied, "Now don't that sound about half silly! Down here in the South, we just say, 'we're shore glad y'all come! And y'all come back.'"

Ben Estes was listening and when Ola said that he bent over, slapped his leg and laughed and laughed. DeWitt, Aubrey and Ola went over to the Nutt Hotel on the square and rented adjoining rooms. It was a pretty old-fashioned hotel. The likes of which Ola hadn't been in since she was a child. The room had an old time Simmons type bed, an old-fashioned dresser, wash stand with bowl and pitcher, two chairs and there was a small lavatory on the wall.

There was a screen door leading out into the hall and it had a curtain over the middle part of it, thereby giving privacy when the wood door was open. The room had one window and it looked out on the Sheriff's Office next door. Ola laughed and told Aubrey, "We can't be better protected than being close enough to the sheriff to just holler out the window if we need help." Their room there was on the second floor and the stairs were narrow and almost straight up. But it was a very nice old-fashioned hotel. The kind you just never forget staying in. It was built of rock and the walls were 18 inches thick.

DeWitt came into the Everhart's room and they talked for a good while. He didn't like or trust Howk any more than they did and he thought it was awful to have pictures of Jesse all in the funeral home but he and Ola both knew and agreed that in the funeral home was not the place or the time to say or do anything about it.

Ola was sitting on the bed. DeWitt sat down by her, pulled her hat off, pushed her hair back, looked at her a few minutes and said, "My God! No wonder Jesse thought so much of you. Of course, you're kin. I can see the favor easy now. Sure you favor the Dalton's."

The next morning when they went back to the funeral home Harriet and her daughter, the women from Kentucky and several others were there and of course

Howk was walking around so everybody would be sure to see him. Now that poor old Jesse was dead and couldn't tell old Howk that he was lying, he not only claimed he was a grandson but even started claiming that his name was Jesse James the third. And he even twisted Jesse's death certificate. Ola had it corrected since then.

Ola had asked Jesse back in 1948 if Howk was any kin to him and he very firmly replied, "Absolutely not! No kin whatsoever! Never was and never will be!"

The funeral was held in the funeral home chapel at 2:30 in the afternoon on August 19, 1951. DeWitt, Aubrey and Ola sat together. A number of people were in the chapel. Someone played the piano Ola couldn't recall the song or songs that were sung. Reverend Plez Todd, a Methodist minister preached the funeral. Jesse was the son of a Baptist preacher and was, himself, a Baptist and Ola found it hard to understand why the Methodist preacher was called on to preach the funeral.

The service started and the phone rang. Someone said, "Ola Everhart is wanted on the phone." The preacher stopped the service as she went to the phone. She came back, sat down; the preacher started again and in a little bit the phone rang again and Ola was called to the phone again. Again, the preacher stopped until she came back and sat down. There was so many starts and stops during the service that she really didn't know what the preacher said.

When the service closed and the body had been viewed, Aubrey, DeWitt and Ola rode together in the procession out to the Granbury Cemetery where Jesse was laid to rest near his friend Sam Rash.

If your curious, no, Howk, who claimed to be a grandson, did not pay the funeral bill. DeWitt Travis who knew more about Jesse's business than anybody, paid all of it himself.

After his burial DeWitt, Aubrey and Ola went to the Rash home where Jesse had died. When they drove up, they got another shock! Old Howk had signs on the house like it was a cage at a zoo, about poor old Jesse. Howk went out to the house too. They took pictures of the house and of themselves with DeWitt and Howk. Ola thought she might need a picture of Howk in the future or her might, if something happened to her. But she really wanted a picture of her good friend DeWitt. She and Aubrey liked him a lot.

Old Howk made money off poor old Jesse, made the funeral home look like a carnival after his death then took his hat, guns, watch and chain, scrapbooks, photo albums, clothes and what he had in the way of personal things.

CHAPTER SEVENTEEN

One Sunday afternoon, Aubrey and Ola went to Centerville, Texas to visit Jesse or, Uncle Frank, as they called him then as that was back before he came out with his true identity. Old Howk was there in the room and sitting by the waste basket tearing up a lot of mail, papers and some pictures of Jesse's which might have been very valuable to him.

When they were there one time Jesse showed them some of his pictures. There was one of him and Indian Chief Geronimo together, an enlarged picture of him and his wife together when he was young and several others. But the three Ola remembered the best were the ones just mentioned and one of his mother, Frank and Jesse together. Jesse gave Ola copies of all of them and signed them J. Frank Dalton, as he was known at the time.

Jesse also said, "Ola, I've got two bullet holes in my left leg. Toward the back of my leg between my knee and my hip. And I've got this bullet hole in my left shoulder from back in my outlaw days." But he didn't say when or where he got them.

No one knows what old Howk did with the albums and scrapbooks of Jesse's but Ola heard that he pawned the guns and watch. What a shame! Well, Jesse was gone. His suffering was over. No longer would he be hounded by treasure hunters for treasure that wasn't there. Or drug from place to place by Howk so Howk could make money.

On April 3, 1882 when Charley Bigelow was killed by Bob Ford, his body accepted as being that of Jesse James and was buried as being Jesse James, then legally, Jesse James the outlaw was dead. Legally, yes. But in truth, the real Jesse James was very much alive as a good many people knew. He used many alias names down through the years and done many different things as he went many places but lived a law-abiding life. Then, in 1948 after he had passed his one-hundredth birthday on September 5, 1947, he kept his promise to his mother that if he lived to be a hundred, he would come out with the true facts of who he was. That he was in truth and fact, the real Jesse James, who once much wanted and hunted outlaw. That the man killed in 1882 was Charley Bigelow and he was buried as being Jesse James.

Down through the years, other men have claimed to be the real Jesse James, which he heard about but they were all proven to be fakes.

When he and Ola were talking one day, he said, "Ola, my great desire is to be buried under the name I was born with, Jesse Woodson James. With one foot in the grave and the other on the brink, do you think I would lie about who I am? Certainly not! I am Jesse James. I don't give a damn whether some people believe it or not. I know who I am. And I know that because of what happened in 1882, when I was supposedly killed, which was a hoax I have lived almost seventy extra years."

He was buried under his true and correct name, just as he desired. Today there is a tombstone at his grave to prove it. From May 19, 1948 until his death on August 15, 1951 NOBODY was able to prove him wrong beyond all shadow of doubt. The following copied from an article in *The Literary Digest* for October 29, 1927:

To understand the later career of Jesse James, it is necessary to picture the Missouri-Kansas border of Civil War days. Kansas Jayhawkers under the Union flag were making forays across the State line, shooting men who sympathized with the Southern cause, driving off horses, burning houses over the heads of women and children and outraging civilization.

Southern men made reprisals in kind, and with good measure. Here the young Jesse James went to school and learned his lessons. It was irregular and disagreeable, but it was war.

When General Lee surrendered at Appomattox a great many young Southerners did not consider themselves demobilized. There had been such fringes of persistent belligerence at the close of all wars. Young Jesse James, full of patriotism and fight, simply refused to haul down his flag. There were bitter grievances which the defeat of the South did not cure, and he applied himself industriously to them.

He was received gladly by hundreds of his opprest neighbors, just as Robin Hood had been in his day. Elderly folk in the Missouri border counties still remember Jesse James with affection, telling how he was brought up religiously, never swore, was devoted to his family, generous to the poor, gallant in battle, honest in personal dealings. He was the hunted quarry in a war of extermination. His mother was wounded and almost killed when his pursuers bombed his home. He took the only means of self-defense left open to him.

For a younger generation to whom Jesse James is a kind of eternal verity – the super-train-robber, just as Sherlock Holmes is the super-detective – It is hard to realize that he was and still is a moral issue and that he might be living today, a man eighty years old. Fully half of his alleged robberies, his biographer Robertus Love says, were committed within a hundred miles of his home at Kearney, where he was born, where his mother continued to live, and where he frequently returned to see her.

How he and his masked band were pointing their Colt 44s at a stagecoach in Hot Springs, Arkansas. How their blood-curdling guerrilla yell of Civil War days echoed through a bank in Columbia, Kentucky. Now they snatch the strong-box with its $10,000 gate receipts from the door-keeper at the Kansas City Fair. And every time save one they galloped away from the midst of hundreds, without a trace, in the full glare of day. To the police then, as well as to the readers of the dime thrillers, Jesse James was a figure of magic. They never had a picture by which to identify him and no dependable description of his features.

He was, as Robertus Love has pointed out, presumably the inventor of both daylight bank robbery and of the train hold-up. Yet, like most inventors, he must have realized comparatively little from his product.

It must be admitted, however, that Jesse James had some grounds for resentment against life in general and perhaps, Northerners in particular. He was born at the beginning of a troublesome time at one of the most troublesome spots in America – on September 5, 1847 in Missouri, near the Kansas border, not far from Kansas City. His almost equally famous brother Frank preceded him into the world by four years.

Before Jesse was four years old his father suddenly determined to quit both gospel and farm and go to seek the family fortune in California, where within a few weeks he sickened and died.

A few years later, Mrs. James married Dr. Samuel a physician from Kentucky. The James children and their half-brothers and sisters stayed and grew up in Kearney in the ominous shadow of the Civil War.

When it came, they were already inured to raiding and plunder. Across the border from Kansas came bands of Jayhawkers or Red Legs – Abolitionists who carried off Missouri slaves. Meanwhile, Missouri border ruffians returned the compliment by counter raids into free Kansas. When the war broke out these bands enlarged into regiments of guerrilla fighters. One of these in Missouri was called Quantrell's band, named after their noted desperado leader. This band, Frank James, Jesse's older brother joined.

Experiences that embittered the life of Jesse James followed swiftly.

One day in 1863, while Jesse was still at home plowing, Northern regulars came to the Samuel farm, demanding the whereabouts of Quantrell. Believing that the doctor knew more than he would tell, and that the family was at any rate notorious in its secessionist sympathies, the soldiers drove the doctor at the point of the bayonet to a tree. There they bound him, strung him up by a rope, and left him for dead. But Mrs. Samuel cut him down and revived him.

Meanwhile the soldiers had found Jesse and had given him a sound lashing with a rope end as he ran between his furrows. When he got home his back was gashed with bleeding welts.

The boy was only fifteen, round-faced and blue-eyed, but his mind was made up. He, too, would join Quantrell's guerrillas. He did, and fought as well as any man. On one occasion with four comrades, he is said to have killed fifty-two men.

But he was wounded most painfully, in the right lung. When the war was nearly over, he, with a few of his troop, bore a white flag to a northern camp to surrender. As they were marching out, some soldiers suddenly attacked them, and Jesse was shot again in the same lung.

The next year the bank robberies began and they continued at the rate of two or three a year.

At first, in the town of Liberty, a dozen miles from their home, in February, 1866, the local bank was held up in broad daylight, an innocent bystander killed, and $72,000 taken. The James family asserted that Jesse could have had no part in this, as his wound at that time kept him in his bed.

By October the bank in Lexington had been robbed, and a few months later an armed posse came out to capture Jesse James at his home. Jesse rising from a sick bed, fired at them through the door. While they retired for reinforcements, their quarry fled. From that time on he was a hunted man, living in curious parts of the country under various names, but never recognized, never captured.

The year before, Pinkerton agents, taking a brutal revenge on the Jameses for the killing of one of their force, threw a lighted bomb through a window. As luck would have it, Jesse and Frank were not at home. The bomb killed their eight-year-old half-brother Archie and blew off their mother's right arm. All through these years the story seems to describe a private war between the Pinkertons and the Jameses, with little government interference.

The James gang could never have existed as it did were it not for the shelter and help given to it by the residents in the region between Kearney, Independence, St. Joseph and Kansas City. The James boys were heroes to them, and that was one element in the favor shown them. Another was pure expediency and discretion. Anyone who failed to give such help as was needed, to say nothing of showing open antagonism, would have swift reason to regret it.

Concerning Frank James, a tale is told as coming from an old farmer near St. Joseph, where Democracy has all the sanctity of a religious creed. The old man was reminiscing one day somewhat along this line.

"*Yes, I knowed them James boys when they were just boys sure enough, and I knowed them when they growed up. They wasn't bad fellers, but Frank James sure did disappoint me. I would never have believed it of him if I didn't actually know it myself. After he was pardoned and he settled down and 'lowed he was goin' to be respectable for the rest of his life. I never knowed Frank to say anything he didn't mean, and when he did go to live in Kearney, I thought he was goin' to do as he said sure enough, and yit spite of all he said and spite of all we 'spected of him, durned if he didn't go and vote the Republican Ticket!*"

CHAPTER EIGHTEEN

I do not recall who wrote the following, but it will give you some insight into a little of Frank James' life and will show how fast thinking he was, as was Jesse, when they needed it for survival. As Jesse said and they both lived by, "Self-preservation is the first law of nature."

In 1874, Miss Annie Ralston, the very pretty seventeen-year-old daughter of Samuel Halston who was a prosperous farmer in Jackson County, Missouri, eloped with the slim and sinewy outlaw Alexander Franklin James. Her father was amazed and outraged when he learned that his beautiful daughter had run off with Frank James, a dozen years her senior.

It was more than eight years before they could be safe in calling themselves Mr. and Mrs. Frank James. In the meantime, they went by various surnames, Woodson being their favorite. It was a family name in the James connection, and by a Kentucky cousin who was to become a member of the outlaw band and to die miserably at the hands of another member.

Robert, the only child of this union, namesake of the Reverend Robert James, never knew his real surname until his father unstrapped the faithful Remington's and handed them over to the Governor of Missouri late in 1882. Those years "on the dodge" were passed in several states, including Missouri, Texas, Kentucky, Tennessee and Maryland. In each of these states Frank James engaged in legitimate business or employment, working hard when he found it practical and possible. Fear of discovery and capture, or of being killed in a running fight for his life, was the hypothetical wolf that howled always at his door.

But Frank James was possessed, in degree approaching the superlative, the presence of mind which was his temporal salvation. Mr. Samuel E. Allender of St. Louis, at one time Chief special agent for the St. Louis – San Francisco Railway Company and formerly Chief of detectives in the St. Louis police department, told some years ago, at his desk at police headquarters, this story in illustration:

"No doubt you recall that sometime after Frank James surrendered to Governor Crittenden in 1882 and stood trial and was acquitted by a jury of Missourians, he came to St. Louis and was employed by the late Colonel Ed Butler, owner of the Standard Theater, as doorkeeper at that celebrated home of variety. When he was employed, I was a young city detective, and I became well acquainted with the ex-outlaw. The neighborhood of the theater, as you know, was fertile for detective work.

"One night when the show was on, I stood outside the door of the theater, chatting with Frank James. The curtain went down for an intermission, and the major part of the male crowd filed out to patronize the bar. In the crowd I spied a police character, some petty thief or pickpocket. I stepped aside, led him away, called the patrol wagon and sent him in. A few minutes later the audience returned, the curtain went up and the door was closed. As I stood there with James, he remarked that he had seen me do an unwise thing when arresting the suspect. 'Why didn't you cover the fellow with your gun?' he asked me. I explained that such a procedure was not practical in a city like this, where forty thousand arrests were made annually; if every officer whipped out a gun whenever he made an arrest, he would be considered a nut, in fact, he wouldn't remain very long on the job.

"'That's all right,' Frank James said, 'but the officer always gets it when he least expects it.'

"He then illustrated the point by relating a little experience he had had at a time when, as he put it, 'they thought they wanted me.' He said he was stopping in Baltimore, had a room in a house built in a solid block of dwellings with no space between. One night he wanted something to eat, so he picked up a basket and went to an all-night market close by. On his way back to his lodging with the laden basket on his left arm, his coat collar turned up and his hat brim turned down, he noticed a number of policemen walking up and down in front of his house, as it appeared from a short distance.

"'I could think of nothing else,' said James, 'than that the officers had been tipped off to my rooming there, and that probably some of them had been searching the house and they were waiting for me to return. I was too close to them to turn back without arousing their suspicion. Directly across the street from the policemen I noticed a white horse hitched to a buggy; the street was lighted by gas-lamps and the horse showed up quite visibly in the mellow gleam. I decided quickly upon my plan of action. Probably the officers, I thought, had the block surrounded. My plan was to walk straight on past them if they didn't interfere with me; I would not go into my room at all. If they attempted to capture me, I would try to reach the horse and buggy by shooting it out with the officers, and then drive away as fast as the horse could travel.'

"James said he walked along with his right hand on his six-shooter, which was harnessed under his left arm. His right hand thus was concealed under his coat and under the arm on which the basket hung. Approaching the bunch of officers, he edged out toward the curtain, intending to walk around them as though he had not noticed them especially. When he was opposite the officers, one of them reached out a hand to stop him. James sprang backward into the street, off the sidewalk, toward the horse and buggy, pulling his pistol from its place but not quite getting it out – not so that it was visible to the policemen.

"'Well, sir, what is it? – What is it?' James asked the officer who had tried to stop him. 'Don't be so scary,' said one of the other policemen, with an oath; 'We're not going to hurt you.' James again said, 'What is it?' expecting every second to find it necessary to open fire and "get" as many of them as he could, when another officer, in a rather gentle tone, said, 'Say, don't be afraid of us, we're not going to harm you, man; we simply want to get men enough to serve as a jury in a coroner's case where a man in the house next door to my own house had died without medical attention, by natural cause or otherwise.'

"James then saw, he stated, that the policemen were in front of the house adjoining the one where he roomed, instead of immediately in front of that house. That seemed to end his story,' continued detective Allender, 'but my curiosity prompted me to ask how he got along on the jury.'

"'I simply told them,' Said James, 'that I was not a citizen of Maryland, that I lived in Washington, D.C., and I walked on into my house. That was the end of it so far as I was concerned.' Frank James told his story to illustrate the narrow escape those Baltimore policemen had. I was struck by his great presence of mind as indicated by his rapidity in planning his escape, but more especially by his explanation that he was not qualified to serve as a juror."

Copied from the *Houston Chronicle* Magazine:
By Garland Farmer, Special writer, Sunday, March 28, 1948

FRANK DALTON FINDS PEACE
Veteran Civil War Fighter, nearing 100
Finally Accepts Pension as Quantrell Raider.

Tucked away inside many newspapers, the following little news story recently was printed, unnoticed by many:

QUANTRELL RAIDERS ADDED TO CIVIL WAR PENSION LIST.
"First to qualify for a pension was Frank Dalton, an uncle of the Dalton boys of Missouri and cousin of Frank and Jesse James."

To those who know the real story of this man, now approaching his 100th birthday, this above news item marked two events: The final recognition of Quantrell's Militia as a formal part of the Confederate Army, and the final decision of Frank Dalton to accept a pension.

For many years this old pioneer has been a familiar character to hundreds of people around Henderson, Longview, Gladewater and other East Texas points.

With long hair, tied in a knot, and tucked up beneath his white 10-gallon hat; mustache and goatee that reminds you of such frontiersmen as Buffalo Bill, Frank Dalton has crammed more excitement and adventure in one lifetime than a dozen average persons.

Until he fell and broke his leg, he stood erect and clear-eyed. Even in his 80s, Dalton thought nothing of walking eight or ten miles in a day. The approaching century mark, however, finds those eyes dimming and his feet faltering.

A veteran of the Spanish-American War, the Civil War, the Sioux Indian War and World War I, Frank Dalton knows what it is to be a hunted man with a name which struck terror to the hearts of hundreds of people, particularly along the Missouri-Kansas border.

The Younger brothers were his kinsmen; the James brothers, in addition to being his cousins were his comrades while they served under the private flag of William Quantrell.

He does not hesitate to tell you about each of them, and how the young gangs went wrong after the Civil War. He grows pensive – almost sentimental, however, when he speaks of two people who greatly influenced his life; Bill Quantrell and Belle Starr, two names which Frank Dalton believes have received little justice at the hands of historians.

"The real name of William Quantrell was Charles Hart," explained Dalton. "He graduated from a Military School in 1860 ad went to Lawrence, Kansas, where he opened a school for boys."

Then Dalton told of the affair which resulted in this mild-mannered young professor becoming the most-feared man in several states.

It happened one evening in 1862. Nat Hart, his brother, had gone south to enlist in the Confederate Army, but young Charles had decided he would continue his school for boys.

At his boarding house on this particular evening, however, six stern-faced men called on the young schoolteacher.

"Well, Hart," the spokesman said, "You know our stand on the slavery question here, and the other things which brought on this war. You have not expressed your sentiment either way, so we have come to demand you sign an oath of allegiance to the North."

Charles Hart was plainly surprised. He studied only a moment, then answered: "I believe the educating and training of boys is very important, and I would like to remain neutral."

"That is impossible! You've got to show your colors!"

"In that case," Hart answered, calmly, "I must side with the South, for my brother and many other relatives are already serving in that army."

Charles Hart was placed in jail that night, Frank Dalton says, and the next day he was tied to a tree in the business section of Lawrence, publicly whipped and told to leave town.

It was then that Charles Hart went to Missouri, changed his name to William Quantrell and organized, "Quantrell's Militia," an organization that was soon fervently hated or intensely loved, according to the viewpoint.

Dalton says the burning of Lawrence, Kansas, was in retaliation for the burning of Lexington, Missouri. One attack called for another, and the tragedies of war went on, with Quantrell's band striking like lightening where it was least expected.

"He thought he had a rightful cause for everything he did while carrying on his guerrilla warfare. Even though the Confederates did not recognize us, because most of us were only kids, or for other reasons, we kept right on fighting for the South."

But, like his "Chief", Frank Dalton came through all his hard experience a mellowed man. For years he has been living in peace, mostly in Texas. Facing the century mark, however, the once-supple body has naturally slowed down, hence his willingness to accept the $100 per month pension allowed him as a veteran of Quantrell's Militia.

The second person about whom Frank Dalton speaks very kindly – but more reluctantly – is a woman. The world remembers her as the straight-shooting "Gun Moll" of yesterday – Belle Starr.

Dalton remembers her as Myra Belle Shirley, whose adventurous spirit took her face from the profession of teaching school through days as a woman spy for the South; as the wife of a hunted man, and back to teaching, part of which was spent in a school near Dallas.

"In the spring of 1863," Dalton recalled, "I was shot in the left leg during a skirmish near Warsaw, Missouri, and took refuge in a nearby farmhouse until I was able to ride again.

"Skirting Osceola, county seat of St. Clair County and home of the Younger brothers (two of whom were in my company), I came to a school house. Here I stopped to get a drink at a nearby spring and to let my wounded leg rest.

"I had torn my shirt into strips and tied them around my leg, and I guess I had lost more blood than I thought, for I passed into unconsciousness. When I finally awoke, I was lying on a soft bed in a room filled with sunlight, looking up into the face of Myra Belle Shirley."

The young schoolteacher, afterwards known far and wide as Belle Starr, nursed Frank Dalton back to health.

The fighting heart of Dalton has calmed into a poetic soul. Serenely, those days, he looks back upon a turbulent life, during which he fought in many wars.

As you have read the preceding article, remember, it was written before Jesse James came out with his true identity in May 1948. Therefore, he was still living under the cover of the alias name of Frank Dalton and J. Frank Dalton. He was already one hundred years old at the time. He was one hundred on September 5, 1947 before this article was written in March 1948.

He had proven beyond doubt that he did serve in the Civil War with Quantrell's Raiders and when Quantrell's Raiders were added to the Civil War pension list he was then eligible to draw a pension of $100 a month and was the first one to qualify.

Carl Breihan contends that Frank Dalton was not the real Jesse James. Which he wrote to the department who issued the Confederate pension checks in Austin, Texas. Well, the man who looked over the proof and handled all the paperwork that J. Frank Dalton did serve as a Quantrell man, was retired Military Major, a top-notch attorney at law and a friend of Ola's. Now here is something else Breihan did *not* know. After Frank Dalton came out with his true identity that he was in fact, Jesse W. James, he never accepted another Confederate pension check.

After Frank Dalton came out with his true identity the Major checked the Quantrell list and state that there *was* a Jesse James with Quantrell but no Frank Dalton. In the above article the, then known, as Frank Dalton stated that he knew what it was to be a hunted man, with a name that struck terror to the hearts of hundreds of people. That, of course, was Jesse James.

In the above article Jesse stated that he was an uncle of the Dalton boys, because, at that time, he could not say they were his cousins. He also said that the James boys were his cousins because, he could not say at that time that he was Jesse James and Frank was his brother. But he did say they were comrades while with Quantrell. Which they were.

Now I have read articles written by another historian – at least he says he's a historian and he is trying mighty hard to prove, that the man who used the alias name of Frank Dalton and J. Frank Dalton was *not* the real Jesse James. However, he also states that he does *not* know who J. Frank Dalton really was. Then he says he's written many articles about the Daltons and James's and knows lots about them.

This does strike me as strange, because the James's, Daltons and Youngers were a people who never talked much. They kept their mouths shut about their families and their kinsmen. As Ola's grandfather and my mother always said, "Don't be taking your head off."

So, it is strange that Phillip Steele knows so much about the James's and Daltons but he doesn't know who J. Frank Dalton really was.

CHAPTER NINETEEN

Jesse told Ola about him and Frank going out to California and staying a while with their uncle Drury James where he took the baths in an effort to help his injured lung.

The following article is from a book originally written in 1883.

JESSE'S VISIT TO NEW MEXICO

In 1870 or 1871 Jesse James started for California. He had, to some measure, gotten better in health and strength through the care and kind nursing he'd gotten in Kentucky but still had a terrible cough accompanied by hectic fever. Journeying to New York by easy stages so as not to overtax his strength.

Resting a few days before taking passage, he took in the principle objects of interest in the great city; and it speaks well for the natural character of the man that his visits were oftener to the libraries, art museums, etc., than to the abodes of gilded vice and sin. Temperate by nature, easy, self-possessed and gentlemanly in his demeanor, his dress was as modest as the man himself and he would never have been selected, so far as any outward indication went, as a bandit and desperado. In one thing only, did he give way to temptation. Like most men of generous impulses, he was a born gambler. His nerve and judgment were both excellent, and in all games of chance he played with great skill. In New York, finding time to hand heavily on his hands, he visited the palatial rooms of John Chamberlain and made several large winnings.

After a few days rest and following a faro game in which he left with between $4,000 and $5,000, he boarded the steamer bound for the Isthmus of Panama. Here he relaxed his vigilance and gave way thoroughly to social pleasures. He was the life of that little world, and never seemed to tire in his attempts to contribute to the amusement of the rest.

At last, they reached the Golden Gate at San Francisco. There he lingered a few days then took his leave for the health-giving springs at Paso Robles where he stayed with his uncle, Drury Woodson James, younger brother of Jesse's father, a gentleman of wealth, culture and refinement.

Frank was already there and together, the two brothers, who, despite all tales toe the contrary, were always loving and affectionate towards each other, enjoyed for the first time in years the sense of perfect peace and security. And while here the boys could, and did, use their correct names.

Their stay with their uncle, the baths and treatments did wonders for their health and when they decided to return to Missouri after a lengthy stay, they decided to return on horseback.

Seeing many of that adventurous class called "prospectors", making their way into the mountains, their "burros" loaded with blankets, tools and supplies, the boys concluded to try their luck. Purchasing an outfit, they pushed on to Battle Mountain, just then the new excitement amongst miners. Here they went into camp and began to work in earnest, for it was always one of their characteristics that whatever they took hold of, they did with great energy. Rapid posting themselves as to the best mode of "prospecting", or searching out the hidden treasures of nature, they soon became proficient, and might have settled down into hard-handed, honest miners, or become mighty millionaires, but for an unlucky incident. – But that's another story. This is about Jesse's visit to New Mexico.

Knowing they could return to Battle Mountain they rode southward and after several adventures, rode into Arizona. Here they had a brush with a small band of Mescalero Apaches who were out on a horse-stealing mission, but not averse to a murder if a small party of white men fell in their way. Amazed at the temerity of men who could dare to pass in couples through their country, they made an attack upon them. This was met rather more than half way by Frank and Jesse, who with defiant yells answered the savage war whoop of their enemies, and bursting in full career upon their line killed one savage and mortally wounded another. Turning in swift flight from these daring brothers, the Indians fled in dismay, and the boys, content to "let well enough alone," resumed their journey without pursuing the flying enemy. As far as they could see, looking back over miles of blooming cactus and intervening plain, the Apaches still formed an admiring but respectful group upon a slight eminence.

In the Western part of New Mexico, not far from the line of Old Mexico, lived a wealthy ranchero named Armijo. Of near kin to the Armijo's of Spain, this old gentleman belonged to the blue-blooded families of Castile. His wife, long since dead, had left him a beautiful daughter, Juana, or, as the old gentleman always affectionately called her, Juanita. At two o'clock of the morning of the visit of the James's to the hacienda of Don Miguel Armijo the Apaches, under the lead of one of the noted Victorio's warriors, had struck the hacienda, driving off the large herds of stock, and having found Juana Armijo out riding with one of her maids, had captured them and ridden off to hold them for ransom or worse fate.

Everybody at the hacienda was in tears. Frank, who was an accomplished linguist, soon ascertained the state of affairs.

"Have you made any pursuits?" he said to Don Miguel.

"None," said the old gentleman, "there is no one here to lead them, and of themselves the vaquesoes are too cowardly to pursue the Indians."

"Did they get your horses?" asked Frank.

"No; they were being driven in to be branded, so they missed them."

"How many Indians were there?" Frank asked again.

Ascertaining that there were about eight or ten Indians, and that he could get five or six cowboys, who, for Mexicans could fight rather well, he and Jesse got fresh horses and started in rapid pursuit, the old gentleman showering blessings upon them but muttering at the same time, "Pero ellos son Apaches – ellos son Apaches! ("But they are Apaches – they are Apaches!") No doubt thinking that any other man might be over-come, but the Apaches never.

One of the Mexican vasqueros knew of a trial leading to a pass where the Indians might be intercepted as they were encumbered with a large drove of cattle and must keep to the broader valley trails. Arriving at the pass at four o'clock in the afternoon they formed an ambush, and waited for the Indians to come up.

About six o'clock, unsuspicious of danger, they entered the pass, driving the cattle in advance, and some distance in the rear an old Indian was guarding the captives.

"Now," said Jesse to Frank, "as I'm the best shot, I'll take care of the old fellow in the rear, while you and your Mexicans give it to those in front. If I miss the old devil, up go the girls to a certainty."

"Ready," said Jesse, who had leveled on the old Indian, a hundred yards distance; while the rest of the band were in the pass just abreast of the ambush.

"Son Vds. Listo," whispered Frank to his men.

"Fuego, hombres!" he shouted.

At that sound the volley roared out. Jesse looked at his men, saw him fumble at his gun, then fall from his saddle, and then turned his attention to the others.

Taken completely by surprise, and retreat cut off up the pass by dense masses of cattle and in the rear by their enemies, every Indian was killed in the narrow canyon, and left for the beast of prey and carrion birds. The Senorita Juana welcomed them as angels of deliverance, and the next afternoon she, her maid and his herds were delivered into the hands of old Don. His gratitude knew no bounds, and it is said that a somewhat warmer feeling than that of gratitude had already taken possession of his daughter toward the man whose deadly aim and dauntless courage had saved her from a fate a thousand times worse than death; but Jesse, sighing only for a pair of blue eyes that he knew were ready to smile upon him in Missouri, insisted on getting back home once more. Refusing princely offers of remuneration, the old Don at last prevailed upon them to accept the sum of $5,000, and they rode off, never again to see the face of the kindly old Don and his lovely daughter.

Jesse James was in his twenty-seventh year when he married Miss Zerelda Mimms, his first cousin, who was about his age. When the wounded young guerrilla was brought home from Nebraska early in August 1865. He was carried *on a stretcher from a Missouri River steamboat to the home of John Mimms, at Harlem, now north Kansas City. Mimms had married a sister of Reverend Robert James. The elder daughter of the Mimms's was the wife of Charles McBride, a well-to-do builder of houses in Kansas City. The youngest daughter, Zerelda, named for the mother of Jesse James, helped to nurse the suffering boy back toward health. It was late in October before the patient was able to be taken, by wagon, from Harlem to the old homestead near Kearney.*

As in the case of the Frank James's, the Jesse James's necessarily concealed their identities. Howard was the favorite surname under which they lived in more than one state; but there were other aliases, chosen to fit the changing environment. The two children of theirs were Jesse Edwards and Mary.

The home life of Jesse James' family, discreetly aliased always, was in many respects of the great American average, in spite of everything. Neighbors in Nashville, in the Big Bottom country west of Nashville, in Kansas City and in St. Joseph, said "The Howards" were by no means undesirable neighbors. They were hospitable people, particularly when they lived in Tennessee. On the Big Bottom farm there was much entertaining of neighborhood folk.

One thing noticed by the neighbors was the chivalrous attitude of Mr. Howard toward women and children. Upon occasion, when a member of a stag party, he would utter a mild oath; but when women or children were present his language was as circumspect as that of a Sunday-school superintendent in active service.

Mr. Koger said, "Part of my business was to visit certain outlying towns for the firm. These duties took me frequently to Waverly and Humphreys counties, to the towns of Waverly and Box Station on the Nashville, Chattanooga and St. Louis Railroad. Box Station is now called Denver. It was a small village, and J.D. Howard lived for a time on a rented farm in the Big Bottom region close by. He got his mail at Box Station. I met him often there, and sometimes at Waverly, when I was on my business trips. As he was a customer of our firm, I cultivated his acquaintance to some extent.

Howard had some racehorses on his farm, and he had fixed up a sort of temporary track on which races were run. He associated with some gamblers of notorious reputation, who also were interested in horse racing. I recall that one of them tried to cheat Howard out of a race in which the water was $500. Howard got hopping mad. He rode up to the miscreant and plucked out a big pistol.

'Hand over that money,' he demanded, 'or you'll be a dead man in two seconds!'

The cheater handed over the cash, and Howard cooled down.

Howard also played poker with the gamblers and frequently with neighbors. Then men he played with said he always played on the square, and if anybody tried to cheat, Mr. Howard got quite indignant.

When I learned of Howard's intimacy with the crooked gambling fraternity I didn't approve of his cronies and I told Mr. Rhea that I didn't think he ought to have much to do with that man Howard. A good while after I had warned Mr. Rhea not to trust him too much, the man from the Big Bottom came to Nashville. He was leaving the farm, and as it turned out he was leaving Tennessee – for reasons known now to history but not suspected at the time. Mr. Rhea met him on the street.

'Mr. Rhea,' said Howard, 'I owe you $265, and I'm a little hard up just now, but you're about the only man around here that has treated me like a gentleman, and I made up my mind some time ago that I'd pay you every cent I owe, even if I had to go out and work on the streets at a dollar a day.'

Thereupon Mr. Howard pulled out his pocketbook, extracted $265, handed the money to Mr. Rhea, and walked away smiling.

Here now was an additional bit of evidence to bolster the present narrator's conviction that the late Jesse James was an honest man!"

"I can give you another instance – out of many – bearing upon the same point. K.R. Ross, a farmer in Cass County, Missouri, was a family friend of the James's and the Youngers – related by marriage to the Younger family. From time to time the outlaws visited his home. He entertained them but had nothing to do with them as a freebooting gang. His friendship for the fellows made him unpopular with the police authorities, and so he notified 'the boys' that he'd much prefer they didn't come around his place any more.

Well, the boys understood the situation and kept away from the Ross place. Ross made the statement that not long before Jesse James was killed a man called at his farm with a note addressed to him, signed 'David Howard'. Ross knew that 'David Howard' was Jesse James. The message carried a request that Ross go to a certain place in the woods, as the writer wished to see him. He went, and there he found Jesse James lying on the ground with his coat folded under his head and a pistol in each hand, his arms being crossed on his chest. He told Ross he had been down in the Mississippi River-bottom and was suffering from malaria fever; and he looked it.

'When I started back to Missouri,' said Jesse to Ross, 'I thought of everybody I might trust, and I figured I couldn't trust anybody but you. I have no money, and I'm very sick.'

James then opened his shirt and showed Ross where in the spring of 1865, a federal bullet had entered the right side of his chest; the place of the wound was 'all inflamed' as Ross described it.

'I need a horse, too,' said Jesse.

Ross provided him with a horse, saddle and bridle, and with $40. Jesse mounted the animal, with assistance, and rode away.

In less than a month, so Ross declared, he returned the horse, saddle and bridle and repaid the money.

'Well, anyhow,' said Mr. Kroger, 'Jesse James was honest about what he owed.'"

THE NASHVILLE BANNER NEWSPAPER

Nashville, Tennessee

Friday, July 8 1949

IF "DALTON" WASN'T THERE HE WAS THEREABOUTS

THE HOAX THAT LET JESSE JAMES LIVE

By Robert C. Roark

STANTON, MO., July 8 – The old man who looks, acts and talks like Jesse James, and who claims, at 102 years of age, to be Jesse James says that the man who was killed and buried as Jesse James was a fellow named Charley Bigelow.

The suspicion among the people who have unearthed him is that the killing was a cold frame-up, designed to allow Jesse to escape, and that there was plenty of political help in the operation.

WON'T ADMIT MURDER

But the white bearded old invalid will not admit much along those lines. He will not attempt to explain the murder of the man named Bigelow by the frères Ford, nor will he venture an opinion as to why both Fords and his brother, Frank, were immediately pardoned by Governor Tom Crittenden of Missouri.

"But if that'd been me Bob Ford shot," he said, "Frank would have killed him and Charlie both."

The old man says he had him a string of runnin' horses, and two came down with distemper. "I fetched 'em to St. Joe to isolate 'em," he said. "I had a house there I wasn't usin' for a spell – not until after some runnin' races at Excelsior Springs.

This fellow Charley Bigelow looked enough like me to be my twin, and he was huntin' a house. I told him and his wife they could use my place for a spell, until after the races, and he moved in.

One day I was out in the barn doctorin' my horses when I heerd a gunshot in the house. When I heerd that gun go off I knowed it wasn't no play-party, because we argued with guns in them days. I run into the house and there was Bob Ford, standing over Bigelow with a gun in his hand and blood on the floor.

I said to Ford, 'Looks like you killed him, Bob,' and Bob says, 'Looks like I did, Jesse.' Then I says, 'This is my chance, Bob. You tell 'em it's me you killed.

You tell my mother to say so, and you take care of that Bigelow woman. I'm long gone.'"

WENT TO SOUTH AMERICA

The old man sasys he got on one of his horses – a good horse, a four-mile horse – and he lit out. He says he went to Kansas City to Memphis to New Orleans, where he took a boat for Brazil. He kicked around South America for a spell and came home, and then went to Mexico. He settled later in Oklahoma, and he claims to have been elected under the name of J. Frank Dalton, to the territorial legislature. He later moved to Texas.

Mr. Dalton, or Mr. James, says it was real easy to escape detection, since he had either been in Quantrell's Raiders or had lived the restricted life of an outlaw for 19 years, from his 15th birthday on. Few people knew his well, many were dead, others had their mouths sealed, and it was vast country. He says he visited his son only once, when the boy was about 20 and working in a Kansas City cigar store. The son is now in an institution in California.

BRISTLES AT LEGEND

The fiery old boy's white goatee bristles when he speaks of the enlargement on the Jesse James legend. "I went to see a movie about me, once," he says, "I left after 15 minutes. And that damn silly business about me standing on a chair to hand a picture. You've all been in that house in St. Joe," he said to a surrounding circle. "You know what a low ceiling it's got. Why should a man as tall as me be standing on a so and so chair to hand a picture when I could do it easier standing on the floor?"

Ancient Jesse James, if that he be, does not seem to care whether anybody believes him or not, and often sulks up and will talk to no one. Only the people around him – Frank Hall, his discoverer, and Lester Dill, a kindly man who provides the old gent with a home and medical attention, seems fanatically interested in nailing down the legend.

If the old man has not been proven, he has not yet been disproven, and there is certainly a chance that he is all he says. I prefer to hope that he is telling the truth. For Jesse James or no Jesse James, that old boy in the Ozark cabin had a tremendous life. He didn't buy those bullet scars at the store, or his skill with a six-gun out of a dime novel. Nor did the son of the late Governor of Missouri have J. Frank Dalton write the history of the James gang just because he liked the name Dalton. If the old man wasn't there, those 67 years ago, he certainly was thereabouts.

CHAPTER TWENTY

Now I'll go back to 1881 for a little bit and the last robbery in which Jesse James was involved. A little past 3 p.m. on Friday, March 11, 1881, three armed men on horseback robbed Alexander G. Smith the U.S. Army Engineer Paymaster for the Muscle Shoals Canal Project, about two miles east of Florence (Ala.) on the tow-path that parallels the old Muscle Shoals Canal. William L. McDonald writes of this episode:

Smith had picked up the payroll at a Florence bank and was on his way back to the camp at the mouth of Bluewater Creek, some fifteen miles up the canal. These men, later identified as Frank and Jesse James and aother henchman Wild Bill Ryan had planned this robbery for several months, having heard about the laxity of the payroll handling.

Frank and Jesse James had been living incognito in the Nashville-Waverly vicinity in Tennessee for several years, Frank known as B.J. Woodson, was renting the Josiah Walston place on White Creek in Davidson County. Jesse, known as J.D. Howard, was living at nearby Denver. Wild Bill Ryan, known as Tom Hill, was a native of Nashville.

These three men, with drawn guns, robbed Smith of his saddlebag, his personal watch and $221.00 from his purse. The saddlebag contained the government payroll: $500.00 in gold and $4,500.00 in 50-dollar bills, 20-dollar bills and smaller currency. They tied Smith and forced him to accompany them until about midnight at which time they released him; returning his watch, overcoat and $21.00.

Wild Bill Ryan was arrested in Nashville on March 26, in a drunken brawl. He had $1,300.00 on his person that he could not explain. Frank and Jesse afraid now that Bill would talk, moved their families secretly to St. Joseph, Missouri. This time, Jesse assumed the name of Tom Howard.

Following Jesse James' assassination by Bob Ford, Frank James turned himself in to Governor Crittenden of Missouri. After standing trial and acquitted for killing a trainman in Missouri, Frank was sent to Huntsville, Alabama to stand trial for running the Muscle Shoals Canal payroll. The trial began April 17, 1884, and ended the next day, he was found 'not guilty'.

During this trial Frank James was represented by four of the South's best lawyers: General Leroy Pope Walker, a graduate of Princeton and Columbia Universities, Richard W. Walker of Huntsville, R.S. Sloan of Nashville, and James W. Newman of Winchester, Tennessee. General Walker dramatically closed his plea for 'not guilty' by telling of Jesse's and Frank's service in the Confederate Army. He told how the Yankees hanged Frank's step-father and, with a pistol, severed his mother's arm. Although the jury found him not guilty, seven or eight of the 20 witnesses from Muscle Shoals area positively identified him as one of the three bandits who robbed the paymaster.

Although incidental to the case, there is an old McDonald family story connected with these three men. About ten o'clock on the morning of this robbery, three men rode up to the Anderson McDonald farm at Rawhide (now Cloverdale). He operated a sawmill on his farm some distance from the house. McDonald's sixteen-year-old boy, John, was helping his father with some logs. One of the men, after a cordial greeting, asked John if he would take the three horses to the barn and feed them. After John returned the horses the men mounted, and the man who had requested the service, pitched John a five-dollar gold piece. One of the men, possibly Wild Bill Ryan, hesitated, and after the others were several hundred feet away, told John: "Boy, when you are grown, you can tell folks that Jesse James gave you that gold."

John McDonald treasured that coin until his old age... He died in 1942 and is buried near Corinth, Mississippi.

THE HOUSE AT NO. 1318 LAFAYETTE STREET IN ST. JOSEPH, MISSOURI WHERE CHARLEY BIGELOW WAS KILLED IN 1882 AS DESCRIBED AT THE TIME BY A JOURNAL REPORTER.

This house was formerly the property of Councilman Aylesbury. This house is a one-story cottage, painted white, with green shutters, and is romantically situated on the brow of a lofty eminence west of the city, commanding a fine view of the principal portion of the city, river and railroads, and adapted by nature for the perilous and desperate calling of Jesse James. Just east of the house is a deep gulch-like ravine, and beyond that a broad expanse of open country backed by a belt of timber. The house, except for the west side can be seen for several miles. There is a large yard attached to the cottage, and a stable where Jesse had been keeping his horse, which were found there this morning.

Charles and Robert Ford have been occupying one of the rooms in the rear of the dwelling.

The house rented for $14 a month and when the real Jesse James rented it, he gave the name of Thomas Howard.

The above description of the house is exactly as the real Jesse James described it to Ola. He said, "I rented the house and paid two months rent in advance on it. Then I went to Kansas City, met Bigelow and we got to talking and Bigelow told me that he wanted to move to St. Joe but had no place for his family to live. So, I told him that I had rented the house at 1318 Lafayette Street there and that he could take his family and move in and stay until he found a place, but that I would reserve the stables for my racehorses. So, they moved it. I never lived in that house. But I kept my horses in the stables."

AUTHENTIC STORY OF THE real JESSE JAMES
Police Gazette files of 1882 produce conclusive evidence that the famous Western Outlaw was never killed.

Jesse James still rode in 1950! Ripping aside the musty camouflage of the years, The Police Gazette has conclusive evidence that the most famous desperado of the old West was not killed in 1882, but spent 68 secret years hiding under an alias while another man's body moldered in the grave under his tombstone!

It is a tale of chicanery and double dealing which proves that truth is stranger than fiction. And there is incontrovertible evidence that the young killer whose bloody trail started with Quantrell's Guerrillas and stretched through 18 years of western lawlessness is the same white-haired man of 102 who appeared in 1950 to claim his legendary legacy.

Why, after all those years, did the crippled, dying, J. Frank Dalton come out of Stanton, Missouri to claim his rightful name?

The truth is that Jesse James knew he was reaching the end of the trial which started in the callous days of the Civil War. He had little to gain. But all of the old enemies were gone who might exact retribution. In his condition, he is beyond the vengeance of the dusty laws of the past – and he wanted to clear the name of young Bob Ford, a friend who was accused of shooting him in the back for a $10,000 reward.

Backing those startling and almost fantastic claims were four important facts:

1. The pale blue eyes still flamed as in a hoarse, rasping voice, James told in detail facts and figures which tallied exactly with historical accounts of his depredations – accounts which could not have been memorized and related with such startling clarity by a man of his age.

2. Physical characteristics are undeniable when compared with exclusive photographs carefully preserved for year sna brought to light by the Police Gazette.

3. The testimony of Mrs. Nellie Shevlin, wife of John Shevlin, one of the most honest and fearless law officers of the frontier, as related to this writer.

4. The sworn testimony of retired Union Army officer, Colonel James Russell Davis of Nashville, Tennessee, a 109-year-old, life-long friend of the James family.

Who then was buried at St. Joseph (Kearney), Missouri, in 1882?

It was a man named Charles Bigelow. A one-time confederate of the James gang who planned to betray them to the Pinkerton Agency.

And Jesse James sang in the church choir, with Colonel Davis guarding his back, the day they buried "Jesse James!"

The saga of the slaying of Jesse James is known to all: how Ford supposedly shot him in the back for the reward as Jesse straightened a picture on the wall.

Actually, it was a cover-up so that the harried Jesse could leave his reputation in a coffin with another man's bones and begin life over again in a new land. By innuendo, you gather a weird tale of political double dealing which helped fill the campaign coffers of Governor Thomas Crittenden of Missouri. Afterwards, Jesse slipped away to South America and returned later to wander through Texas and Missouri as a farmer, teacher and lawyer named J. Frank Dalton.

Here is his own story, told to me as he lay in bed waiting to make his final ride:

"I was only 15 years old when I joined my brother, Frank as a member of Quantrell's troop. About the war, I don't like to talk. It was war, and we perpetrated all the cruelties, I suppose, which soldiers have in all war. We were no different.

But when the war ended, we hoped to be allowed to live in peace. I wanted to settle down and I started to study medicine, but it was too much for me. So I began to study law.

But they wouldn't let us alone.

We were accused of treason, irregular murders and just about everything else. They hounded us and our only recourse was the things we did.

So, we were driven into the life we lived – my brother, Frank, and our cousins, the Youngers, and the rest of our gang. I suppose we are accused of many things we didn't do. But on the other hand, there were a lot of things we did which were never blamed on us, so I guess it's about 50-50. I was only 16 years old when we held up our first train, at Blue Cut, just east of Independence, Missouri. From there we just kept on going."

Son of a Baptist minister, Jesse was born in Clay County, Missouri, in 1847. They were turbulent times but he said he "has no alibi because we did plenty of wrong things." Naturally, he would not admit participation in any holdups where law officers or citizens were killed. But he ran through the list of bank and train robberies glibly.

Among the first were Clay County Bank at Liberty, Missouri, where the gang got $70,000 on February 14, 1866; The Lexington, Missouri, bank holdup on October 30, 1866, and the Savannah, Missouri, robbery on March 2, 1867.

The band then moved to Russell, Kentucky, in 1868, and in December, 1869, murdered a cashier in Gallatin, Missouri.

"I wasn't there," old Jesse rasped. "But I was at Corydon, Iowa, and at Columbia, Kentucky, when a cashier was shot."

Driven out of the territory, the gang for the next few years terrorized northern Mexico and the Rio Grande area of Texas. Then, in 1874, the desperadoes turned up at the Kansas City Agricultural Fair and held it up for $10,000.

"What if I was to say I was Jesse James and told you to hand over that money box?" Jesse related he told the startled young cashier at the fair.

"I'd see you in hell first!" the man replied.

"Well, that's just who I am," Jesse said, leveling a revolver. "And you'd better hand it over."

The man did.

"Nobody knows why we did it, though," Jesse grinned painfully. "I had a great horse and I'd entered him in the races at the fair. One of the judges pulled him out of the race, disqualified him. So I said to Cole Younger: 'C'mon we're going to get our money anyway!' And we did."

After that came the daring holdup at Gads Hill, where they ran the train onto a siding and leisurely stripped the passengers as well as the express car; another at Muncie, near Kansas City, and then an expedition by the gang to Huntington and Northfield, West Virginia, where a large posse was supposed to have wounded Jesse.

"They didn't though," he said.

But the heat was on and the gang broke up for two years. Then in 1879 came the sudden robbery of the Chicago and Alton train in Jackson County, Missouri, and in July of 1881 the holdup of the Rock Island and Pacific Railway at Winston, Missouri.

"I wasn't there on the last one," the aged Jesse insisted. 'But it was right after I settled in St. Joe with my wife and Crittenden offered a $10,000 reward for me."

POLITICAL DOUBLE DEALING

And that, apparently, is where the political double-dealing began. For Colonel Davis reveals that on the night before "Jesse James" was slain – the night of April 2, 1882 – the much-sought Jesse had a secret rendezvous with Governor Crittenden.

"They sat on a log in the woods, with me on guard against surprise, and talked or more than an hour," Davis related. "I know what they said, but I'll be damned if I'll tell. Let's say it was mostly political."

But Colonel Davis swears that of the $10,000 reward, Ford, the killer of "Jesse James," received only $600. The rest, it is intimated, found its way into a political campaign fund – the payoff on escape from a reputation. James and Davis both insist that the first time Crittenden ran for governor, the notorious Jesse contributed $35,000 to his campaign funds.

It is significant that the next day after the James-Crittenden rendezvous, Bigelow, who was known to be working for the Pinkertons, disappeared and never was heard from again. And all concerned identify old pictures labeled "Jesse James' corpse," as a picture of Bigelow.

THE HOAX THAT LET JESSE JAMES LIVE

Colonel Davis arrived at the James, or "Howard" cabin shortly after the news reached St. Joseph that Jesse had been shot by Ford.

"A little later," the Colonel related to this writer, "Jesse's mother arrived. She came and looked down at the body and said: 'That's not my son.'

So, I took her out in the kitchen and told her, 'Zerelda, come here and let me talk to you.' I told her there was a $10,000 reward on Jesse's life. I said, 'Let this fellow pass for Jesse and that will get the law off his trail and give him a chance to live a decent life.' She thought a few seconds and said: 'I am going to take your advice.' Then she went in and said: 'I haven't seen my son for a long time, let me look at him again.'

She stared at him for a three or four minutes and then put a handkerchief to her face, started to cry and screamed: 'That's my son.'

But when she came out in the kitchen, she was dry-eyed and she winked at me.

"Not only that, but Jesse insisted on going to the funeral and singing with the choir. I sure was nervous, I'll tell you, and stood back to back with him to keep an eye on everybody. After that, he went to New Orleans and shipped to Buenos Aires."

The testimony of Mrs. Shevlin, whose husband broke up the "Wild Bunch" and other bands of desperadoes, also bears weight.

"John and I were in a town near Colorado some years later and he pointed out two men to me," she said. "He told me they were Bob Ford and Frank James and said: 'That's a queer one, all right. It makes me wonder.'

My husband told me that Jesse and Frank had both vowed that if either of them was slain, the other would avenge his death. John said: 'I can't imagine Frank consorting and hobnobbing with Ford. It just doesn't make sense."

It does in the light of recent developments – for Ford did not kill Jesse James. Somebody, whether it was Ford, Jesse or another of their idle band, cut down Bigelow, the man who was preparing to betray them to the Pinkertons. They then passed the body off as that of "Jesse James."

The 1882 files of the Police Gazette, which featured a special edition on Jesse James at the time the Ford brothers, Bob and Charles were making personal appearances, reads in part: "The death of the noted outlaw was witnessed by none but the Ford brothers." And again: "The two Ford brothers immediately delivered themselves to the authorities and were confined in jail, charged with murder... They refused to be interviewed, but these facts ... were elicited. In July 1881, Robert engaged in the detective business in Kansas City. He soon got his credentials as detective and engaged in the hunt for Jesse James. Charles engaged to help, and aided by their victim's confidence in them, they carried out the plot..."

So it was that the feared bandit rode out of his sordid life to a chance at respectability – and finally has ridden back to clear the name of a friend accused of treachery and finish his long, violent journey under his own banner, the once feared name of Jesse James!

JESSE JAMES'
"IDENTIFICATION MARKS"

1. Rope burns on neck.
2. Evidence of severe burns on feet.
3. Bullet hole through left shoulder.
4. Bullet hole in lower belly.
5. Bullet scars under left knee.
6. Bullet scar under right eye.
7. Bullet hole along hairline of forehead.
8. End of index finger 'chewed' off.

Jesse James told Police Gazette Investigators that the widely circulated photo of himself is actually that of Charles Bigelow.

Authentic Police Gazette portrait of Jesse James shows long slender ears, drooping right eyelid and broad nostrils, which match physical characteristics of 102-year-old J. Frank Dalton.

THE NATIONAL POLICE GAZETTE

APRIL 1950

Pages 5 and 26

As written by George Moirath

Special investigator for the Police Gazette

MORE PROOF – MURDER OF JESSE JAMES A hoax!
STARTLING NEW EVIDENCE UNEARTHED BY POLICE
GAZETTE PROVES THAT J. FRANK DALTON IS THE
real JESSE JAMES, BANDIT OF THE OLD WEST!

By George McGrath

Special Investigator for the *Police Gazette*

"Jesse James still rode in 1950!" Thus did the Police Gazette in its April issue recognized 102-year-old J. Frank Dalton as the real Jesse James.

This exclusive disclosure created a nationwide furor which now has produced even more evidence that this feeble, white-haired man with the bullet-scarred body is the most famous outlaw of the old west, a ghost out of the bloody past for whose safety and chance at decency another man was slain.

It is a slaying fabled in song and story; how young Bob Ford shot Jesse James in the back for a $10,000 reward at St. Joseph, Missouri, on April 3, 1882.

But it is just that – a fable!

And it was a legend which left a spreading stain on the name of Jesse's comrade in bandit arms. So, after 68 years of stealthy living, James came out of obscurity to make grateful payment by cleansing Ford's tarnished name before he died.

There was a tremendous uproar when the Police Gazette became the first publication to establish, by almost incontrovertible proof that the man known for almost seventy years as J. Frank Dalton was in reality Jesse James. But those who leveled scorn and criticism could offer no provable facts to substantiate their denials!

Meanwhile, additional evidence continued to pile up that the Police Gazette had been right when it supported the claims of the silvery-thatched old fighter that he was the most famous – or most infamous – bandit in the gory history of the six-shooter frontier.

LET'S REVIEW BRIEFLY facts on which the first recognition was based. Those included Jesse's detailed accounts of James' gang depredations, impossible for one of such advanced years to have memorized and which checked exactly with accounts available only in old Police Gazette files; characteristics and bullet scars, and the sworn testimony of Colonel James Russell Davis of Nashville, Tennessee, and Mrs. Nellie Shevlin, wife of John Shevlin, one of the most honest and fearless law officers of that roaring era,

Now to be added to these facts are:

1. The testimony of Henry M. Priest, a Nashville, Tennessee storekeeper who identified Dalton as the man once known as "Mr. Howard," the alias used by James when he supposedly was shot by For.

2. Identification of Jesse by John Trammel, 110-year-old former cook for the James gang who was still living at this writing.

3. Jesse's own admission that his outfit perpetrated the Huntington, West Virginia, bank robbery in 185, a surprised even to the historians of that section and a "Job" missed by other chroniclers of the gang's depredation.

4. The testimony of DeWitt Travis of Longview, Texas, of "Dalton's" continued association with the family of Missouri Governor Thomas Crittenden. Jesse alleges they connived politically so that Charles Bigelow, a gang traitor, could be slain and his body passed off as that of Jesse to give the bandit leader an alibi of death.

5. Jesse's continued ability to name incidents and take doubters to the exact spot despite his advanced age.

6. Revelations of how the name J. Frank Dalton was devised as an alias when "Mr. Howard" met his fraudulent end.

7. The inability of opponents to prove that Dalton was no Jesse James at a Missouri probate court hearing.

8. Testimony of Robert E. Lee, 75, of Baton Rouge, Louisiana, one time bodyguard for William F. (Buffalo Bill) Cody, that the famed scout identified Dalton to him in 1893 as Jesse James.

All of these are sworn and certified proof and substantiations.

Yet a certain circle is inclined to discredit Jesse's claims without offering constructive proof. One school of detractors is composed of those who would ask Jesse leading questions concerning unreliable family word-of-mouth tales handed down from father to son. Added to this are indications of promotional squabble which threatens to ruin Jesse's dying gesture of gratitude to his old sidekick Ford.

Priest, 90-year-old retired Nashville storekeeper, provided clinching evidence when he recounted an incident out of "Mr. Howard's" past which was so trivial as to be remembered only by himself and "Howard." Yet it was told in detail by Dalton when Priest confronted him.

"Howard lived in Nashville in 1881 and I often heard his two children speak of 'Uncle Frank,' Priest related. (That would be Frank James, Jesse's brother.) "One day I was in the store and boy brought me a note asking me to bring some money to Mr. Howard at a card game. Just as I got there with the money, Howard arose from the table, pointed a six-shooter at a man in the game, and said: 'don't let me catch you cheating again!" Howard took the money without looking away from the man and the game continued. A short time later Howard came into my store and gave me back the money."

When Priest confronted the man who for 68 years has been hiding under the alias of Dalton, old Jesse listened while Priest asked him if he recalled that Nashville card game. Then Dalton recounted the same story.

Trammel, the former James gang cook, attested that he was at the "Howard" home in St. Joseph on the day of the killing and knew in advance of the plot to slay Bigelow. He added that he saw Jesse "for a day or two after the funeral and many times after that."

It was Trammel who provided more corroborating evidence when he revealed the slaying of the seven Chisholm brothers by the James boys because the Chisholms were thought to be stealing James's cattle.

"They hung them from a big old oak tree near Guthrie, Oklahoma, and then shot them through the head," Trammel recalled.

Jesse not only corroborated this – but led a party straight to the old oak with its "hanging branch" in the wild brush country, about 16 miles outside Guthrie.

Jesse's revelation that he had led his men in robbing a Huntington, West Virginia bank of $20,000 on September 6, 1875, was news even to the people of Huntington.

"The Police Gazette cleared up several snarls in the facts," wrote Squire Mauck, associate editor of the Daily Tribune, Gallipolis, West Virginia." For 75 years people in this area have wondered if Jesse and Frank were included in the quartet of bandits who robbed the bank of Huntington. Jesse was not suspected of being there.

"J.K. Oney, the cashier, was reported to have interviewed Frank James when the latter came to Huntington with a circus after the turn of the century. Frank denied he knew anything of the robbery or had ever been there before. Of course, Frank may have thought it expedient to lie on the cashier Oney. I received a letter recently from the old bandit leader and he told me that he and Frank had been all over West Virginia and Virginia."

So, again, the duty files corroborate old Jesse's story.

The testimony of Travis is of particular interest. Travis, a descendant of Captain Travis who defended the Alamo and a nephew of Neil and Jim Patterson who served in Quantrell's Guerrillas with Jesse James, corroborates old Jesse's tale of political double dealing.

According to Jesse, he contributed $35,000 to Crittenden's campaign coffers the first time Crittenden ran for governor of Missouri. By innuendo, he avers that the $10,000 reward money which Governor Crittenden posted for the death or capture of Jesse James found its way back into the Crittenden coffers when Ford killed Bigelow. The body was passed off as that of "Mr. Howard," the name used by James when he was in hiding.

Substantiating Jesse's claim of a clandestine meeting with the governor the night before the murderous hoax was perpetrated, Travis revealed that he was with "Dalton" at the Bray Hotel in Kansas City in 1935 when old Jesse spend long hours with H.H. Crittenden, son of the governor.

Travis, whose mother identified "Dalton" to him as the old family friend, Jesse James, said that the Crittenden obtained from "Dalton" most of the facts he used in the chapter "Outlawry in Missouri" for his book, The Crittenden Memoirs. And he asserted that when H.H. Crittenden first met "Dalton" in Kansas City he greeted him:

"Old Jesse, my goodness alive, you don't look much older than you used to!"

Lee, Buffalo Bill's one-time bodyguard said, "Dalton" visited Buffalo Bill in his private railroad car at the Chicago World's Fair in 1893 and the two "talked long" about their association.

"If the world knew what they talked about, people would be dumb-founded," Lee insists. "At that time 'Dalton' discussed with Buffalo Bill whether he should reveal his true identity of being Jesse James and the famed scout advised him to 'leave well enough alone!'"

It is Mauck, the Gallipolis historian, who charts the transformation of Jesse James, alias "Mr. Howard", to the pseudonym of J. Frank Dalton.

"There is nothing strange about the name he assumed after the shooting at his home – J. Frank Dalton," Mauck writes. *"That 'J.' was a fragment of the name he received from his Baptist minister father after his birth on September 5, 1847. The name of Frank may have been favored out of deference to his brother. And the name Dalton was a 'natural' because were not the James's and the Daltons of Oklahoma related?"*

Actually, they were cousins. As told in the Police Gazette in a recent issue, the Dalton gang was nearly annihilated in a bank holdup at Coffeyville, Kansas, a decade after the hoax at St. Joseph, Missouri.

Many readers have inquired whether old Jesse's identification marks included a left index finger from which the tip had been shot. Jesse recalls he was just a tot when he got hold of s six-shooter and with a child's inquisitiveness, pulled the trigger. The bullet "chewed" off the tip.

The Police Gazette has been flooded with mail defending and attacking its stand in support of old Jesse. But when he applied to the Missouri probate court for the name to be returned to him legally, there was no proof available that he wasn't Jesse James.

True, the court did not restore the name. But only because, Judge Ranson E. Breuer ruled, there was nothing to give back because old Jesse never changed his name legally to "J. Frank Dalton." So old Jesse can use his original name freely, where, if the evidence had been against him, the court certainly would have ruled that he could not use the name Jesse James.

And old Jesse, rapidly running out of seconds, flashed fire from those blue eagle eyes and demanded:

"With one foot in the grave and the other on the brink, do you think I would lie as to who I am?"

For one, the Police Gazette doesn't think so!

The National Police Gazette

August, 1950

The following is statements made by Robert E. Lee, 76, of Baton Rouge, Louisiana in the courtroom in Union, Missouri:

Robert E. Lee said, "I have known Jesse James 56 years. I first got acquainted with him in Chicago, Illinois during the World's Fair in 1893. I was bodyguard for Buffalo Bill in that circus. Jesse James came there to see Colonel Cody. I was doorkeeper and carried two six-shooters. I told Jesse James, 'If you tell me your name and what you want, I'll let you in.' He wouldn't do it.

He says, 'I don't believe Buffalo Bill would want me to tell a kid like you, my business.'

I said, 'Mister it's just too bad, I'm afraid you can't get in.'

Jesse James said, 'It's funny, an old prairie friend can't see his friend when he is right in there. They told me he is in there.'

I told him, 'You sit and wait a minute.'

I went and told Colonel Cody, 'There's a strange man out here, and he won't tell me what he wants.'

Bill was good-natured, you know, and he said, 'Well Robert, you follow that fellow right down the aisle. We'll see what he wants.'

I walked him ahead of me down the aisle. He was all shaved, smooth shaved. I never seen him before in my life. He walked in and stuck out his hand to Colonel Cody. Cody wouldn't stick out his hand but looked at him and says, 'Who are you? What do you want?'

Jesse James says, 'Colonel, don't you know me?'

Well, when this Jesse James was 3 years old, he had his finger shot with an old cap and ball pistol. Cody knowed that, and he says, 'Open your shirt a minute, I want to see something else.' So he opened his shirt, and Cody looked at he scars of the rope burns on his neck and says, 'My God man! You ain't nobody but Jesse James!'

'That's right.' replied Jesse.

'And this is the same man that is here in the court?' Lee was asked.

'This is the very man right there. That's the man. Jesse James stayed there a week,' said Lee. 'We ate together right there in the car. I know the scars on that man as well as anybody living. I am an old show and circus man, and I've traveled all over the United States and Canada. I've met that man and seen him several times after that, in Fort Worth, in Dallas, and in Longview, Texas. Well of course I knowed he was an outlaw, I had no business to approach him, I had no business with him or nothin', so I just kept my distance and kept away from him. But I have been telling people for 56 years all over Louisiana and Texas and Oklahoma that Jesse James was never shot in St. Joe, Missouri in 1882.

Lee owned a museum at Baton Rouge and could be seen free.

The following is statements made by John Trammel of Guthrie, Oklahoma, in the courtroom in Union Missouri regarding Jesse James:

John Trammel, 110-years-old, "I saw Jesse James in Dallas, Texas at Sanger Brothers Store. Frank James was floorwalker there."

When asked, "Are you sure, that the man you met the year you were freed, and were with for 16 or 17 years, then man you met in Dallas, the man you saw up at Meramec Caverns and the man here in this courtroom are the same man?"

John replied, "The same man, yes sir, the same man. The same man I cooked jonny cakes for."

When asked if he was ever around St. Joe, Missouri, he said, "Yes sir I was around there with him. I didn't know what place it was until he told me."

He was asked, "Did you see a dead man there?"

He replied, "I seen a man laying there dead."

When asked, "Who was that man?"

John said, "I don't remember that man, but I knowed I had seen him, and to me he looked to be the – just lookin' at the dead man I taken it to be Bigelow."

"Well, it wasn't Jesse James the man you had been with for 17 years?" He was asked.

He replied, 'No sir, Jesse ain't never died."

"Are you positive of that?" He was asked.

John replied, "I know, that he never died."

"Was Jesse James in the house?" John was asked.

He replied, "Jesse wasn't in the house."

When the lawyer said, "He wasn't in the house, unless that was he who was killed."

John said, "Well, I know he never did die."

John was asked, "Where did you go after you saw this individual there in the house?"

He replied, "I just went out across the country."

He was asked, "Did you know whose residence it was?"

He said, "I know whose they said it was."

"You know whose they said it was. How did you happen to go there?" he was asked.

John replied, "Being around wherever my boss stopped at, I stopped there, and he tell me to cook him some hoe cakes, I did it, I didn't care where it was at, how dark it was, or what time of night."

The lawyer said, "If that was your boss that lived there, why would you continue to travel over the country and not stay there?"

John said, "My boss was done gone, my boss went off and left me, rode off. If I had stayed there the boss would have come back and found me there. But I left because I don't stay where no dead man was."

"Was Jesse James your boss?" he was asked.

John said, "Yes sir. He went off and left me there. If I had stayed there he would have come back and got me, because I don't stay where no dead folks are at."

The following was stated by Colonel James R. Davis in the courtroom at Union, Missouri.

Colonel James Russell Davis, 109-years-of-age, of Nashville, Tennessee said, "I knew Charley Bigelow for 16 years. Knew he was an outlaw and that he was with the Slade gang. I saw Bigelow around St. Joe, Kearney and down around the country there.

After Bigelow was killed, Jesse went to South America to Buenos Aires, to the Argentine country and was buying and selling cattle.

It wasn't Jesse James that was buried. It was Charley Bigelow. I saw Jesse James at the funeral."

NEW REVELATIONS IN THE DOUBLE LIFE OF JESSE JAMES
March 1951

While he recalls details of holdups and other events with vivid, checkable accuracy, he clamps thin, withered lips in unbreakable silence when treasure is mentioned.

So the search goes on.

Meanwhile the Police Gazette uncovered still another development in the sensational saga of Jesse James.

This was that Bob Ford, the supposed "killer" of Jesse James, finally was liquidated by the James's when Ford was almost disclosed in 1892 that Jesse was still alive, thus giving the daring desperado another half century of life.

For it wasn't Jesse James who perished before a flaming pistol fabled in song and story. It was a member of the James gang named Charles Bigelow, who had been working traitorously with the Pinkertons, planning to betray the much-wanted outlaw chieftain.

The Police Gazette disclosed last April that after 68 years of living under the life-prolonging alias of Dalton, James came forth to clear the record before taking his last ride.

This disclosure created a nation-wide furor, and several factions since have attempted to discredit the bed-ridden bandit who started his nefarious career as a member of Quantrell's border raiders at the age of 15. But there charges and counter-charges now have brought to light the search for the bandits loot – and the strange delayed end of Ford, the supposed shot-in-the-back "killer" of Jesse James.

Former U.S. Marshal John Shevlin, one of the old west's leading peace officer, revealed to the Police Gazette the deadly payoff of Ford.

It was Shevlin who helped to clinch "Dalton's" claim to his rightful name of Jesse James by exposing the continued friendship of Frank James, Jesse's brother, and Bob Ford. Frank publicly had vowed, after Jesse's supposed slaying to "get" Jesse's killer. But Shevlin saw Frank and Bob Ford hobnobbing intimately in 1889 at Colorado City, Colorado – seven years after Jesse's supposed death.

Jesse since has confirmed that Frank and Bob were not only friendly but were partners in the operation of the Grove Theatre in Colorado City.

Everything went smoothly, Shevlin recalls, until the Cripple Creek gold field opened – and then Ford began to talk while drinking.

"Ford sold the Grove Theatre, pocketed the money and opened a gambling house and saloon," Shevlin disclosed. "His idea was to cut Frank James out of the money received from the sale of the theatre, which they owned jointly. Also, Ford had been drinking heavily and, in his cups, began talking of secret matters known only by himself and the James boys."

The "secret matters" supposedly included the top-secret fact that the much-wanted Jesse still was alive, hiding behind the buried remains of the traitorous Bigelow.

"Jesse told me that when this happened, 'Ford didn't last long,'" Shevlin revealed.

"A gunman was hired to kill Ford, but he got drunk and gambled away the money and muffed the job. Another man named O'Kelly then was hired and he

accomplished the death of Ford. O'Kelly was convicted and sentenced to 40 years in Canon City Penitentiary, but was pardoned within 30 days by Governor Waite."

There was whispers of the gang having high political connections.

Shevlin also disclosed that while he was chief of the government reservation at Hot Springs, Arkansas, he licensed "Dalton" to run a shooting gallery there.

"At that time 1901 to 1904, Jesse James had been 'dead' for 20 years and no one was looking for him, but there he was, the most publicized outlaw of the century, right under my nose for at least three years," Shevlin professes with awe. "And here he was, 50 years later, telling me the story of the greatest hoax ever perpetrated."

One of the most ardent disclaimers is Carl W. Breihan of Lemay, Missouri, president of the Missouri division of the Longstreet Memorial Association. Breihan wrote a biography of Jesse James.

An able historian, Breihan has gathered much evidence attempting to disprove Police Gazette recognition of "Dalton" as James.

These include a Photostat of "Dalton's" application for a Texas Confederate pension; another showing that Robert James married Zerelda Cole; another of a telegram from Fort Smith, Arkansas, on November 30, 1887, outlining the slaying of one Frank Dalton; an affidavit from DeWitt Travis, alleging that the aged, silver-haired man who came forth in 1950, rode with Quantrell as "Frank Dalton"; a letter from the U.S. Adjutant General that there was no record of Dalton enlisting at Fort Harker as "Dalton" claimed in a 1941 magazine story; a letter from the Veterans Administration that "Dalton" applied for a pension under that name, and a letter from Mrs. C.J. Danielson, operator of a rest home, disclaiming that "Dalton" was Jesse James.

While Breihan is honestly convinced that this is not the real Jesse James, as are others, the Police Gazette does not find his evidence strong enough to over-balance the proof which gained Jesse his recognition.

Concerning the application for a Texas pension, and also to the Veterans' Administration, James openly admits that ever since his supposed death he lived under the alias of Dalton. There was no question as to whether, where or when his parents were wed. The ancient telegram from Fort Smith proves only, that a man using the name "Frank Dalton" was killed.

Mrs. Danielson's testimony proved only that James used the name "Dalton," as admitted, and she could not have known the real Jesse or even the real Dalton as she was not born until two years after Jesse purportedly was killed. Concerning the vagaries of "Dalton's" 1941 magazine story, there were many things he still wished to keep covered at that time and, being 93 at that time, a few irregularities come under the heading of poetic license.

Those irregularities also could have come from old Jesse's fear of prosecution, still with him even on his deathbed.

As for Travis' affidavit, this is the same man who in another sworn statement three years after the one given to Breihan, testified concerning "Dalton's" continued association with the family of Missouri Governor Thomas Crittenden. Jesse alleges that they connived politically so that Bigelow could be slain and his body passed off as that of Jesse James to give the bandit leader an alibi of death.

It is important that the first Travis affidavit, the one held by Breihan, was made on March 10, 1947. That was when Jesse still hid behind the life-saving "Dalton" masquerade and the long arm of the James gang still might strike at betrayers – just as it had at Ford. But Travis changed his tune when Jesse came out in the open himself.

There is another mysterious item in Breihan's purported proofs. When the historian applied to the General Services Administration of the National Archives and Records Service in Washington, he was advised:

"The data and information contained in Mr. Dalton's file is deemed privileged and confidential and may not be disclosed."

Privileged and confidential because it truly reveals that "Dalton" actually is Jesse James?

After an exhaustive investigation, the Police Gazette believes that Dalton indisputably is Jesse James. There is too much substantiating proof – physical characteristics and scars; his ability to relate unerringly at his advanced age details of his crimes; the testimony of John Shevlin, a noted peace officer; identification by John Trammel, 110-year-old cook for the James gang, and by Robert E. Lee, former bodyguard of Buffalo Bill Cody, who heard the famous scout greet "Dalton" as "Old Jesse", and Travis' admission that he heard H.H. Crittenden, son of the former Missouri governor, use the same greeting when he met "Dalton".

The evidence thus would indicate that the daring desperado finally reached trails' end under his own bloody banner.

National Police Gazette

By George McGrath

Special Investigator for the *Police Gazette*.

Jesse James thought lots of Sam Rash, and it was his desire to go back to Granbury, Texas to the old Sam Rash home once again before he died.

A friend gave me the following information:

Sam and Lee Rash both lived at Granbury. Lee was Sam's son and there was another son, Walter.

Lee Rash married Eva Huggins and when her mother died, her 7-year-old brother, Harry Huggins went to live with his sister Eva and her husband Lee. He also spent much time at the Sam Rash home. The home was located just a little south of the present post office in Granbury on Lambert Branch, by the railroad tracks.

Another sister of Harry Huggins, Ella Huggins, married Dan James, a first cousin of Jesse James. They lived on the old "Wilson Huggins" home place just west of Action.

It was here that Harry Huggins seen Frank James ride up on a horse, never dismounting and staying in the edge of the woods. Dan went out to Frank but neither Harry or Ella heard what was said.

This was around 1905. It was through this relationship that Jesse James and Sam Rash met.

It was at the Sam Rash place that the James gang would hop off the train and stay for a while. Whatever Sam Rash knew concerning the gang, he kept to himself. But he was not involved in any of their robberies. No names were ever mentioned during these visits. But all of a sudden, the visits stopped. Harry Huggins grew up never hearing any more until Sam Rash's daughter Goldie Rash in 1951, brought the old man to Granbury to die. Harry Huggins did NOT believe it could be the one and only Jesse James. Knowing he would be well over a hundred and, also knowing some were not beyond using the situation to make money.

He thought on the matter for several days and decided to go visit the man. But before going he thought of several questions to ask him. Questions that no one could prompt beforehand. Questions that the real Jesse James could answer and no one else.

Upon arriving at the Sam Rash home, he found a very sick, but alert, old man. The "Mr. Dalton" was very glad to see him, telling him what had transpired since he and his gang used to hop off the train there, and his return to die there.

But the real shocker came when, during the course of their conversation, the old man answered every pre-thought up question.

Harry Huggins left there feeling he had just talked with the real Jesse James, alias Frank Dalton.

Which of course, he had.

Copied from an article in the Police Gazette. Written by George McGrath. Special investigator for the Police Gazette January 1952:

The searing Texas heat converted the tiny room into a scorching oven but the frail, white-haired man shivered. Gnarled hands clutched at the scarred, old six-shooter at his side and hoarse whispers clawed their way out of his throat in the rasping rattle which precedes death.

It was August 15, 1951, and the old man who had lived almost 104 years was dying. He knew it. But his steel-blue eyes still glittered unafraid and for the last time, through thin almost bloodless lips, the old man sneered at those who questioned his identity.

"I am Jesse James," he declared.

Then, grating out the words with painful effort, the man who had perpetrated the hoax of the century by masquerading for 68 years reiterated in a deathbed confession his claim to being the infamous outlaw supposedly slain by Bob Ford at St. Joseph, Missouri, on April 3, 1882.

"What they believe does not matter now," he panted as he faced his last ride. "Let them think what they will. But this I know – because of what I did, I lived 70 extra years."

What he did was to murder with premeditation a Pinkerton agent named Charles Bigelow. The body was palmed off as that of "Mr. Howard," Jesse's alias in St. Joseph, Missouri. And Jesse, the most feared and hunted outlaw of the Old West, thus was free to live openly as "J. Frank Dalton" until 1950 when, nearing the end of the trail, he came forth finally to clear Bob Ford of blame.

Face to face with death he had meted out to many a holdup victim, old Jesse knew, as the afternoon waned and the shadows closed in, that now he had nothing more to gain by either truth or falsehood. So on this last day at Granbury, Texas, he talked of things which he had never before revealed.

He spoke without remorse. To the end he was Jesse James, King of the outlaws.

"Following my supposed death at Ford's hands," Jesse said, "I worked with my brother Frank, who ran the Groves Theatre in Colorado City. Then I went to

Hot Springs, Arkansas, and opened a shooting gallery. But I didn't do very well as far as money goes."

As Jesse jay breathing his last in the Texas heat, witnesses still were coming forth to substantiate his claims to one of the greatest masquerades in criminal history.

John William Pierce, of Orrick, Missouri, another of those "in the know", signed an affidavit that, as a confidante of the James gang, he knew Bigelow was to be slain instead of Jesse.

"I was laying stone on a piece of ground about 200 feet from the house where the shooting took place at St. Joseph. That morning Jesse was supposed to have been killed," he asserted.

"When I heard the shots, I ran tot eh house and saw the dead man lying on the floor. That man was the one I knew as Charley Bigelow."

Pierce revealed that Jesse came furtively to his home around noon, and told him, "The job has been done. Now I will have to leave the country."

The Missourian said that he saw Jesse again in 1893, and that James confided he had just returned from South America.

Another substantiating witness was Clarence N. Bouyer, of Fort Worth, Texas. He swore, in an affidavit, that his father rode with Quantrell's Guerrillas – where Jesse James first began his bloody career – and there became acquainted with Jesse. The elder Bouyer, prior to his death in 1919, told Clarence in strictest confidence that Jesse was not dead because he had seen the outlaw leader in West Texas some years after he was believed to have been killed.

Added evidence piled up continually as Police Gazette investigators continued their search for corroborating evidence. One such incident involves the use of the old Salt Peter Cave near Stanton, Missouri, as a hideout for the James gang. It was while riding with Quantrell that Jesse first became familiar with the caverns – and only last year told the people operating the caverns as a tourist spot about a secret exit.

In 1865, the Union Army was using the caverns as an ammunition dump and powder factory. Quantrell's men were ordered to infiltrate the Union camp as workmen and learn the lay of the land. This they did so successfully that the Confederate forces destroyed the Salt Peter vats and munitions.

In later years, Jesse and his men found the caverns invaluable.

"One time, while making a get-away, we were being pressed close by a posse of Pinkertons and we made for the caves with them at our heels," old Jesse recalled. "They didn't try to come into the caves after us. They figured we would have to come out eventually because they thought there was only one entrance.

"They holed up at the mouth of the cave for our days," he added.

"But I knew the cave like the back of my hand for I had been there with Quantrell and many times afterward. We knew of an exit, about eleven miles back from the mouth of the cave, which came out on the other side of the mountain. The opening was just big enough to allow a man and a horse to squeeze through single file. We all escaped."

The operators of the caverns at that time, in 1950, knew nothing of another exit from the caves. Old Jesse made a crude map of the interior of the caves for them and, after considerable exploring, the exit was found hidden in underbrush and rubble – just as the old man had explained.

It was episodes such as this which convinced the Police Gazette in 1950 that "Dalton" actually was the supposedly long-dead Jesse James. There was too much substantiating proof – physical characteristics and scars, his amazing ability to relate unerringly at his advanced age the details of his crimes, and identification of the aged man by numerous witnesses.

Those include John Shevlin, a noted peace officer who intimately knew Frank James, Jesse's brother; John Trammel, 110-year-old former cook for the James gang; Robert E. Lee, former bodyguard for Buffalo Bill Cody, who heard the famous scout greet "Dalton" as "old Jesse"; and the admission of DeWitt Travis that he heard H.H. Crittenden, son of the former Missouri governor who knew the James boys, use the same greeting when he once met "Dalton".

There were others, as the Police Gazette revealed recently, who kept silent for hope of profit. For there were those who believed that someday, old Jesse would reveal the location of secret caches of money and jewelry which he took from his hapless victims.

But none of that information passed the old man's grim lips as he lay dying last August. Instead, he reiterated defiantly his ghostly claim to the bloody legend of the past:

"I am Jesse James."

Those were his last words as, with the sun fading in the western horizon, he died at 7:30 p.m. on August 15, 1951.

They laid old Jesse, cold and still seventy years later, in a grave beside the unnamed and unmarked spot which holds the moldering bones of Belle Starr, the "Outlaw Queen".

Some will always wonder whether this hard-eyed, defiant old man was really Jesse James. For those who have delved into his claim there can be little doubt. For those who saw him and heard him on that last day in the tiny, oven hot room in Granbury, Texas, there can be no doubt that he was, indeed.

The following was written to Henry J. Walker. I had the pleasure of meeting and visiting with him a few years before his death:

Joseph, Oregon
June 25, 1956

I was born and raised at Bigelow, Missouri, and seeing your letter in the Mound City paper, I thought I might have some information that would interest you. While I'm no young man, the James boys were before my time. Although I remember Frank James and when he died.

When I was twelve or fourteen years of age, Frank Bridgman, an old timer, told me that the town was named after a family by the name of Bigelow and they had a son, Charles. His sister told me many times that she had carried meals out in the timber for Jesse James, that seemed to be his stomping ground, but I never heard of him living there.

In 1921, an old fellow, who was 69 years old, a John Hutton, who was raised at Mound City, told me that he had heard from reliable sources that Bob Ford shot Charley Bigelow, and not Jesse James, but they looked so much alike that he got the reward, and Jesse James got away.

Very Truly, and good luck
Charles Mallon

In a letter from The Historical Society of Missouri at Columbia in 1985, was the following:

No one, to this day, knows who J. Frank Dalton really was.

I will never forget what Jesse James, alias J. Frank Dalton told me.

"Ola, my great desire and hope is that I will be buried until my true and correct name, JESSE WOODSON JAMES."

He is In the Granbury Cemetery at Granbury, Texas.

THANK YOU FOR READING!

If you enjoyed this book, we would appreciate your customer review on your book seller's website or on Goodreads.

Also, we would like for you to know that you can find more great books like this one at www.CreativeTexts.com

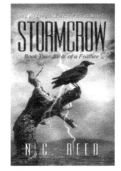

Milton Keynes UK
Ingram Content Group UK Ltd.
UKHW041407110923
428463UK00004B/276